BEYOND METHODS

COMPONENTS

OF

SECOND LANGUAGE
TEACHER EDUCATION

The McGraw-Hill Second Language Professional Series

(FORMERLY "THE McGRAW-HILL FOREIGN LANGUAGE PROFESSIONAL SERIES")

General Editors: James F. Lee and Bill VanPatten

Directions in Second Language Learning

(FORMERLY "DIRECTIONS FOR LANGUAGE LEARNING AND TEACHING")

Primarily for students of second language acquisition and teaching, curriculum developers, and teacher educators, *Directions in Second Language Learning* explores how languages are learned and used and how knowledge about language acquisition and use informs language teaching. The books in this strand emphasize principled approaches to language classroom instruction and management as well as to the education of foreign and second language teachers.

Beyond Methods: Components of Second Language Teacher Education. Edited by Kathleen Bardovi-Harlig and Beverly Hartford (both of Indiana University)
Order number: 0-07-006106-8

Communicative Competence: Theory and Classroom Practice, Second Edition, by Sandra J. Savignon (The Pennsylvania State University)
Order number: 0-07-083736-8

Making Communicative Language Teaching Happen, by James F. Lee and Bill VanPatten (both of University of Illinois, Urbana-Champaign)
Order number: 0-07-037693-x

Workbook to accompany *Making Communicative Language Teaching Happen*, by James F. Lee and Bill VanPatten
Order number: 0-07-083736-8

Perspectives on Theory and Research

Primarily for scholars and researchers of second language acquisition and teaching, *Perspectives on Theory and Research* seeks to advance knowledge about the nature of language learning in and out of the classroom by offering current research on language learning and teaching from diverse perspectives and frameworks.

Breaking Tradition: An Exploration of the Historical Relationship between Theory and Practice in Second Language Teaching, by Diane Musumeci (University of Illinois, Urbana-Champaign)
Order Number: 0-07-044394-7

BEYOND METHODS

COMPONENTS
OF
SECOND LANGUAGE
TEACHER EDUCATION

EDITED BY

KATHLEEN BARDOVI-HARLIG
INDIANA UNIVERSITY

BEVERLY HARTFORD
INDIANA UNIVERSITY

Boston   Burr Ridge, IL   Dubuque, IA   Madison, WI   New York
San Francisco   St. Louis   Bangkok   Bogotá   Caracas   Lisbon   London
Madrid   Mexico City   Milan   New Delhi   Seoul   Singapore   Sydney
Taipei   Toronto

McGraw-Hill

*A Division of The **McGraw·Hill** Companies*

This is an  book.

BEYOND METHODS
Components of Second Language Teacher Education

This book is printed on acid-free paper.

2 3 4 5 6 7 8 9 0   BKM BKM   9 0 9

ISBN   0-07-006106-8

This book was set in Palatino by The Clarinda Company.
The editors were Thalia Dorwick and Gregory Trauth.
The production supervisor was Michelle Lyon.
R.R. Donnelley & Sons was printer and binder.

Library of Congress Cataloging-in-Publication Data
Beyond methods : components of second language teacher education /
  [edited by] Kathleen Bardovi-Harlig, Beverly S. Hartford : general
  editors. James F. Lee, Bill VanPatten.
      p.   cm. — (The McGraw-Hill second language professional
  series / directions in second language learning and teaching)
    Includes bibliographical references and index.
    Contents: The case for psycholinguistics / Bill VanPatten — The
  place of second language acquisition theory in language teacher
  preparation / Kathleen Bardovi-Harlig — Why syntactic theory? /
  Maria-Luise Beck — Phonology in language teaching / Martha C.
  Pennington — Sociolinguistics in language teacher preparation
  programs / Beverly S. Hartford — The role of pragmatics in language
  teacher education / Gabriele Kasper — A world language perspective:
  English, French, and Spanish / Kimberley Brown — Non-native
  reading research and theory / James F. Lee — The writing course /
  William Grabe and Robert B. Kaplan — Assessment and second language
  teaching / Harry L. Gradman and Daniel J. Reed.
    ISBN 0-07-006106-8 (pbk.)
    1. Language teachers—Training of.   2. Language and languages—
  Study and teaching.   I. Bardovi-Harlig, Kathleen. 1955–
  II. Hartford, Beverly.   III. Lee, James F.   IV. VanPatten, Bill.
  V. Series.
  P53.85.B49   1997
  407—dc21   96-53163
                                                            CIP

http://www.mhcollege.com

CONTENTS

FOREWORD

Directions in Second Language Learning is a series that addresses not only questions about the current and future status of language teaching but also issues surrounding the education and training of language teachers. To this latter end, we are pleased to present *Beyond Methods: Components of Second Language Teacher Education*. In this volume, Kathleen Bardovi-Harlig and Beverly Hartford have collected an impressive set of contributions from various scholars that offers students and their educators an overview of the different disciplines that inform language teaching. Some twenty years ago, a collection of this kind might have contained articles only on structural linguistics and psychology. Today, however, owing chiefly to the impact of second language acquisition research on language teaching, this volume reveals the breadth and complexity of learning another language. The editors and authors have worked to create a volume accessible to advanced undergraduates and graduate students, and we believe it will be a useful companion to other texts and readings on language learning and teaching.

J.F.L.
B.VP.

PREFACE

When new graduate students enter a language teacher preparation program, they often want to take their methods course first. They are understandably eager to embark on what they see as the most relevant (or most interesting) course early in their training. They are ready to get down to business and discover what language teaching is all about.

The preparation for teaching language is as much about understanding language as it is about how to teach it. In fact, making decisions about methods, syllabus design, and assessment (just some of the decisions teachers make regularly) must be made from a base of knowledge of language. This knowledge of language should include more than specific knowledge of the particular language one will teach, whether the language is one of the familiar English, French, Spanish, or German, the increasingly popular Japanese or Chinese, or the less commonly taught languages such as Swahili, Hausa, Hungarian, or Uzbek. Whether teachers are native speakers or non-native speakers of the language they teach, training in grammar, phonology, and use of the language is relevant. This knowledge must also include an understanding of how people process language (oral and written), how language is acquired, how language is used in various social settings, and how social variables affect language use. Such a knowledge of language is also key to interpreting crucial claims made by various methods regarding the "best" or most "efficient" means of teaching a language.

Thus, much of the preparation for language teaching takes place in courses other than in methods courses. Yet, if there is one course all teacher preparation programs have in common, it is the methods course (although the content may be quite different in different programs). In any display of books at professional meetings for language teachers, such as TESOL (Teachers of English to Speakers of Other Languages) and ACTFL (American Council on the Teaching of Foreign Languages), one will find a seemingly endless selection of books concerned with the methods of language teaching.

This book is not another methods book. Instead, this book addresses the preparation of language teachers in their understanding of language. *Beyond Methods* introduces language teachers to findings from language research that are directly relevant to the language classroom. This volume presents a view of language that is pertinent to all instructional settings, whether a second language or foreign language and whether teachers are native or non-native speakers of the languages they teach.

We sought to include what we consider to be the core areas of knowledge for second-foreign language teachers. For each of the ten chapters, we selected topics that are likely to be covered in their own course or as a substantial portion of another course in Master's level programs dedicated to the education of language teachers. Although no single program is likely to be fortunate enough to have separate courses for all of these areas, we see these topics as a desiderata for language teacher education. We have invited specialists in different areas of language who are active teacher educators to discuss the relevance of their research areas to teacher preparation. The contributors teach courses and give lectures on the topic of their chapters at universities around the world.

AUDIENCE

The chapters are designed to answer the question students most often ask: "Why should I take such a course?" In answering this question, the authors address three types of readers: prospective teachers enrolled in MA programs, practicing teachers in formal programs or engaging in self-study, and teacher educators and program planners.

As a book for prospective students engaged in coursework, this volume can be used as a main textbook in a course that surveys the field of applied linguistics as it pertains to language teaching or as a supplement to a methods course. As a main textbook in a survey course, it moves the readers from theory into practice by laying the theoretical and research foundations for teaching practice. All of the authors have included explicit discussions of the application of their areas of inquiry to the second foreign/language classroom, moving from theory to practice. As a supplement in a methods course, this volume helps readers understand the theoretical foundation which underpins teaching practices which are the focus of a methods course, helping readers to move from practice to theory.

Practicing or novice teachers working individually for professional development will also find this book informative. We have included thought-provoking questions throughout the chapters to encourage readers to relate the discussion to their own language teaching and learning experiences. In addition, each chapter identifies key terms, which are defined in the text, and makes suggestions for further reading in books and relevant journals to help readers pursue areas of interest in greater detail. These features will also be useful for readers who are using the book for a course.

Teacher educators and program planners may also wish to use this book as a reference for planning courses or for establishing teacher preparation programs. The volume provides an outline of a language-teacher education program in which language is the central focus. Each chapter explores the main issues in the field of research and may be used profitable as a reference. In addition, educators will discover that the self-study questions—which ask the reader to "pause to consider" a particular interpretation or application of the reading—lend themselves to class discussion.

xiii

PREFACE

CONTENTS AND ORGANIZATION

Readers will find that certain issues that are central to the learning of second-foreign languages are addressed across chapters. The role of input, the first language, motivation, language attitudes, and the role of instruction are some of the issues treated from the multiple perspectives of the chapters in this volume.

Each of the ten chapters covers a single discipline or subdiscipline within the study of language and associated with a distinct program of research. The first two chapters on psycholinguistics and second language acquisition deal with the processes underlying comprehension and acquisition, processes that are basic to all language classroom activities. The next two chapters, on syntax and phonology discuss the structure of language. Although the specific languages we teach differ in the details of their grammars and sound systems, certain organizing principles are common to all languages, and these chapters examine those principles. Next, we describe language in its larger setting: the social context of language use as explored in the disciplines of sociolinguistics and pragmatics, and in the framework of world languages. The chapters on reading and writing show how far we have come from viewing these as areas of mere skill development, to an understanding of these as areas affected by psycholinguistic and acquisition processes. The final chapter draws together the issues raised throughout the book in a discussion of language assessment.

"The Case for Psycholinguistics" is made in Chapter 1 by Bill VanPatten. This chapter sets the tone for the volume, highlighting the learner's contribution to the language learning endeavor by exploring the mental processes underlying language comprehension and language use. Through a review of sentence processing and parsing of sentences, VanPatten demonstrates how psycholinguistics contributes to an understanding of the concept of "comprehensible input." The presentation of the principles of developmental psycholinguistics, or child language acquisition, reveals the close relationship between psycholinguistics and second language acquisition research discussed in Chapter 2. The chapter closes with a review of specific pedagogical applications of psycholinguistically informed processing instruction.

Kathleen Bardovi-Harlig discusses "The Place of Second Language Acquisition Theory in Language Teacher Preparation" in Chapter 2. The author makes a strong case for the centrality of understanding how learners contribute actively to the process of acquiring languages. She presents evidence for the engagement of a language acquisition device, active during this process, which is reflected in common acquisition patterns across learners, regardless of their native languages. By drawing on work on the acquisition of tense and aspect in a variety of target languages, she shows how learners proceed through similar developmental stages even with different L1s. In addition, she addresses factors, especially classroom factors, that may influence acquisition. However, she shows that this influence is mainly on rate of acquisition, not on order of developmental stages. She also discusses the role of classroom instruction and the relevance of understanding second language acquisition processes to the selection and evaluation of classroom materials and curriculum design.

Chapters 3 and 4 deal with the structure of language. In Chapter 3, Maria-Luise Beck answers the often-asked question: "Why Syntactic Theory?" As she presents the grammar-related concepts with which teachers should be familiar, she introduces the reader to the organization of language and the principles that shape it. Beck deals with the theory of grammar as a representation of the mental grammar of language, not with pedagogical or traditional grammars. She also introduces the reader to generative grammars and how they are evaluated in terms of how well they account for the language they seek to describe (or more technically, their *level of adequacy*.) She shows how grammars attempt to account for native-speaker intuitions and how a theory of grammar can help account for stages observed in language acquisition.

In Chapter 4, "Phonology in Language Teaching: Essentials of Theory and Practice," Martha C. Pennington reviews the area of phonology in language teaching and teacher education. She demonstrates that although focus on pronunciation in language pedagogy had declined throughout the 1970s and most of the 1980s, phonology is an important aspect of the language curriculum in a communicative framework. Pennington claims that a learner's pronunciation is key to comprehensible output and to interaction with other speakers. She argues further that teaching practice should be grounded on knowledge of the phonology of the languages concerned, both the native and target language(s) of the learners, as well as on language learning theory. Her chapter focuses on establishing links between the larger area of second language acquisition, phonological theory, and teaching practice.

Chapters 5, 6, and 7 discuss language as related to cultural and societal issues. All three authors encourage teachers to reflect on the concept of the "native speaker" by suggesting that a range of targets may be appropriate for instructional settings depending on the goals of the students. In Chapter 5, "Sociolinguistics in Language Teacher Preparation Programs," Beverly S. Hartford presents a broad overview of the field of sociolinguistics. She discusses the need for the language teacher to understand the nature of linguistic variation and the factors that may influence it. This requires the understanding of language in use and the various socio-psychological parameters that influence users. She discusses the role of learners as social beings, as members of speech communities, and how this bears on their acquisition of second/foreign languages. From the point of view of the speech community, she shows how multilingualism plays a part in language variation and change, and how learners are part of this process. She also presents the socio-psychological factors which are believed to be involved in learners' motivations and ultimate success in language acquisition and which the language teacher must take into account. Finally, in a discussion of language planning, she shows how the language teacher may be expected to play not only the role of a classroom facilitator, but also be involved in social and linguistic change by being asked to participate in language planning activities.

In Chapter 6, "The Role of Pragmatics in Language Teacher Education," Gabriele Kasper explores the relevance of pragmatics to teacher preparation from two perspectives: as forming the basis of what language learners need to know about language in use and as informing a teacher's perception of his/her own classroom as a domain for meaningful discourse. The ability to use appropriately situated speech is part of communicative competence. Kasper discusses the role that native speaker intuitions and observation play in determining pedagogical targets, the development of pragmatic competence, and classroom activities for increasing pragmatic competence. The first part of the chapter helps us understand what learners need to know about language in use and how they learn it; the second part of the chapter helps teachers understand student-teacher and student-student interaction as a real part of culture which is reflected in the classroom. Patterns of turn-taking, the success of group work, the responsibility of listeners, and the choice of register by language students in the classroom can all be understood from the perspective of pragmatics. Kasper demonstrates how awareness of cross-cultural communication has a direct bearing on how teachers structure and interpret the outcomes of a range of classroom activities.

In Chapter 7, "A World Language Perspective: English, French, and Spanish," Kimberley Brown addresses a relatively new topic in the preparation of language teachers. She looks at the growth of a small number of languages used extensively as second/foreign languages around the world, in particular, English, French, and Spanish. The rapid spread of these languages as instruments of education, economics, and technology has brought into question the role of the native speaker as a target for language learners. Brown suggests that although teaching materials are most frequently built on the notion of a native speaker target, this may not be the best choice. She points out that these particular languages have become locally established, with local norms that may differ from native speaker norms. She also calls our attention to the fact that such languages may more often be used as common communication systems among non-native speakers than between non-native and native speakers. Given these facts, Brown cautions language teachers to evaluate the actual needs of their learners in the probable uses of one of these world languages, setting goals and selecting and designing materials that reflect those needs. Such goals and materials, she suggests, may be to meet local norms or to achieve mutual intelligibility among non-native speakers, but not, perhaps, to aspire to the norms of the native speaking communities.

Formerly, reading and writing in language classes were treated only as skills. However, current research has revealed that reading comprehension in a second/foreign language is the result of psycholinguistic processes, just as it is in the native language. Likewise, research in writing has shown that psycholinguistic and social processes are also factors in second/foreign language writing. In keeping with the thread that runs throughout this volume, James F. Lee, in Chapter 8, "Non-Native Reading Research and Theory," argues for the active role of the learner in the acquisition of reading. Rather than viewing reading and its acquisition as a passive activity, Lee shows how the learner-reader and the text interact in order for meaning to emerge. Learner-readers bring rich backgrounds to reading tasks and utilize this knowledge ("schemata") in order to understand the text. They bring both knowledge of how texts may be constructed ("formal schemata"), knowledge of the language (i.e., lexical, syntactic, orthographic, and semantic), and knowledge of what the content might be. This helps in their ability to make inferences and assign meaning. He shows how what might at first appear to be "errors" in reading from the teacher's point of view may actually be a result of the application of these various knowledge sources to the understanding of the text by learners. The language teacher—by understanding how the learner applies such knowledge in the process of reading—can better understand how learners approach their tasks, can modify their own expectations of learners' reading behaviors and, in particular, select and design reading materials that both draw on the reader-learners' existing knowledge sources as well as expand them.

In Chapter 9, "The Writing Course," William Grabe and Robert B. Kaplan show how a theory of writing and writing instruction must be understood in the larger context of language and language use. Grabe and Kaplan argue that a theory of writing cannot by limited to the development of writing as an isolated skill, but must integrate a theory of language, input processing, social context, and affective influences. Examples of theories in each of these areas are evaluated for what they contribute to our knowledge of the development of writing. A range of theories of writing development are reviewed in detail. Finally, approaches to the teaching of writing are evaluated against the theories of writing and language use to illustrate which of the aspects of language acquisition they address in their practices.

Chapter 10, "Assessment and Second Language Teaching" by Harry L. Gradman and Daniel J. Reed, explores the principles and current practices of language testing. Gradman and Reed show how the views of language discussed throughout this volume have influenced the theory and practice of language assessment. As views of linguistic competence have shifted from exclusively grammar-based or syntactically-oriented views to include oral and written communicative competence, assessment practices have broadened to include innovative exercises that meet the traditional testing criteria of reliability, validity, and practicality. In addition, the field of language testing has introduced areas of consideration in its own right, including issues of measurement, reporting to stakeholders, and the collection of multiple language samples through portfolio assessment. This chapter brings together the issues raised in this volume by exploring the assessment of various competencies discussed throughout.

ACKNOWLEDGMENTS

We would like to thank the students of the Survey of Applied Linguistics at Indiana University, summers of 1995 and 1996, for helping us pilot this book, and for contributing questions from the perspective of the reader. We would also like to thank our colleague, Daniel Reed, who co-taught the course with Beverly Hartford. Thanks are also due to Dudley Reynolds, Yi Yuan, Tom Salsbury, and Karla Bastin for their assistance in preparing this volume. Finally, we thank Bill VanPatten and James Lee, the series editors, for their unfailing guidance and wisdom through the many stages of bringing this book to press. We are grateful to the Program in TESOL and Applied Linguistics and the Center for English Language Training at Indiana University for its support of this project.

K.B.H., B.S.H., Bloomington, IN, October, 1996

CHAPTER 1

The Case for Psycholinguistics

Bill VanPatten
University of Illinois at Urbana-Champaign

INTRODUCTION

In the heyday of behaviorism, language acquisition was seen as a relatively simple process similar to other kinds of learning.[1] Linguists could describe the surface features of language to be learned and those features constituted the new habits that the second language learner was to acquire. Teaching was equally simple; all one had to do was drill students on the appropriate structures of the language and avoid errors. Teacher education, then, was limited to understanding the tenets of habit formation and how to conduct drills efficiently.

But if the research in second language acquisition since 1970 has shown us anything, it is this: Language acquisition is a complex and multi-dimensional phenomenon. Language acquisition is not simple and, by extension, what teachers need to know is no longer simple. Language acquisition can be studied from linguistic, cognitive, social, and educational perspectives, each lending important insights into the nature of how language is acquired. The present chapter is about psycholinguistic insights and their implications for second language acquisition. After a brief definition and overview of the field of psycholinguistics, I will discuss how psycholinguistics is relevant to understanding second language acquisition, and I will conclude with what second/foreign language instructors should know about psycholinguistics and second language acquisition.

WHAT IS PSYCHOLINGUISTICS?

Traditionally, psycholinguistics has been defined as "the study of the mental mechanisms that make it possible for people to use language. It is a scientific discipline whose goal is a coherent theory of the way in which language is produced and understood" (Garnham 1985, p. 1). That is, with *native speaking adults*, the questions that have driven classic psycholinguistic studies are

1

"How do people use their linguistic competence to *comprehend* utterances or discourse?" and "How do people use their linguistic competence to *produce* utterances or discourse?" Juxtaposed to formal and theoretical linguistics, which aim to describe language as an object or knowledge system, psycholinguistics is about underlying *processes*. A perusal of standard psycholinguistic textbooks shows this quite clearly (Table 1.1). Typical chapter titles in books that offer an overview of psycholinguistics focus on perception of language, memory and comprehension, accessing the lexicon, parsing (or the "on-line" processing of the structural relationship among elements in a sentence), processes in production, the relationship of comprehension to production, and so on.

TABLE 1.1. Example Tables of Contents from Three Texts on Psycholinguistics, Arranged Chronologically

Foss & Hakes (1978)
  The Study of Language
  Aspects of Linguistic Competence
  Perceiving Speech
  The Process of Comprehension
  Memory and Comprehension
  Sentence Production
  Producing Speech After it is Planned
  Learning to Produce Utterances
  Acquisition Processes and Learning to Understand Utterances
  Becoming Linguistically Competent
  Reading
  Language and the Brain
  Language and Thought in the Context of Language Diversity and Linguistic Universals

Garnham (1985)
  Introduction: How to Study Language Understanding
  The Contribution of Linguistics
  Recognizing Words
  Parsing: The Computation of Syntactic Structure
  Introduction to the Concept of Meaning
  Word Meaning
  Understanding Discourse and Text
  The Structure of the Language Processor
  Language Production and its Relation to Comprehension

Garman (1990)
  Characteristics of the Language Signal
  The Biological Foundations of Language
  Sources of Evidence for the Language System
  Processing the Language Signal
  Accessing the Mental Lexicon
  Understanding Utterances
  Producing Utterances
  Impairment of Processing

As an example, we can examine one of the questions that psycholinguists have investigated over the years: What role does semantics play in the comprehension of an utterance and what role does syntax play? In the following utterance, semantics would seem to play a major role in comprehension:

(1)   *Juan watched Roberto.*

The verb *watch* carries with it certain semantic notions that constrain the meaning of the sentence once the verb *watch* is encountered in the utterance. For example, there must be an animate being who performs the activity, *watch*, and there must be something (not restricted to an animate being) that is *watched*. To put this in other terms, once the processing mechanisms access the semantics of the verb *watch*, certain possibilities for the completion of the utterance are expected while others are ruled out. Thus, the process of comprehending a sentence like (1) involves calculations by the language processor that rules out certain other possibilities.

Pause to consider . . .

how semantics works during comprehension. After the beginning of each sentence below, what can you expect to follow and what kind of things would you rule out?

John's tennis coach said that he needs to learn to keep his eye on . . .

The frog jumped across the . . .

Fanny baked a . . .

John was startled when the phone . . .

Imagine that the following were actual sentences in English. What kind of interpretation would you give each. Why?

Cat dog chased.

Pig slop ate.

Tickled child parent.

We can contrast the simple active sentence (1) with the following passive sentence:

(2)   *Roberto was watched by Juan.*

In this case, it seems clear that syntax figures more prominently into comprehension. Although it is true that the processing mechanisms must still access the verb, *watch*, the syntax of the utterance is particularly important to ensure comprehension of "who saw whom." As the internal processors encounter, *was watched*, a series of syntactic consequences occurs, ruling out the possibility that Roberto was the one who did the watching. The function word, *by*, confirms this interpretation and correct syntactic relationships of the various nouns to the verb phrase is achieved. In a certain sense, the syntax of the sentence helps us to correctly uncover the intended meaning of the speaker. In contrast to the comprehension of (1) then, the processes involved in the comprehension of (2) rely more heavily on syntax during the on-line (or real-time) processing of meaning.

Pause to consider . . .

how you use syntax during comprehension. Match each phrase in column A with a corresponding phrase in column B. Then, explain what made you rule out certain semantically possible phrase combinations.

A	B
Mary baked a . . .	to be quiet.
John baked some . . .	is a nice guy.
I think John . . .	cookies.
I want John . . .	pie.

This same relationship between semantics and syntax can be seen when contrasting the following two utterances:

(3)   *Maria has money.*

(4)   *Maria has spent her money.*

As it accesses the semantics for the verb *have*, the processing mechanism may encounter two options: (1) *have = possess* and (2) *have =* auxiliary verb. Comprehension of the sentence is not complete until the words following *have* are computed and analyzed. The processing mechanism must determine the function of *have*. This is a syntactic issue.

As these simple examples illustrate, linguistic knowledge or competence implies that users of a language must also possess some kind of mechanism that mediates between the speech signal and their linguistic knowledge. Clearly, the processing of sentences during the act of listening happens at astonishingly fast speeds. The computation of the sentences (1) and (2) happens for most native speakers within the blink of an eye. The nature of the processing mechanism becomes even more important and the question of processing speed more critical when longer and more complex sentences, such as (5), are involved.

(5)   *Ramón was the one who said that Manuel was punched in the face during the fracas between Julieta and Gloria.*

One of the primary goals of psycholinguistic inquiry has been to develop a model of speech comprehension. Over the years, debate has centered on two issues: The first issue is whether the model should be semantically driven or syntactically driven. In a largely semantically driven model, the relationship between elements in an utterance (e.g., nouns to verbs) is based on the semantics of the verb and the listener's knowledge of the real world. The processing mechanism first responds to an incoming speech stream by accessing lexical and real-world information and making a tentative decision about the meaning of the utterance. Thus, with sentence (2), the listener first ascertains the meaning of *watch* and then computes who is more likely to see whom based on what he/she knows about Juan and Roberto (e.g., Juan is a private detective and Roberto is being tracked down). In a largely syntactically driven model, the processing mechanism would first code and tag the nouns as subjects/objects (syntactic categories) and also determine whether the sentence is active or passive (based on syntactic markers). With sentence (2), the processors would first determine that Juan is the agent of *was watched* and that the sentence is passive because of the *was . . . by* markers. The processors would then use this information to determine the correct meaning of the utterance (i.e., who did what to whom). In both models, semantics vs. syntax is not an either/or dichotomy in that the model is not based solely on one or the other. When we say "largely semantic" we mean that the semantics and context of the situation are computed first and that syntax serves as a back-up for confirmation. When we say "largely syntactic" we mean that the syntax of the utterance is computed first and that the semantics and context of the situation serve as a back-up for confirmation.

The second issue in psycholinguistics has been whether the processor works in a serial or parallel manner. In a serial manner, the processor tags and accesses each sentential element from the linguistic system one at a time during on-line comprehension. Thus, with sentence (4), when the processor encounters, *has,* it must access its meaning and grammatical function. When the processor incorrectly determines that *has* is a full verb that means *possess,* then the function of the verb and its meaning will have to be reassigned when the processor accesses information on *spent.* In parallel processing, however, the processor tags and accesses various things at once. In sentence (4), for example, both *has* and *spent* could be processed at the same time, with the information on *spent* influencing the accessing of *has* before the meaning of *has* has been determined. This type of processing is obviously more efficient.

---

*P**ause to consider . . .*

why parallel processing is more efficient. Develop flow charts that represent serial and parallel processing for the sentence *Maria has spent her money.* Which flow of information would invite more errors and thus involves potentially longer processing time?

Psycholinguistics is not limited to what adult native speakers do. In fact, a branch of psycholinguistics known as "developmental psycholinguistics" is concerned with child language acquisition.

> ***Pause to consider . . .***
>
> what comes to mind when you think of the language of children. What are some of the characteristics of children's speech?

Historically, the study of child language acquisition began as an attempt to describe children's utterances, to discover how they differed from adult utterances, and to determine whether acquisition developed systematically. Researchers asked: "Is child language simply 'flawed' adult speech? Or does child language have its own 'grammar'?" Research soon revealed that child language is indeed not flawed adult speech. Instead, child language appears to evolve over time, each stage uniquely characterized by particular constraints and rules. If we take LC to mean "linguistic competence," then acquisition research reveals that children's linguistic competence moves developmentally in the following way:

$$LC0 \rightarrow LC1 \rightarrow LC2 \rightarrow LC3 \ldots \rightarrow LC \text{ adult-native}$$

At each point in time (0, 1, 2, 3 . . . adult-native), the child's linguistic competence can be described and is different from the point before and the one after. Each stage does not suggest a mere accumulation of linguistic information; it appears that linguistic rules may actually change from stage to stage. For example, when children acquire past-tense forms, their language reveals particular stages as summarized in Table 1.2. At first, children do not mark verbs for tense. This is followed by a stage in which high frequency irregular past-

TABLE 1.2. Stages in the Acquisition of Past-tense Forms in English by Child First Language Learners

Stage 1: no past tense markers
Daddy go

Stage 2: some common irregulars
Daddy went
but
Daddy talk

Stage 3: regulars appear, previous irregulars drop out and are regularized
Daddy talked
but
Daddy goed/Daddy wented

Stage 4: irregulars reappear
Daddy talked
Daddy went

tense verbs are marked for tense. This second stage is followed, in turn, by one in which the regular past-tense ending is acquired and also applied to irregular verbs through overgeneralization. The final stage involves the "reacquisition" of the irregular past-tense verb forms.

tense verbs are marked for tense. This second stage is followed, in turn, by one in which the regular past-tense ending is acquired and also applied to irregular verbs through overgeneralization. The final stage involves the "reacquisition" of the irregular past-tense verb forms.

In this example, the child is not merely adding past tense to his/her linguistic competence. At each stage he/she is also *adjusting the rule of application* for past-tense forms. Rule adjustment may be due to a variety of factors or processes, and these must be inferred from the observed production data. Some psycholinguists have suggested that children possess at birth particular constraints on how language data can be organized. Thus, as language is processed, these internal mechanisms operate on the data in particular ways to organize it. One result may be overgeneralization of a rule or form as exemplified in the third stage of the acquisition of the past-tense markers. It may also be assumed that at each stage the learner is processing the input data differently than during a previous stage, such that particular features of the language are more or less "in focus" during on-line comprehension. Thus, in stage one, the learner may not even "catch" past-tense forms in the input during comprehension but instead focuses on content words.

> ## *Pause to consider . . .*
>
> that acquisition of form is not simply cumulative but is qualitative in that rules are adjusted, not merely augmented, at various stages. Can you think of any other examples (See Bardovi-Harlig, Ch. 2)?

Developmental psycholinguistics has not limited itself to child language production; it has also looked at how children comprehend speech and the role of syntax in that comprehension. For example, while adults easily comprehend passives, children do not. Let's take our passive sentence from before.

(2) Roberto was watched by Juan.

In the early stages of acquisition, children have a 50% chance of correctly identifying that Juan did the watching and Roberto was the one watched in sentence (2). In the subsequent stage, children reveal a marked increase in *miscomprehension* of the sentence and incorrectly interpret Roberto as the "watcher" and Juan as the "watched." Later, they show marked improvement in correctly interpreting the sentence, and by age 6 or 7 always seem to interpret passives correctly. At about this same time, they begin to produce passives themselves.

To summarize, psycholinguistics studies the processes underlying speech production and comprehension.[2] Its goal has been to develop a model of language processing. Developmental psycholinguistics is the study of children's linguistic systems and how these systems are used in language production and comprehension.

P*ause to consider . . .*

the example of children's processing of passive sentences. Why would children at a certain age consistently misinterpret sentences, such as *John was watched by Roberto*, *The cow was kicked by the horse*, and *Jeffrey was knocked over by Alex*? Are children relying on syntax or semantics to process these sentences?

HOW IS PSYCHOLINGUISTICS RELEVANT TO SECOND LANGUAGE ACQUISITION?

As we have noted, psycholinguistics concerns itself with how children acquire language and with what factors are involved in the comprehension and production of language. Clearly, then, second language acquisition theory and research has a great deal in common with psycholinguistics, for it is concerned above all with how individuals internalize a second (or subsequent) linguistic system and with what factors are involved in the comprehension and production of non-native language. Although many teachers may see second language acquisition in the classroom as an issue of instruction and practice, researchers and theorists recognize that certain processes and factors independent of instruction and practice govern second language acquisition. In fact, research has fairly consistently shown that second language learners pass through developmental stages in the acquisition of grammatical features and that these stages are the same whether the learner is in a classroom or not. Thus, whatever psycholinguistic processes may be responsible for second language acquisition, they do not change from context to context. As Susan Gass, a noted scholar in second language acquisition, states:

> It is difficult to imagine a situation in which the fundamental processes involved in learning a non-primary language would depend on the context in which the language is learned. In particular, the psycholinguistic tasks learners are faced with, the abilities that learners come to the learning situation with, the potential motivation they bring to the learning task do not depend on the learning situation, whether it be a foreign language classroom, a second language classroom in a second language environment, or so-called naturalistic "street" learning in a second language situation. . . . The task facing a second language learner is to come up with a grammar of a second language (grammatical competence) and to develop the ability to put that knowledge to use (Gass 1990, p. 35).

We can illustrate Gass's point easily by beginning with the notion of input. Based on Krashen's (1982, 1985) claims, it is widely recognized—if not universally accepted in second language acquisition research and theory—that learners, regardless of context, need access to comprehensible meaning-bearing input in order to acquire a grammatical system. By comprehensible meaning-bearing input, we mean language that learners hear (or see when reading) to which they attend for its propositional content: That is, the language encodes a message or messages that the learner is supposed to understand. At the same time, the learner must be able to grasp that message: that is, to decode it in some way so that the message is understood. We can characterize the input-dependent nature of second language acquisition in the following way:

input → developing system

Implied in this scheme is the notion that acquisition is inextricably bound to comprehension. Although acquisition of a grammar may not be completely dependent on comprehension, comprehension is surely the starting point for acquisition. As pointed out previously, one of the principal domains of inquiry in psycholinguistic research is the factors and processes involved in language comprehension. Because comprehension is an area of psycholinguistic inquiry, psycholinguistics is relevant to second language acquisition.[3]

It would seem, then, that second language acquisition theory and research would have a great deal to gain by a careful study of how learners process input data. What mechanisms and psycholinguistic strategies do learners use to tag and decode an input string during the act of comprehension? Do second language learners process input data as they process sentences in their native language? Do they process input data like child language acquirers? Do they use both native and childlike processing mechanisms? Or do second language learners have unique ways of processing input data?

The answers to the above questions are important for they will help us understand how second language learners create intake data. "Intake" refers to that subset of the input that learners actually process in some way during comprehension. It has been hypothesized that not all input data get attended to, that the data are filtered in some way, resulting in intake. It is the intake that forms the actual data made available for acquisition by the developing system. Thus, the scheme above needs to be altered in the following way:

input → intake → developing system

Pause to consider . . .

the relationship of intake data to input data. Intake is defined as "that subset of the input that learners actually attend to process in some way during comprehension." The term, *subset*, however, invites a purely quantitative distinction between input and intake: That is, the latter is simply construed to be a reduced part of the former. Is it possible that intake may be *qualitatively* different from the input? That is, is it possible to attend to input data but to misinterpret it in some way? (Hint: Review the brief discussion above about children's interpretation of passive structures in English.)

Recent research reveals the importance of understanding input processing from a psycholinguistic perspective (see, for example, VanPatten 1996). If the input that a learner gets contains abundant examples of a linguistic feature, why doesn't that feature appear immediately in the learner's output? The answer may be that the learner does not initially perceive and process the linguistic feature in the input. This can be illustrated with an example of tense processing in Spanish.

Like English, Spanish inflects verbs for present/past tense distinction: *toma* 'she takes' vs. *tomó* 'she took.' Unlike English, Spanish does not rely on modal verbs for other tenses or moods (e.g., future *tomará* 'she will take' and subjunctive *tome* 'she might/may take'). That is, Spanish inflects the verb for all tenses and moods and does not rely on modals, such as *will* or *may*. Also unlike English, Spanish inflections are syllabic and nonpresent inflections carry strong stress, hence the written accent in the examples given here. In short, Spanish has a relatively clear and consistent verb-final marking system for tense. Now, one could argue that second language learners of Spanish are confronted with these forms in the input and that they should be able to acquire them relatively easily. However, a closer look at how learners process input data reveals that this may not be the case. VanPatten (1996) develops a series of processing principles regarding the manner in which learner attention is directed during on-line (real time) comprehension:

P1. Learners process input for meaning before they process it for form.

P1(a). Learners process content words in the input before anything else.

P1(b). Learners prefer processing lexical items to grammatical items (e.g., morphological markings) for semantic information.

P1(c). Learners prefer processing "more meaningful" morphology before "less or non-meaningful morphology."

In these principles, it is postulated that the learner's processing mechanisms are driven by communicative efficiency: that is, how to get the most meaning with the least effort. This is predicated on a key aspect of comprehension, namely, the limited capacity of an individual's working memory.[4] Processing and accessing the semantics of lexical items is a key function of the learner's internal processors. Of most relevance to the present discussion is P1(b). Note that tense, while marked by grammatical inflections, may also be indicated by adverbs of time.

(6) *¿Qué leyó Juanita anoche?*

'What did Juanita read **last night?**'

(7) *Mi madre me llamó el sábado pasado.*

'My mother called me this **last Saturday.**'

In these examples, the grammatical inflections for tense are redundant. In various studies conducted at the University of Illinois (Musumeci 1989; Cadierno, Glass, Lee & VanPatten, forthcoming), we are finding that learners rely primarily on lexical indications of tense and not grammatical inflections when processing input, both at the sentence level and at the paragraph level. Put another way, the processing mechanism is apparently not picking up the grammatical features of the language and thus the intake data do not contain the relevant grammatical information. Independent research on the output of second language learners reveals that tense is first marked in the output via lexical means, that is, by adverbs of time (see, for example, Bardovi-Harlig 1992). This seems to indicate that—at least in the early stages of acquisition— learners' processing mechanisms are causing the intake data to be more lexically rich than grammatically rich. The developing system is apparently not getting the inflectional morphology in the early stages.

Eventually, many learners do acquire tense inflections. This may be accounted for by another processing principle.

> P2. For learners to process form that is not meaningful, they must be able to process informational or communicative content at no (or little) cost to attention.

With this principle, we postulate that as learners get better at real-time comprehension, their processors are less taxed than in earlier stages. Attention is "freed up" to capture elements of the input string that were skipped over in previous stages. The resulting intake data are grammatically richer. Returning to examples (6) and (7), in the earlier stages of acquisition, as learners process input data they are most likely attending to content words (e.g., *yesterday, last week, tomorrow*) as indicators of tense. This is predicted by P1(a) and (b) and corroborated by the research cited earlier. The past-tense markers are most likely no more than "noise" in the input in this stage. Later, as learners become better at comprehending utterances, processing space is freed up and the "noise" of previous input (in this case past-tense markers) can become a candidate for processing. In the later stages, the effort needed to comprehend utterances is not as great as in the earlier stages. Effort can now be directed toward features in the input that were previously skipped over during processing.

---

*P*ause to consider . . .

that language learners may not process formal features of language when comprehension is effortful and resources are drained. In what ways does the output of early-stage second language learners suggest that they are attending mostly to content words in the input? Is this any different from what children learning their first language do?

This is just one example of how the psycholinguistics of second language input processing is relevant to understanding second language acquisition. Input processing is, of course, more complex than indicated by this relatively simple example. Input processing also concerns how learners compute the structural relationships among elements of an utterance. Although the adult native speaker may clearly recognize what the subject, object, and so on is, when processing an input string this may not be the case for the language learner. Language learners may think they understand but may, in fact, not and consequently miscompute the relationships. LoCoco (1987), VanPatten (1984), Lee (1987), for example, found that learners of Spanish may ignore prepositional case marking and miscompute the grammatical function of non-subject nouns and pronouns that occur before the verb.[5] In the following example, a typical learner's misinterpretation is asterisked:

A Juan	*no*	*lo*	*admira María*	*para nada.*
Juan-OBJ	doesn't	him-OBJ	admire Mary-SUBJ	at all.

'Mary doesn't admire John at all.'

"*John doesn't admire Mary at all."

Me	*llamó*	*mi hermana*	*anoche.*
Me-OBJ	called	my sister-SUBJ	last night.

'My sister called me last night.'

"*I called my sister last night."

The consequence of incorrect input processing should be clear. As learners incorrectly process input sentences, the developing system is given incorrect intake data with which to work. This is confirmed by the output of learners of Spanish when they often use object pronouns as subject pronouns, the lack of object case marker *a*, a rigid adherence to subject-verb-object word order, and the overuse of subject marking.[6] Clearly, the intake the learners are deriving from the input is not what many teachers think it is.

In short, the creation of a linguistic system can be studied from a psycholinguistic perspective. In fact, it could be argued that, at some level, second language acquisition must be studied from a psycholinguistic perspective. How learners process input strings may reveal a great deal about why their linguistic systems develop the way they do.[7]

Is Psycholinguistics Relevant to Language Teaching?

It is fair to say that most instruction in the grammar of a second language is structurally and not psycholinguistically motivated (Garrett 1986). This is particularly true of instruction in foreign language classrooms in the United States. Features of grammar are taught and practiced in a sequence inherited from the Latin grammarians of the Roman Empire. In terms of practice, emphasis is placed on manipulation of forms and structure in learner output. At no point in explicit grammar instruction do the practices seem to reflect understanding of language processing: That is, explicit instruction and practice in grammar do not consider how learners attend to grammatical information in the input. In this section, I describe how psycholinguistics can make a significant contribution to language teaching practice.

First, we should acknowledge that the research on explicit instruction in grammar has tended to focus on one of two issues: (1) whether grammar should be taught and (2) what aspects of grammar should be taught. The consensus has been that instruction can speed up acquisition, but not alter the fundamental stages that a learner must traverse en route to developing a nativelike system. In addition, it is not clear that instruction is necessary and, at least in some instances, it has been reported that premature instruction may be detrimental. In all this research, an important question goes unasked. If we were to know something about how learners get grammatical information from the input, may not the more pertinent question be *how* we should teach grammar? In asking this question, we are also asking *what psycholinguistic processes the instruction seeks to affect.*

A series of investigations (Cadierno 1995; Cheng 1995; VanPatten & Cadierno 1993; VanPatten & Sanz 1995);[8] has taken an input processing perspective on grammar instruction. That is, the question is asked: "How do learners process input data?" and then "Can instruction alter the way in which learners process input data to make their intake grammatically richer?" and "Would such instruction be better than traditional instruction?" If grammar acquisition is linked to comprehension, then traditional output-based instruction should have at best, limited effects.

Using subjects from Spanish, several studies conducted at the University of Illinois have compared traditional output-based instruction (explanation plus drills and communicative activities) to what we called *processing instruction* (explanation plus *structured input activities*). Structured input activities are those in which learners hear and see a grammatical feature in the input and must use it to process the utterance for meaning. In one experiment on past tense (Cadierno 1995), adverbials are absent from all structured input activities. Learners rely on the grammatical inflections to get tense when comprehending the utterances. In another experiment (VanPatten & Cadierno 1993) learners are taught not to rely on a processing strategy of "first noun = subject" and must correctly interpret preverbal objects and object pronouns as well as postverbal subjects. During processing instruction, learners are not required to produce anything: only to respond to input utterances in some way. For example, learners may respond by indicating "true/false," "possible/impossible," "applies to me/doesn't apply to me" or by using other binary options. Learners may add information to an input utterance (e.g. fill in a name, a time, a place, and so on). They may match some kind of visuals to input utterances or match input utterances with logical follow-up utterances (see Lee & VanPatten 1995, Ch. 5). In these experiments, we compared both traditional instruction and processing instruction to a control group that was not instructed on the items in question.

Using a design in which the subjects' knowledge and performance are measured both before instruction and afterwards, we tested their ability to both *interpret* and *produce utterances* in the second language. In one experiment, we added a narrative task to see how learners could handle connected discourse in production. Our results have been clear and consistent. Subjects in the processing group make significant gains in both comprehension and production, while the traditional group makes significant gains in production only. This is important in that subjects in the processing groups never once produced the targeted grammatical items during instruction. This suggests that processing instruction, because it is linked to comprehension and, because we know that comprehension is related to acquisition, is providing better intake to the developing system. Traditional instruction is not tied to comprehension and, therefore, does not affect the developing system in the same way.

What needs to be underscored here is how our research on grammar instruction is psycholinguistically motivated. In researching processing instruction, we began with the accepted claim that input drives acquisition. We then fashioned instruction out of what we believed about how *learners process input data;* we did not fashion it out of some preconceived idea of how language is structured and what learners need to know. Thus, our experimental instruction was informed by prior psycholinguistic research. Our pedagogical research confirmed that our question concerning how to teach grammar is a valid one. It is not enough to ask whether or what one should teach; one must also ask on what processes instruction seeks to have an impact.

---

*P*ause to consider . . .
_____

the idea that grammar instruction should affect processes. How is this different from more traditional conceptualizations of grammar instruction? How does "affecting processes" differ from or how does it overlap with "affecting knowledge"?

CONCLUSION

It is not my intention to turn instructors into psycholinguists engaged in research and development of new approaches to grammar instruction. My aim is rather to point out how psycholinguistics can inform the practice of language instruction. Because much of second language acquisition is psycholinguistic in nature, language teachers can benefit greatly by having knowledge about input processing. To this end, I suggest that teacher education for second language instructors include a substantial formal component that focuses on language comprehension as it relates to acquisition. Knowing that some features of language are more difficult to process in the input than others, knowing that the learners' processing mechanisms may predispose them to tag the input in particular (and possibly incorrect ways), knowing that comprehension cannot be equated with acquisition will give the instructor insight into why learners sometimes have difficulty acquiring grammar. With this knowledge comes a greater appreciation for the complexities of the task facing second language learners. With this knowledge comes a better sense of one's role in helping learners with that task.

Pause to consider . . .

what you think are the most important ways that knowledge of psycholinguistics will help you as a language teacher.

NOTES

[1] I would like to thank the editors, Kathleen Bardovi-Harlig and Beverly Hartford, for comments on a draft of this chapter. I would also like to thank the following people who read all or parts of the chapter throughout its development and made comments: Sally Magnan, James F. Lee, Cristina Sanz.

[2] For simplicity, we have focused only on spoken language in this discussion.

[3] The present discussion ignores the role that culture and sociolinguistic issues may bear upon meaning in comprehension.

[4] A discussion of capacity and memory would take us far beyond the focus of the present chapter. See VanPatten (1996) for detailed discussion.

[5] Unlike English, Spanish does not have rigid subject-verb-object word order.

[6] Spanish does not require subject pronouns and, in many cases, it is wrong to use them.

[7] Speech production has not been addressed here because, as a psycholinguistic phenomenon, it is relatively unexplored. It would seem, however, that issues in access and retrieval during speech production would prove to be important in understanding how learners create utterances (cf. Schmidt [1992] for a discussion of the development of fluency and accuracy in output).

[8] See VanPatten (1996) for a summary of these studies.

KEY TERMS, CONCEPTS, AND ISSUES

psycholinguistics
  speech comprehension
  speech production
  role of semantics
  role of syntax
  on-line processing
  serial vs. parallel processing
developmental psycholinguistics
  adjusting rule of application vs. simple accumulation
the relevance of psycholinguistics to SLA
  context of learning
  input vs. intake

developing system
acquisition is inextricably linked to comprehension
processing principles
processing mechanisms may not pick up grammatical features
the relevance of psycholinguistics to language instruction
structurally- vs. psycholinguistically-motivated grammar instruction
processing instruction and structured input

EXPLORING THE TOPICS FURTHER

1. *General Psycholinguistics.* A good, short, and accessible introduction to major developments in psycholinguistics from a historical perspective is Tanenhaus (1988). For a more complete and updated overview of the field of psycholinguistics, see Garman (1990) and the various chapters of Newmeyer (1988).

2. *Psycholinguistics and Second Language Acquisition.* One of the first works to appear on the psycholinguistics of second language acquisition is Hatch (1983). This is a very readable book but has not been updated since its original publication and perhaps should be read in conjunction with Garman (see above) or a similar comprehensive text. For a model of input processing and its relationship to second language grammatical development, see VanPatten (1996).

REFERENCES

Bardovi-Harlig, K. (1992). The use of adverbials and natural order in the development of temporal expression. *IRAL, 30,* 199–220.

Cadierno, T. (1995). Formal instruction from a processing perspective: An investigation into the Spanish past tense. *Modern Language Journal, 79,* 179–193.

Cadierno, T., Glass, W.R., Lee, J.F., & VanPatten, B. (Forthcoming). The effects of lexical and grammatical cues on processing past temporal reference in second language input. *Applied Language Learning.*

Cheng, A. (1995). *Grammar instruction and input processing: The acquisition of Spanish ser and estar.* Unpublished doctoral thesis, University of Illinois at Urbana-Champaign.

Foss, D. & Hakes, D. (1978). *Psycholinguistics: An introduction to the psychology of language.* Inglewood Cliffs, NJ: Prentice Hall.

Garman, M. (1990). *Psycholinguistics.* Cambridge: Cambridge University Press.

Garnham, A. (1985). *Psycholinguistics: Central Topics.* London: Methuen.

Garrett, N. (1986). The problem with grammar: What kind can the language learner use? *The Modern Language Journal, 70,* 133–148.

Gass, S.M. (1990). Second and foreign language learning: Same, different, or none of the above? In B. VanPatten & J. F. Lee (Eds.) *Second Language Acquisition-Foreign Language Learning* (pp. 34–44). Clevedon, UK: Multilingual Matters.

Hatch, E.M. (1983). *Psycholinguistics: A second language perspective.* Rowley, MA: Newbury.

Krashen, S. (1982). *Second language acquisition and second language learning.* London: Longman.

Krashen, S.D. (1985) *The input hypothesis.* London: Longman.

Lee, J.F. (1987). Morphological factors influencing pronominal reference assignment by learners of Spanish: Dedicated to Joseph H. Matluck. In T.A. Morgan, J.F. Lee, & B. VanPatten (Eds.) *Language and language use: Studies in Spanish* (pp. 221–232). Lanham, MD: University Press of America.

Lee, J.F. & VanPatten, B. (1995). *Making communicative language teaching happen.* New York: McGraw-Hill.

LoCoco, V. (1987). Learner comprehension of oral and written sentences in German and Spanish: The importance of word order. In B. VanPatten, T. Dvorak, & J.F. Lee (Eds.) *Foreign language learning: A research perspective* (pp. 119–129). Cambridge, MA: Newbury House.

Musumeci, D. (1989). *The ability of second language learners to assign tense at the sentence level: A cross-linguistic study.* Unpublished doctoral thesis, University of Illinois at Urbana-Champaign.

Newmeyer, F. (Ed.) (1988). *Linguistics: The Cambridge survey. Volume III. Language: Psychological and biological aspects.* Cambridge: Cambridge University Press.

Tanenhaus, M. K. (1988). *Psycholinguistics: An overview.* In Newmeyer. (Ed.) pp. 1–37.

VanPatten, B. (1984). Learners' comprehension of clitic pronouns: More evidence for a word order strategy. *Hispanic Linguistics, 1,* 57–67.

VanPatten, B. (1996). *Input processing and grammar instruction: Theory and research.* Norwood, NJ: Ablex.

VanPatten, B. & Cadierno, T. (1993). Explicit instruction and input processing. *Studies in Second Language Acquisition, 15,* 225–243.

VanPatten, B. & Sanz, C. (1995). From input to output: Processing instruction and communicative tasks. In F. Eckman (Ed.) *Second language acquisition and pedagogy* (pp. 169–185). Hillsdale, NJ: Earlbaum.

CHAPTER 2

The Place of Second Language Acquisition Theory in Language Teacher Preparation

Kathleen Bardovi-Harlig
Indiana University

INTRODUCTION

In the professional language teaching journals of the 1970s and early 1980s, linguistic analysis of pedagogical grammar points provided the link between the language teaching profession and "science."[1] Recurrent in these articles was the assumption that the better or more accurately we could describe language, the easier it would be for learners to learn it.

Such a view reveals at least two things about the language teaching profession at the time: (1) The field viewed linguistics as providing legitimacy,[2] and (2) Teachers were seen as the central figures in classroom language learning, and their explicit linguistic knowledge and their presentation of that knowledge was seen as a key to the success of their students.

Much has changed. The linguistic descriptions found in the various journals of applied linguistics have been gradually replaced by articles that focus on second language acquisition, investigations not into the formal representation of linguistic constructs, but investigations into how learners come to acquire a second language in and out of classrooms. The grounding of pedagogical innovation now includes knowledge of how learners learn language. This increasing focus on the language learner as the central figure in the classroom is an important step in the development of the field (cf. VanPatten, Ch. 1; Beck, Ch. 3; Tarone & Yule 1989). Presentations of the learner as language processor or the learner as "knower," preprogrammed for language, serve as evidence of the shift in approach. With this shift comes the recognition that language students are primarily language *learners*, not primarily *students*.

With the shift in the field to the recognition that the learner—not the teacher—is the central figure in language acquisition, a gradual shift also has occurred toward including or requiring a course in second language acquisition in many language teacher preparation programs, whether in masters degree programs in foreign languages or in Applied Linguistics/TESOL. It is the contention of these programs that it is no longer sufficient for language teachers to be knowledgeable solely in the structure and use of the language they teach; they should also understand the process by which linguistic knowledge develops.

Because not every language teacher preparation program has a course on second language acquisition, required or optional, it is relevant to ask: "Why include a course in second language acquisition in a language-teacher education program?" I suggest that second language acquisition research:

1. Defines the process and product of second/foreign language acquisition;
2. Identifies factors that influence acquisition;
3. Suggests certain areas of instruction (which is different from methods);
4. Helps teachers to evaluate methods and materials;
5. Dispels myths;
6. Contributes to the definition of the roles of the learner and teacher; and
7. Increases a teacher's access to the professional literature.

I discuss each point individually, although evidence for the various points overlaps somewhat.

Before continuing, I would like to point out what appear to be limits on second language acquisition research to inform classroom teaching practice. Second language acquisition research does not determine method; it is not the "answer" for language teaching. It is one discipline among many with which language teachers should become familiar during their preparation. The goal of studying second language acquisition should be to learn ways of viewing the acquisition process. Teachers should be better prepared for and should better understand the successes and limitations that they and their learners encounter in language classrooms.[3]

WHAT IS SECOND LANGUAGE ACQUISITION?

The study of language acquisition has interpreted language in a broad sense, beyond pedagogical interpretations of the notion of grammar. Thus, language acquisition research addresses not only the acquisition of morphology and syntax (which are typically thought of as comprising grammar from a pedagogical perspective), but also phonology (pronunciation), lexicon (vocabulary), and semantics (meaning). In addition, pragmatics (language use) is often studied as is the construction and organization of conversation and writing.

I use the term, "second language acquisition" to encompass the learning of a second or foreign language with or without instruction. The term *second* is used broadly to mean any language learned after the first language(s) and may include second-, third-, or fourth-learned languages. Whereas investigations of first language acquisition exclusively involve children (hence the term *child language acquisition*), investigations of second language acquisition often focus on adult language learners, but may also include teenagers and children. The term, *second* is also used to distinguish *host* environment experiences, where learners learn the language spoken in the area (such as learning English in the United States or Canada, or Spanish in Latin America), from *foreign* experiences where learners learn a language not commonly spoken in the area (such as learning English in Japan, or French in the United States). Host, or second, language experiences may take place in or out of the classroom (i.e., they may be instructed or uninstructed), whereas foreign language learning is generally instructed. The study of acquisition in the host and foreign settings can be narrowly referred to as second language acquisition (SLA) and foreign language learning (FLL), respectively (cf. VanPatten & Lee 1990). Second language acquisition is also used as a general term, which includes both environments (VanPatten 1990); this is the way it is used here.

Defining the Process and Product of Language Acquisition

Second language acquisition takes a learner-centered view of the language acquisition process. This view assumes that the main activity in a second/ foreign language classroom is language acquisition. Under this view, understanding second language acquisition is an attempt to understand what learners are doing in the instructional setting. Understanding what learners *do* in the instructional setting can be further divided into understanding the process of acquisition (i.e., the stages or sequences observed across time or across levels of proficiency) and understanding the outcome (i.e., the language produced by learners at any one stage).

Awareness of acquisitional processes and developmental stages can help teachers assess linguistic development in a more insightful manner than can be done by an external measure, such as a course syllabus or a textbook sequence. The acquisition of a morpheme or a syntactic construction generally proceeds in a series of stages. The stages are not taught to classroom learners, but they nevertheless emerge in the course of acquisition. Before considering how recognizing developmental stages relates to evaluation, consider two examples of developmental sequences, one each from the acquisition of tense and the acquisition of word order.

Although it is treated pedagogically as a single grammatical point, the past tense is acquired in a series of stages. Three stages common to both tutored and untutored learners (see Table 2.1) can be identified (Bardovi-Harlig 1992b, 1993; Meisel 1987; Schumann 1987).

In the earliest stage of temporal expression, no systematic use of tense/aspect morphology occurs. Another term for tense/aspect morphology is *verbal inflections*. In English, for example, tense/aspect morphology includes past (*-ed*, as in *talked*) and non-past (Ø, *-s*, as in *we go* and *he goes*), progressive

**TABLE 2.1. Stages of Acquisition of Temporal Expression in
Tutored and Untutored Learners**

Untutored Second Language Learners of German, English, French (Meisel 1987; Schumann 1987; Véronique 1987; Noyau 1990)	Tutored Second Language Learners of English (Bardovi-Harlig 1992b, 1994)

1. No explicit reference to time
  a. scaffolded discourse
  b. implicit reference (context)
  c. contrast of events
  d. chronological order
	1. No explicit reference to time
	  a. scaffolded discourse
	  b. implicit reference (context)
	  c. contrast of events
	  d. chronological order

2. Temporal reference established exclusively by adverbials	2,3. Temporal reference established primarily by adverbials; emergence of verbal morphology (unsystematic use)
3. Emergence of verbal morphology (unsystematic use)	
4. Increasingly systematic use of verbal morphology	4. Increasingly systematic use of verbal morphology; decline in use of adverbials
	5. Highly systematic use of verbal morphology
	6. Violations of chronological order ("Reverse Order Reports")
	7. Use of pluperfect

(*be + ing,* as in *is/was playing*), and perfect (*have + en,* as in *have/had seen.*) Without tense/aspect morphology, learners establish temporal reference in four ways:

1. By relying on the contribution of their fellow-speakers (scaffolded discourse);
2. Through reference inferred from a particular context (implicit reference);
3. By contrasting events; and,
4. By following chronological order in narration (Meisel 1987; Schumann 1987).

In the next stage, reference to the past is first expressed explicitly through the use of adverbial expressions (e.g., *yesterday, then, after*) and connectives (e.g., *and, because,* and *so*).[4] In the third stage, which follows the adverbial-only stage, verbal morphology appears, but is not used systematically. At this stage, learners continue to rely on time adverbials. As the use of tense morphology increases, the use of time adverbials decreases. A fourth stage, common only in tutored learners, is characterized by high rates of appropriate use of verbal morphology (Bardovi-Harlig 1992b).

*P**ause to consider . . .***

in what ways the production of temporal reference corresponds to the comprehension of temporal reference (cf. VanPatten's discussion in Ch. 1). In what general ways might production and comprehension be linked in second language acquisition?

A second example comes from the acquisition of word order in German (Pienemann 1989). In standard German, the subject and inflected verbal elements are inverted after the preposing of adverbial elements. Before learners produce sentences that exhibit inversion of the subject and the auxiliary, as in (1d), they pass through the stages in (1a-c):

(1a) *die kinder spielen mit ball*   [SVO, Stage X]
       the children play with ball

(1b) *da kinder spielen*   [Adverb Preposing, StageX+1]
       there children play

(1c) *alle kinder muss die pause machen*   [Verb Separation, Stage X + 2]
       all the children must the break have

(1d) *dann hat sie wieder die knoch gebringt*   [Inversion, Stage X + 3]
       then has she again the bone bringed

In (1a), learners exhibit the first stage of subject-verb-object word order. In this stage, sentences generally conform to standard German word order. At Stage X + 1, learners acquire "adverb preposing", an optional rule which moves the adverb to sentence-initial position. In standard German, adverb preposing requires the inversion of the subject and inflected verbal element, a rule that is not acquired until Stage X + 3. Thus, at Stage X + 1, sentences with preposed adverbials are ungrammatical. In Stage X + 2, an obligatory rule is acquired: "verb separation" is required whenever the verb consists of an auxiliary plus main verb. The inflected auxiliary and the uninflected main verb are separated by moving the uninflected verb to clause-final position. Before verb separation is acquired, sentences of the type in (1c) have the same word order as those with main verbs only, as in (1a). Finally, "inversion" is acquired (Stage X + 3), and this brings sentences with adverbial preposing into target form.

*P**ause to consider . . .***

how these descriptions of second language acquisition compare to VanPatten's description of child-language acquisition in Chapter 1.

Although many more examples of acquisitional stages exist, these should be sufficient to illustrate that learner language (interlanguage) is not composed of a random collection of mistakes or imperfect utterances, but rather is a system with its own linguistic integrity. The view of acquisition as consisting of sequenced stages influences the evaluation of learner production.[5] At the end of every developmental sequence is potentially a targetlike production, which is formally correct (i.e., it has accurate morphological or syntactic form) and is used appropriately (i.e., used as native speakers would use it in the target language).[6] Between the starting point and the end point may be a series of stages that are prescriptively incorrect, but that indicate progress.

---

*P*ause to consider . . .

other cases in which one nontargetlike production might be "better" than another. Which of the following, *The goose are flying away/The gooses are flying away*, shows more knowledge and why? Can you think of other similar cases?

Returning to the issue of assessing the development of linguistic competence, this view of acquisition allows teachers to view nontargetlike production as progress, where appropriate. To see how this might work, consider three examples. First, taking an example from morphology, consider the case of the past tense in English. In the sentences (2a and 2b) both *tell* and *telled* are nontargetlike:

(2a) *Yesterday I tell Jimmy something.*

(2b) *Yesterday I telled Jimmy something.*

In (2a), *tell* indicates the use of a base form with no use of verbal morphology. In contrast, *telled* shows productive use of the past tense in (2b). The learner recognizes *yesterday* as requiring the use of the past tense. Developmentally, then, the sentence in (2b) contains a better "wrong" form than the sentence in (2a).

Consider again the example of the acquisition of word order in German. The first two stages are repeated here as (3a) and (3b):

(3a) *die kinder spielen mit ball*   [SVO, Stage X]
      the children play with ball

(3b) *da kinder spielen*   [Adverb Preposing, Stage X + 1]
      there children play

In (3a), Stage X learners produce a targetlike sentence with subject-verb-object order. In the next stage (X + 1), the acquisition of adverb preposing results in sentences that exhibit word-order errors because, although learners prepose the adverb, they have not yet acquired inversion which applies in German when the adverb is preposed. Nevertheless, sentences, such as (3b), show evidence of a later acquisitional stage than does the error-free sentence (3a).

Finally, consider another example from syntax, this time from English relative clauses. Again, in this case, error-free production suggests an earlier stage of linguistic development than does production with errors:

(4a) *John is talking to the man. The man is his brother.*

(4b) *The man who John is talking **to him** is his brother.*

Example (4a) shows two error-free single-clause sentences. Example (4b) shows the same informational content in which a learner attempts a relative clause. The use of the emergent relative clause reveals knowledge of subordination, even in the face of the use of the resumptive pronoun *to him* which is nontargetlike. Although acquisitionally, (4b) is more advanced than (4a), any evaluation dependent on error-free production would rate (4a) more highly than (4b), discounting the progress represented by (4b).

---

*P**ause to consider . . .***

how second language acquisition research views learner errors. How does this differ from traditional pedagogical approaches? What kinds of evaluations can be made from learners' errors?

Each of these sequences shows a case where a "wrong" answer shows evidence of a later stage of acquisition than does a simpler "right" answer. Familiarity with acquisitional sequences is not only relevant to the teacher in assessing the progress of individual learners, but is also relevant in evaluating effectiveness of methods and teaching techniques and materials. Thus, it may be important, and more acquisitionally informed, to ask not which classroom procedures give correct answers, but which result in progress toward target-like production.

In addition to contributing to understanding how learner grammars develop, acquisition research also contributes to the understanding of what variables influence the acquisition process.

Factors That Influence Acquisition

So far, I have concentrated on the development of linguistic competence itself. Yet of equal importance to understanding second and foreign language acquisition—and of direct relevance to the classroom—are the factors that influence acquisition. Such factors are often directly manipulated by methods of and approaches to language teaching.

The major difference between first and second language acquisition is the fact that although first language acquisition is uniformly successful, second language acquisition is characterized by variable success: Some learners are very successful, others show only limited success, and still others fall in between. In their review of the literature, Larsen-Freeman and Long (1991) discuss seven variables that influence acquisition: age, language aptitude, social-psychological factors, personality, cognitive style, and learning strategies. The socio-psychological factors can be further divided into the main categories of motivation and attitude (cf. Hartford, Ch. 5). Personality variables include self-esteem, extroversion, anxiety, risk-taking, sensitivity to rejection, empathy, inhibition, and tolerance of ambiguity.

Instruction is also an important factor in acquisition, and a growing body of literature exists which seeks to understand the relationship of acquisition to instruction. Several studies have claimed an advantage for instructed learners, which includes both rate of acquisition (instructed learners may move more quickly through the acquisition stages) and eventual level of attainment (instructed learners may reach higher levels of proficiency [Bardovi-Harlig 1995; Ellis 1990]). In contrast, instruction does not seem to affect the order of acquisition sequences or the order in which rules are acquired (Pienemann 1989). Several new studies have also investigated the interaction of particular presentations and the developing grammar from the perspective of learnability theory (Schwartz & Gubala-Ryzak 1992; White 1991, 1992; White, Spada, Lightbown & Ranta 1991; White & Trahey 1993).

---

*P**ause to consider . . .***

why the term, "instruction" is used instead of "teaching". What possibilities does this open?

From a pedagogical viewpoint it may seem somewhat surprising that second language acquisition researchers would investigate the influence of instruction—which, in fact, means that researchers question whether instruction always has the desired effect of promoting language acquisition. Pedagogically, at least, it is generally assumed that instruction ranges from helpful to necessary. In discussing the influence of instruction on acquisition, I return to each of the acquisitional sequences to which I referred earlier.

German Word Order

Pienemann (1989), Ellis (1989), VanPatten (1987), and Lightbown (1987) present convincing empirical evidence that instruction does not influence the order of acquisition. Pienemann (1989) illustrates this by comparing the changes in the grammars of learners of German at different stages of development in response to instruction. When the learners were given instruction on inversion (Stage X + 3, sentence (1d)), only the learner who had met the developmental prerequisite for acquiring inversion benefited from instruction. That is, only the learner who had reached Stage X + 2, the acquisition of verb separation, acquired productive use of inversion. Although all learners showed use of inversion on a grammar test, only the more advanced learner used inversion productively, whereas the less advanced learners did not. Pienemann argues that learners cannot "skip" a necessary developmental stage and acquire inversion even with instruction. In fact, learners who were only at Stage X + 1 (adverb preposing) retreated to Stage X, apparently avoiding adverb preposing which requires inversion. Pienemann posits the "Teachability Hypothesis," which states that the teachability of language is constrained by what the learner is ready to acquire. It predicts that instruction can only prompt language acquisition if the interlanguage is close to the point when the structure to be taught is acquired in the natural setting.

Reverse Order Reports

A second investigation of instruction comes from a longitudinal study of sixteen adult classroom learners of English as a second language (Bardovi-Harlig 1994). Written samples consisting primarily of daily journal entries were compared to the daily instructional logs completed by the students' grammar and composition teachers to study the relationship between instruction and the productive use of the pluperfect.

The pluperfect is one of the linguistic devices used in English to signal deviations from chronological order (i.e., "reverse-order reports;" Bardovi-Harlig 1994). Other linguistic devices include the use of adverbials, reported speech or thought, and indicators of causation. The pluperfect is commonly found in the background of narratives to present events which happened prior to those in the main story line. A typical example is *John entered college in 1980. He had graduated from high school five years earlier.*

Two ordered prerequisites exist for the emergence of pluperfect: First, a stable use of simple past tense, meaning a rate of appropriate use of past tense in past-time contexts of 80% or more (5a); and second, after the use of past tense stabilizes, the expression of reverse-order reports (5b). The pluperfect emerges later, with slightly higher group rates for the appropriate use of past tense (5c). In the following examples, the bracketed numerals indicate the order of occurrence of the reported events. The examples are from learners' journals (Bardovi-Harlig 1992b, 1994):

(5a)   Stable Use of Simple Past, Use of Chronological Order:
      I fixed the apartment with them [1] *and at 6:30 our friend came* [2]

(5b)   Emergence of Reverse-Order Reports:
      I went back to my apartment [2] ***after*** *I finished washing.* [1]
      My sister played piano very well. ***Before*** *she played* [2], *we were very nervous* [1].

(5c)   Emergence of Pluperfect:
      John and I went to her building [2]. *She had invited her friends.* [1]

Although all sixteen learners in the study eventually used reverse-order reports, only ten learners showed productive use of the pluperfect.

What is the effect of teaching the pluperfect on the interlanguage system? To answer this question, the record of instruction in the teaching logs was compared to the communicative use of the pluperfect in the daily journals kept by the learners.[7] It turns out that the effect of instruction is predictable on the basis of the stage of the individual learner at the time of instruction. If the learner has not satisfied the prerequisite stages, instruction has no apparent effect. The learners fall into three groups: those who used pluperfect before instruction, those who used pluperfect after instruction, and those who did not use the pluperfect in any language sample during the study.[8]

Six of the learners did not use the pluperfect in reverse-order reports in the texts sampled, in spite of instruction. Four of these learners had not reached the requisite developmental stages. Two of those learners had not produced reverse-order reports before instruction. They showed use of reverse-order reports only after both periods of instruction and even then did not use the pluperfect. The other two exhibited reverse-order reports prior to the second period of instruction, but they showed rates of appropriate use of past at 71% and 69%, respectively, for that sampling period, which is under the group mean of 85% for the emergence of pluperfect. These rates appear to be too low to support the emergence of a new tense. Thus, these learners may be said not to have been ready to acquire a new form on the basis of not having satisfied the previous acquisitional stages. The remaining two learners who did not use the pluperfect showed high rates of appropriate use of past and use of reverse-order reports prior to instruction, but did not use the pluperfect. Six learners did use pluperfect reverse-order reports at some time after instruction. Some learners received repeated instruction on pluperfect, but only produced the pluperfect after the prerequisites were met.

The observed effect of instruction supports Pienemann's (1989) Teachability Hypothesis, that learners only benefit from instruction when they are at the stage at which they would have naturally acquired the rule in question (cf. Ellis 1990). The fact that not all learners who met both prerequisites ever attempted the pluperfect even with (repeated) instruction suggests that meeting the acquisitional stages, with or without instruction, is necessary, but not sufficient, for the emergence of the pluperfect. One possible reason for this is that learners use other available linguistic devices, such as time adverbials to express reverse-order reports, and these may be so effective communicatively that learners have no need to expand their grammars formally to express this semantic concept.[9]

Aspectual Classes

A third example illustrates the strength of acquisitional sequences in instructional settings. In the acquisition of *past* morphology, learners show the same pattern of acquisition whether they are learning English, French, or Spanish, whether they are receiving instruction or not, and whether they are learning in a host or foreign environment. Among the forces that shape the acquisition of the tense/aspect system are verbal aspectual categories that have to do with the internal constituency of events or situations. The distribution of the *past*, which includes the English simple past, the French *passé composé*, and the Spanish preterite, shows a decided bias toward aspectual classes. The best-known division of aspectual classes distinguishes between stative and dynamic (or "action") verb phrases (e.g., activities, accomplishments, and achievements). Among dynamic verbs, *past* morphology appears first with achievements, actions which may be thought of as a single point (e.g., *arrive, recognize, realize*), then accomplishments, which have both endpoints and duration (e.g., *build a house, write a paper,* or *read a book*), and finally activities which have no endpoint but do have duration (e.g., *sleep, walk,* or *play*).[10]

Andersen (1986, 1991) first described this acquisitional sequence for two natural child-learners of Spanish as a second language. A number of studies have since corroborated these findings with instructed and uninstructed adult learners of English as a second language (Bardovi-Harlig 1992a; Bardovi-Harlig & Bergström 1996; Bardovi-Harlig & Reynolds 1995; Bayley 1994; Robison 1990, 1995), Spanish as a foreign language (Hasbún 1993, 1995; Ramsay 1990), and French as a foreign language (Bardovi-Harlig & Bergström 1996; Bergström 1993, 1995; Kaplan 1987).[11] The data on which these studies are based come from a variety of sources, including oral interviews and narratives from the untutored learners, and written narratives, expository texts, and controlled elicitation tasks from the instructed learners. Given the evidence that similar patterns hold across languages, environments, and tasks, it seems clear that the particular distributional patterns cannot be attributed to instruction.

---

*P*ause to consider . . .

the ways in which instruction in second/foreign language affects acquisition. What does not seem to be affected by instruction?

Identifying Areas for Instruction

Second language acquisition research can indicate areas where learners show persistent differences from the target language. It may suggest that learners would benefit from a focus on a particular area or may suggest a particular approach to a problem. Areas of difficulty are not always predictable by linguistic measures like regularity (or lack thereof) or by measures of linguistic complexity. For example, this has proved to be the case in the acquisition of the preterite and imperfect in Spanish, and *passé composé* and *imparfait* in French. This mismatch in morphological complexity and acquisitional order was first discussed by Kaplan (1987) in the acquisition of French as a foreign language. In both French and Spanish, the imperfect is regular, whereas this is often not the case with the nonimperfect past tense (the preterite in Spanish and *passé composé* in French). Spanish preterite shows stem changes in frequently used verbs, such as *poner* 'put' (*puse,* 1st sg. pret. 'I put') and *poder* 'be able' (*pude* 1st sg. pret. 'I was able'). In French, the *passé composé* stands in opposition to the *imparfait.* The French *passé composé* is formally compound (containing an auxiliary and a participle, as in (*Jean*) *a chanté,* 'Jean sang/has sung') and thus is morphologically more complex than the imperfect (*Jean chantait,* 'Jean sang/was singing/would sing'). In addition, in the *passé composé,* two possible auxiliary verbs exist, *être* 'be' and *avoir* 'have,' whose use is lexically determined. Thus, in both Spanish and French, the imperfect is morphologically more regular and, in French, it is also morphologically less complex in terms of number of morphemes. Nevertheless, classroom language learners, like their untutored child counterparts (Andersen 1991), show earlier acquisition of nonimperfect past than imperfect past in both communicative and structured tasks (Bergström [1995] and Kaplan [1987] , for French; Hasbún [1995], for Spanish).

Moreover, studies of both university students learning French as a foreign language (Bardovi-Harlig & Bergström 1996; Bergström 1995) and elementary school children learning French in an immersion program (Harley & Swain 1978) show that learners use only a small number of lexical verbs in the imperfect. Thus, research indicates both that the imperfect is acquired late and that its use is limited by learners to certain verbs; however, neither can be predicted from a description of the target language.

In English, another area of difficulty for learners is related to the acquisition of tense and aspect and involves adverbs of frequency. Work done in English as a second language shows that learners pay more attention to local cues of tense, such as adverbs of frequency, than to global cues of tense, such as the established temporal frame of the text (Bardovi-Harlig 1992a; Bardovi-Harlig & Reynolds 1995). Until learners are very advanced, they respond to cues, such as *everyday* or *usually*, with the present tense, even when the context for past is clearly established by a temporal adverb, such as *last year* as in *Last year John usually leaves for school around 8 o'clock.* The acquisitional facts reveal that learners do not generalize the use of adverbs of frequency to past-tense environments.

Both of these situations, the case of the imperfect in Spanish and French and the case of past-tense use in English, highlight areas where learner language shows persistent differences from the target language. The distribution of forms in interlanguage suggests that, in both cases, learners would benefit from continued meaningful input in which the targeted constructs appear. These cases are addressed later.

In addition to specific points of grammatical competence which are problematic for learners, second language acquisition may also identify more general areas of potential instructional focus. One such area which has been recently identified as being in need of instructional support is pragmatic competence. Pragmatic competence can be viewed as the ability of language users to match language with contexts in which it is appropriate (Levinson 1983). A number of studies which form the growing field of interlanguage pragmatics convincingly argue that even advanced second/foreign language learners frequently exhibit nontargetlike norms in such areas as opening conversations (Omar 1991, 1992), closing conversations (Hartford & Bardovi-Harlig 1992), as well as in several different speech acts (cf. Kasper, Ch. 6, for a review).

Evaluation of Methods and Materials

Methods

An understanding of the processes of second language acquisition aids in the evaluation of methods in a nontrivial way. The knowledge of the variables involved provides a principled way of choosing among classroom practices. Any approach to language instruction that puts acquisition ahead of teaching should be more successful than approaches that do not.[12]

One issue that is addressed by almost all language teaching methods is that of correction. Although many methods have taken a variety of positions on correction, from explicit correction to paraphrase and subtle reiteration, second language acquisition research now appears to have some insight into different types of responses to error based on the type of error made by the learner. Overgeneralizations may require a different response or treatment in the classroom than do undergeneralizations. Overgeneralizations result in a learner's using a rule or form too frequently, that is, in environments in which native speakers do not use it. Undergeneralizations result in a learner's not using a rule or form often enough, that is, not using it in environments where native speakers do. According to "subset theory," which is one type of "learnability theory," learners are thought to retreat from an overgeneralization only by negative evidence: that is, examples which show the learner that such strings are not possible in the target language. This suggests one particular type of error treatment in class.

In fact, learnability theory suggests that negative evidence is needed whenever the learner's grammar is not a subset of the target language. A subset grammar would include only a portion of the target grammar. However, everything included in the subset grammar is also included in the target grammar. When the learner's grammar is *not* a subset of the target grammar, it includes rules that the target grammar does not. Subset theory in second language acquisition draws on set theory from mathematics and defines sets in the same way. A case in which the learner grammar is not a subset of the target grammar can be found in the placement of adverbs in English interlanguage by native speakers of French as well as in the placement of adverbs in French by native speakers of English (White 1991, 1992). French and English both allow adverbs at the end of the verb phrase, as in (6a) and (6b), and in presubject position, as in (6c) and (6d). Adverbs may also occur after an auxiliary verb, as in (6e) and (6f):

(6a)   *Jean boit son café **rapidement.***

(6b)   *John drinks his coffee **rapidly.***

(6c)   ***Prudement** Jean a ouvert la porte.*

(6d)   ***Carefully** John opened the door.*

(6e)   *Jean a **souvent** visité la museé.*

(6f)   *John has **often** visited the museum.* (White 1991, p. 134)

However, English and French differ in other respects: In English, adverbs may not appear between the verb and its direct object, whereas they may in French, as in (7a) and (7b).

(7a)   *Marie regarde **souvent** la télévision.*

(7b)   **Mary watches **often** television.*

In contrast, the adverb may appear between the subject and the verb in English, but not in French, as in (8a) and (8b).

(8a) *Marie **souvent** regarde la télévision.*

(8b) *Mary **often** watches television.* (White 1991, p. 135)

The type of evidence needed by the learner of English who produces (7b) or the learner of French who produces (8a) is negative evidence. No amount of positive evidence, nor any number of good examples, shows the learner that the string, which is included in his or her grammar, is not part of the target language.[13]

Undergeneralizations, according to subset theory, can be treated by positive evidence: that is, more input that shows how the target language works by providing good examples. Such input should include examples of the constructions lacking in the learner's interlanguage. This suggests a different type of treatment in the classroom. One such case is the learner of French who does not produce sentences such as (7a) or the learner of English who does not produce sentences such as (8b). Positive evidence containing adverbs in the relevant positions for the respective target languages would allow learners to add such word orders to their grammars.

Another undergeneralization is found in the distribution of past tense in the environment of adverbs of frequency in English. We have already seen that learners do not use past tense everywhere native speakers do. This can be easily remedied by positive evidence that helps learners expand their grammars. In fact, because we want to add to the learner's knowledge, and not replace the knowledge the learner has, positive evidence is the most effective means. That is, we do not want learners *not* to use simple present tense with adverbs of frequency. We want them to be able to use past tense in that same local environment when the discourse context calls for it.

Thus, the general types of responses should not be determined by method, but by language development. However, the specific technique of responding to errors can and should be determined by language teaching method.

---

*P*ause to consider . . .

what type of evidence might be warranted to induce a change in learners' grammars in the case of some of the learner errors that you have observed. First, identify a specific error, then determine whether it is an overgeneralization or undergeneralization with respect to the target language. Finally, decide what type of evidence would best facilitate acquisition and provide a specific example of input that should be presented to the learner to help the grammar develop toward the target language norm.

Materials

On another level, the study of second language acquisition can assist teachers in evaluating materials. To a certain extent, materials are at least partly determined by the method one follows, but an independent question is whether materials constitute the type of input required. This also relates to the identification of potential areas of classroom focus discussed earlier in the section entitled "Identifying Areas for Instruction."

An important link between input and acquisitional stages is made by Andersen (1990) in the "Principle of Distributional Bias." Andersen (p. 58) hypothesizes that there are "properties of input that promote the incorporation of an inappropriate form-meaning relationship into the interlanguage," that is, input may sometimes (mis)lead learners and thus bring about certain acquisitional patterns. For example, a distributional bias toward using *past* with achievements in the input might tell learners that their hypotheses about English (or Spanish or French) which initially limit the past or preterite form to achievements and accomplishments are essentially right. Although Andersen employs the concept of distributional bias to explain the relationship of natural input to acquisition, it is also relevant to instructional input and, thus, to the evaluation of pedagogical materials. Relevant to this discussion is whether language textbooks—if not the sole source of input for language learners, often a high prestige source—codify this distinction between verbs. This would certainly not be done to mislead learners, but rather to give them the clearest possible examples of how grammatical aspect is used. If a distributional bias were to exist in the textbooks, then nonintroductory portions of the textbooks and other classroom input would need to include nonprototypical examples of tense/aspect use to help the learners expand their grammars.

A second case of a distributional bias occurs in the use of adverbs of frequency in English. Adverbs of frequency are typically used pedagogically to cue the use of simple present tense. Native speakers recognize this as a simplification, however, because they can produce not only sentence (9a), to which learners are exposed, but also sentence (9b), to which learners are not exposed in their textbooks:

(9a) *John usually leaves for school around 8 o'clock.*

(9b) *John usually left for school around 8 o'clock.*

Learners, in contrast, apparently do not recognize (9a) as simply a best-case (or prototypical) use of an adverb of frequency.

A combination of research findings from second language acquisition shows that, regardless of the tense that has been established by the discourse and the text in general, beginning and intermediate learners will mark verbs for present tense in the environment of the adverbs of frequency. Examination of a number of ESL/EFL textbooks reveal that textbooks do not explicitly show adverbs of frequency used with past-tense verbs. Pedagogical materials seem to be guilty of a distributional bias that may lead learners to stick with their hypothesis that frequency adverbs "mean" simple present tense. The modification or introduction of materials which provide evidence that sentences of the type of (9b) do, in fact, exist in English is incredibly easy, but not something that is obviously necessary coming from any particular teaching method (Bardovi-Harlig & Reynolds 1995). Results from second language acquisition research point to an area where positive evidence is necessary.

Moving from grammar to pragmatics once again, studies of acquisition have shown that learners often demonstrate substantial differences from native speakers in the execution of speech acts and other conversational moves. Surveys of current ESL materials show that even some common speech acts and conversational functions are not represented accurately and that others are not represented at all (Bardovi-Harlig, Hartford, Mahan-Taylor, Morgan & Reynolds 1991; Billmeyer & Boxer 1989; Williams 1988).

Pause to consider . . .

other areas in which language textbooks that you have used present idealizations or simplifications in grammar or areas of language use which may unintentionally provide insufficient input for the learners to acquire target-like competence.

DISPELLING MYTHS

Students often come into applied linguistics programs with various preconceived notions about how language learning works. I will not attempt to review them exhaustively, but I will briefly mention three. The most widespread myth that education in second language acquisition dispels is that the teacher is in (exclusive) control of the language learning process. When we begin to view acquisition as a sequence of stages which take time, we see the language learner as central to the language learning process. Research in related areas, such as language learning strategies (Oxford 1990; Oxford & Nyikos 1989; Wenden & Rubin 1987) and motivation (Dörnyei 1990, 1994; Gardner & Lambert 1972; Gardner & Tremblay 1994a, 1994b; Hartford, Ch. 5), emphasizes the degree to which acquisition centers on learners, not teachers.

A second pervasive myth is that of the first language or what I call the first-language-is-everything myth. The influence of a learner's first language is complex. A reasonable approach, outlined by Andersen (1983), claims that language acquisition is not exclusively driven by first language or by natural principles to the exclusion of first language, but rather is a mix. This is one area where host environment instructional settings, such as ESL classrooms, may offer a broader view of acquisition than foreign language settings. When teachers work in a foreign language setting where the learners are from a homogeneous language background and all the learners go through similar stages, it is tempting to attribute certain characteristics to the first language. In contrast, the ESL setting, due to its characteristically varied student populations, reveals that many stages are characteristic of language acquisition in general, and not of any first language in particular. The study of second language acquisition helps to distinguish between the universal and the particular.

A related myth is that each language is learned in a different way than other languages. It is clearly the case that languages have unique lexicons and morphology, and that culturally determined ways of using the language may exist. Nevertheless, the fundamental characteristics of language acquisition (the emergence in stages, the need for input, and so on) are the same.

Similarly, although different instructional settings of host or foreign language instruction have obvious differences that must be addressed, principles of language acquisition often cut across differences in settings (Ellis 1990, 1992; Gass 1989; Pienemann 1989). For example, a host environment does not guarantee contact with native speakers outside the classroom, and a foreign language setting does not guarantee impoverished input. Although *ease* of access to input is clearly different, *use* of available input depends on the learner. ESL teachers all know some learners who take such extensive advantage of the host environment that they only rarely come to class. More common, however, are ESL students who come to class daily, but exclusively speak the first language at home and associate only with first-language speaking friends. Foreign language teachers also know about students in junior-year-abroad programs who make very different living arrangements. Some participants elect to stay with native-speaking host families, but others select American roommates and spend their time with English-speaking friends, which greatly limits their exposure to the target language. In contrast, I have met many EFL learners who have gone to great lengths to secure and make use of English-language materials, including books and films, even in countries such as Albania which had been closed to the West for decades. In addition, foreign language programs, particularly among the less commonly taught languages, regularly host events designed to increase the availability of the target languages.[14] What second language acquisition can tell us about all of these situations is that it is not only the availability of input, but the use that learners make of the input, that is a predictor of development.

---

*P*ause to consider . . .

the myths that second language acquisition helps to dispel. What beliefs might underlie these statements?

1. "I met the new French teacher. She really knows French grammar inside and out! Her students are going to learn a lot."
2. "All my students, who are native Spanish-speakers, say *He no go* instead of *He doesn't go*. This is because negation is expressed that way in their native language."
3. "My son is in Japan and he's going to learn Japanese. He'll learn much more over there, even though he spends all his time on the American military base."

Knowing what language learners do helps us to understand what our roles as teachers should be in the classroom. When we know what learners do to learn language in and out of the classroom, we can determine what type of help learners need to facilitate the acquisitional process or to advance from stage to stage.

Recognizing the learner as the central figure in language learning does not diminish the importance of the teacher or the classroom environment. Teachers remain responsible for the planning of classroom activities which aid learners in acquiring the language, whether providing input training (cf. VanPatten, Ch. 1; VanPatten & Cadierno 1993), comprehensible input, focused noticing exercises (cf. Bardovi-Harlig & Reynolds 1995), strategy training, organizing meaningful group work, or any number of acquisition activities.

Learner variables (such as the amount of input a learner seeks, motivation, acquisitional sequences, rate of acquisition) figure heavily in the classroom language learning equation. Whatever their nature, learner variables in large measure determine the results of classroom interaction. This should not be interpreted negatively by language teachers. The study of acquisition shows that the responsibility for success rests with the learner as well as with the teacher, which should relieve some of the pressure on language teachers. In turn, when we language teachers relinquish some of the control we can be more tolerant—not only of the language learners—but of ourselves as teachers, as well.

ACCESS TO THE LITERATURE

Now that we have considered the benefits of including the study of second language acquisition in teacher preparation, I also suggest that each one of these benefits can be attained or maintained through the reading of the relevant literature. Reading the literature is an excellent way to keep abreast of developments in the field. Attending conferences is another, and the skills that are required for listening to professional papers are much the same as the skills required to read the literature. Approaching the literature can be somewhat daunting for those without training, as Crookes (1993) points out. Common to most second language acquisition courses of which I am aware is training in reading and evaluating research articles. Training makes the literature accessible. This preparation also allows teachers to be informed consumers when encountering recommendations for teaching based on research.

Gateway to Research?

I do not expect second/foreign language teachers to be full-time researchers. Exposure to the study of second language acquisition may encourage some language teachers to conduct research of their own and/or to engage in collaborative research with researchers, building partnerships of varying types. One such area is "action research" in which teachers engage in "research on their own teaching and the learning of their own students" (Crookes 1993, p. 131) and which is generally designed to solve a problem or to answer a question in the specific instructional setting in which it is conducted. The collaborative research project of Koenig and Zuengler (1994) is an example of such research in the ESL classroom.[15]

Knowledgeable teachers can provide an important link between research and teaching in the language teaching/acquisition fields. Teachers will be increasingly called upon to interpret work from acquisition research for classroom implementation. Often researchers do not have the skills in materials development that practicing teachers have, and they do not have the situational knowledge that would help them to implement procedures for particular language instruction settings, learner goals, or programs.

CONCLUSION

The study of second language acquisition is a necessary component in the preparation of second/foreign language teachers. Admittedly, it is only one of many such components. The study of second language acquisition provides teachers with an informed view of the very process that they strive to set into motion. It provides a means of interpreting learner language which takes them beyond the realm of errors into the realm of a linguistic system, which has its own rules and patterns, and which takes time to emerge.

---

*P*ause to consider . . .

what you think are the most important ways in which knowing more about second language acquisition will help you as a language teacher.

NOTES

[1]See, for example, DeCarrico (1986), Moy (1977), and Riddle (1986).

[2]I write this paper from an (applied) linguist's point of view. Coming from that tradition, the influence of linguistics has been particularly salient to me. There have been other influences on language teaching as well, including education. VanPatten (1990, p. 23) suggests that educational research has been particularly influential in foreign language teaching, more so than in ESL: "Sometime in the 1960s . . . FL professionals turned their attention away from both what language is and how languages are learned, and focused their attention instead on the manipulation of instructional variables and methodology."

[3]See also Lightbown (1985) and Tarone, Swain & Fathman (1976) for a discussion of other limitations of research in its application to the classroom. See Gass (1995) for a discussion of the intersection of second language acquisition research and teaching.

[4]This early reliance on temporal adverbs has also been identified in a comprehension study by Sanz-Alcala and Fernandez (1992).

[5]The knowledge that acquisition takes place in stages is more important than is learning the specific stages by memory. Once teachers are alerted to the fact that

acquisition proceeds in stages toward target-like use, the recurrence of the stages in learner production makes them recognizable.

[6]I say that potential for targetlike production exists at the end of the sequence because every learner does not necessarily reach that point.

[7]According to the instructional logs, instruction on pluperfect was form-focused. For a more complete description, see Bardovi-Harlig (1994).

[8]Four learners used the pluperfect prior to instruction. They are not directly relevant to this argument and are not discussed here. For a fuller account see Bardovi-Harlig (1994).

[9]In fact, independent ratings by native-speaker judges suggest that this is true (cf. Bardovi-Harlig 1994).

[10]Achievements and accomplishments may also group together (Andersen & Shirai, 1994; Bardovi-Harlig & Reynolds, 1995).

[11]Andersen and Shirai (1994) and Shirai (1991) review the unpublished research of Andersen's students.

[12]For an evaluation of methods based on a particular theory of second language acquisition, see Krashen (1982).

[13]If one were to assume that a grammar that allows SAV (e.g., English [8b]) and a grammar that allows only SVAO (e.g., French [7b]) were mutually exclusive (i.e., no grammar could allow both rules), then positive evidence may be sufficient. See Schwartz and Gubala-Ryzak (1992) and White (1992).

[14]The less commonly taught languages include the largely non-Indo-European languages: Finno-Ugric languages, including Hungarian and Finnish; African languages; and East Asian languages; and the indigenous languages of the Americas.

[15]Crookes (1993) provides a comprehensive discussion of action research.

KEY TERMS, CONCEPTS, AND ISSUES

second language acquisition
second language/foreign language
host/second environment
first language
target language
interlanguage
tutored/untutored learners,
  instructed/uninstructed learners
targetlike production/nontargetlike
  production
developmental stages
  undergeneralization/overgeneralization
  negative evidence/positive evidence
systematic usage

linguistic competence
linguistic complexity
regularity
morphology, morpheme
  tense/aspect
  preterite/imperfect
Teachability Hypothesis
error
correction
discourse
text
lexicon

EXPLORING THE TOPICS FURTHER

1. *Introductions to second language acquisition.* Larsen-Freeman and Long (1991) and Ellis (1994) provide comprehensive introductions to second language acquisition research. Dulay, Burt & Krashen (1982) offer a less ambitious overview from one well-known theoretical perspective. Excellent overviews of second language acquisition with special reference to class-

room language learners can be found in Ellis (1990, 1992.) For readers who are interested in how second language acquisition researchers relate their investigations to pedagogy, *Second Language Acquisition Theory and Pedagogy* (Eckman, Highland, Lee, Mileham & Weber 1995) provides a state-of-the-art collection of nineteen papers.

2. *Positive and negative evidence in classroom instruction.* For a discussion of the effects of positive and negative evidence on the development of interlanguage grammar in classroom instruction, see White (1991), White & Trahey (1993), White, Spada, Lightbown & Ranta (1991), and Trahey (1996). Bardovi-Harlig & Reynolds (1995) also provide examples of texts and activities that emphasize positive evidence in the instruction of tense and aspect.

3. *Experimental and theoretical discussions on error correction and grammar.* For an interesting theoretical discussion on the potential effects of negative evidence on the development of grammar, see the discussion in White (1991), the response in Schwartz & Gubala-Ryzak (1992), and the rebuttal by White (1992). The thematic issue of *Studies in Second Language Acquisition*, 15(2), "The role of instruction in second language acquisition," presents a range of viewpoints.

4. *Journals of interest.* For serial publications with a focus on second language acquisition, consult *Studies in Second Language Acquisition, Second Language Research*, and *Language Learning*. Articles on second language acquisition also appear in *TESOL Quarterly* (where findings are generally related to pedagogy), *Modern Language Journal, Canadian Modern Language Review*, and *Applied Linguistics*.

REFERENCES

Andersen, R.W. (1983). Transfer to somewhere. In S. Gass & L. Selinker (Eds.) *Language transfer in language learning* (pp. 177–201). Rowley, MA: Newbury House.

Andersen, R.W. (1986). La adquisicíon de la morfología verbal [The acquisition of verb morphology]. *Lingüística, 1,* 90–142.

Andersen, R.W. (1990). Models, processes, principles, and strategies: Second language acquisition inside and outside the classroom. In B. VanPatten & J.F. Lee (Eds.) *Second language acquisition/Foreign language learning* (pp. 45–68). Clevedon, UK: Multilingual Matters.

Andersen, R.W. (1991). Developmental sequences: The emergence of aspect marking in second language acquisition. In C.A. Ferguson & T. Huebner (Eds.) *Crosscurrents in second language acquisition and linguistic theories* (pp. 305–324). Amsterdam/Philadelphia: John Benjamins.

Andersen, R.W. & Shirai, Y. (1994). Discourse motivations for some cognitive acquisition principles. *Studies in Second Language Acquisition, 16,* 133–156.

Bardovi-Harlig, K. (1992a). The relationship of form and meaning: A cross-sectional study of tense and aspect in the interlanguage of learners of English as a second language. *Applied Psycholinguistics, 13,* 253–278.

Bardovi-Harlig, K. (1992b). The use of adverbials and natural order in the development of temporal expression. *IRAL, 30,* 199–220.

Bardovi-Harlig, K. (1993). The contribution of classroom language learners to acquisition research: Evidence from a longitudinal study. Paper presented to SLA-FLL III

(Second Language Acquisition-Foreign Language Learning); West Lafayette, Indiana, February 26–28.

Bardovi-Harlig, K. (1994). Reverse-order reports and the acquisition of tense: Beyond the principle of chronological order. *Language Learning, 44,* 243–282.

Bardovi-Harlig, K. (1995). The interaction of pedagogy and natural sequences in the acquisition of tense and aspect. In F.R. Eckman, D. Highland, P.W. Lee, J.L. Mileham, & R.R. Weber (Eds.) *Second language acquisition theory and pedagogy* (pp. 151–168). Hillsdale, NJ: Lawrence Erlbaum.

Bardovi-Harlig, K., & Bergström, A. (1996). The acquisition of tense and aspect in SLA and FLL: A study of learner narratives in English (SL) and French (FL). *Canadian Modern Language Review, 52,* 308–330.

Bardovi-Harlig, K., Hartford, B.A.S., Mahan-Taylor, R., Morgan, M.J., & Reynolds, D.W. (1991). Developing pragmatic awareness: Closing the conversation. *ELT Journal, 45,* 4–15.

Bardovi-Harlig, K. & Reynolds, D.W. (1995). The role of lexical aspect in the acquisition of tense and aspect. *TESOL Quarterly, 29,* 107–131.

Bayley, R. (1994). Interlanguage variation and the quantitative paradigm: Past tense marking in Chinese English. In E.E. Tarone, S.M. Gass, & A.D. Cohen, (Eds.) *Research methodology in second language acquisition* (pp. 157–181). Hillsdale, NJ: Lawrence Erlbaum.

Bergström, A. (1993). The expression of temporal reference by English speaking learners of French: Report on the cloze. Paper presented to the 13th Meeting of the Second Language Research Forum, University of Pittsburgh, Pittsburgh, PA.

Bergström, A. (1995). *The expression of past temporal reference by English-speaking learners of French.* Unpublished Pennsylvania State University PhD dissertation, Pennsylvania State University, State College, PA.

Billmeyer, K. & Boxer, D. (1989). Pedagogy and pragmatics: Theory, practice, and ethics. Colloquium presented at the Twenty-third Annual TESOL Conference; San Antonio, Texas, March 7–12.

Crookes, G. (1993). Action research for second language teachers: Going beyond teacher research. *Applied Linguistics, 14,* 130–144.

DeCarrico, J.S. (1986). Tense, aspect, and time in the English modality system. *TESOL Quarterly, 20,* 665–682.

Dörnyei, Z. (1990). Conceptualizing motivation in foreign language learning. *Language Learning, 40,* 45–78.

Dörnyei, Z. (1994). Understanding L2 motivation: On with the challenge! *The Modern Language Journal, 78,* 515–517.

Dulay, H., Burt, M. & Krashen, S. (1982). *Language two.* New York: Oxford University Press.

Eckman, F.R., Highland, D., Lee, P.W., Mileham, J.L., & Weber, R.R. (Eds.) (1995). *Second language acquisition theory and pedagogy.* Hillsdale, NJ: Lawrence Erlbaum.

Ellis, R. (1989). Are classroom and naturalistic acquisition the same? A study of the classroom acquisition of German word order rules. *Studies in Second Language Acquisition, 11,* 305–328.

Ellis, R. (1990). *Instructed second language acquisition.* Oxford: Basil Blackwell.

Ellis, R. (1992). *Second language acquisition and pedagogy.* Philadelphia: Multilingual Matters.

Ellis, R. (1994). *The study of second language acquisition.* Oxford: Oxford University Press.

Gardner, R. & Tremblay, P.F. (1994a). On motivation, research agendas, and theoretical frameworks. *Modern Language Journal, 78,* 359–368.

Gardner, R. & Tremblay, P.F. (1994b). On motivation: Measurement and conceptual considerations. *Modern Language Journal, 78,* 524–527.

Gardner, R. & Lambert, W. (1972). *Attitudes and motivation in second-language learning.* Rowley, MA: Newbury House.

Gass, S.M. (1989). Second and foreign language learning: Same, different, or none of the above? In B. VanPatten & J.F. Lee (Eds.) *Second language acquisition/Foreign language learning* (pp. 34–44). Clevedon, UK: Multilingual Matters.

Gass, S.M. (1995). Learning and teaching: The necessary intersection. In F.R. Eckman, D. Highland, P.W. Lee, J.L. Mileham, & R.R. Weber (Eds.) *Second language acquisition theory and pedagogy* (pp. 3–20). Hillsdale, NJ: Lawrence Erlbaum.

Harley, B. & Swain, M. (1978). An analysis of the verb system used by young learners of French. *Interlanguage Studies Bulletin, 3,* 35–79.

Hartford, B.S. & Bardovi-Harlig, K. (1992). Closing the conversation: Evidence from the academic advising session. *Discourse Processes, 15,* 93–116.

Hasbún, L. (1995). *The role of lexical aspect in the acquisition of tense and grammatical aspect in Spanish as a foreign language.* Unpublished PhD dissertation, Indiana University, Bloomington.

Kaplan, M.A. (1987). Developmental patterns of past tense acquisition among foreign language learners of French. In B. VanPatten, T.R. Dvorak, & J.F. Lee (Eds.) *Foreign language learning: A research perspective* (pp. 52–60). Cambridge, MA: Newbury House.

Koenig, J. & Zuengler, J. (1994). Teacher/researcher collaboration: Studying student and teacher goals in oral classroom activities. *TESOL Journal, 4,* 40–43.

Krashen, S. (1982). *Principles and practice in second language acquisition.* New York: Pergamon.

Larsen-Freeman, D. & Long, M.H. (1991). *An introduction to second language acquisition research.* London: Longman.

Levinson, S.C. (1983). *Pragmatics.* Cambridge, MA: Cambridge University Press.

Lightbown, P.M. (1985). Great expectations: Second-language acquisition research and classroom teaching. *Applied Linguistics, 6,* 173–189.

Lightbown, P.M. (1987). Classroom language as input to second language acquisition. In C.W. Pfaff (Ed.) *First and second language acquisition processes* (pp. 169–187). Cambridge, MA: Newbury House.

Meisel, J.M. (1987). Reference to past events and actions in the development of natural language acquisition. In C.W. Pfaff (Ed.) *First and second language acquisition processes* (pp. 206–224). Cambridge, MA: Newbury House.

Moy, R.H. (1977). Contextual factors in the use of the present perfect. *TESOL Quarterly, 11,* 303–309.

Noyau, C. (1990). The development of means for temporality in the unguided acquisition of L2: Cross-linguistic perspectives. In H. W. Dechert (Ed.), *Current trends in European second language acquisition research* (pp. 134–170). Clevedon, UK: Multilingual Matters.

Omar, A.S. (1991). How learners greet in Kiswahili. In L. Bouton & Y. Kachru (Eds.) *Pragmatics and language learning,* (Vol 2, pp. 59–73). Urbana-Champaign, IL: DEIL, University of Illinois.

Omar, A.S. (1992). *Opening and closing conversations in Kiswahili: A study of the performance of native speakers and learners.* Unpublished PhD dissertation, Indiana University, Bloomington.

Oxford, R.L. (1990). Language learning strategies: What every teacher should know. Rowley, MA: Newbury House.

Oxford, R.L. & Nyikos, M. (1989). Variables affecting choice of language learning strategies by university students. *Modern Language Journal, 73,* 291–300.

Pienemann, M. (1989). Is language teachable? Psycholinguistic experiments and hypotheses. *Applied Linguistics, 10,* 52–79.

Ramsay, V. (1990). *Developmental stages in the acquisition of the perfective and the imperfective aspects by classroom L2 learners of Spanish.* Doctoral dissertation, University of Oregon, Eugene.

Riddle, E. (1986). The meaning and discourse function of the past tense in English. *TESOL Quarterly, 20,* 267–286.

Robison, R. (1990). The primacy of aspect: Aspectual marking in English interlanguage. *Studies in Second Language Acquisition, 12,* 315–330.

Robison, R. (1995). The aspect hypothesis revisited: A cross-sectional study of tense and aspect marking in interlanguage. *Applied Linguistics, 16,* 344–370.

Sanz-Alcala, C. & M. Fernandez. (1992) "Native speakers' and L2 learners' processing of verbal morphology in Spanish," paper presented 12th Meeting of the Second Language Research Forum, Michigan State University, East Lansing, MI.

Schumann, J. (1987). The expression of temporality in basilang speech. *Studies in Second Language Acquisition, 9,* 21–41.

Schwartz, B. & Gubala-Ryzak, M. (1992). Learnability and grammar reorganization in L2A: Against negative evidence causing the unlearning of verb movement. *Second Language Research, 8,* 1–38.

Tarone, E., Swain, M., Fathman, A. (1976). Some limitations to the classroom applications of current second language research. *TESOL Quarterly, 10,* 19–31.

Tarone, E. & Yule, G. (1989). *Focus on the language learner.* Oxford: Oxford University Press.

Trahey, M. (1996). Positive evidence in second language acquisition. *Second Language Research, 12,* 111–139.

VanPatten, B. (1987). Classroom and naturalistic acquisition: A comparison of two case studies in the acquisition of clitic pronouns in Spanish. In T. Morgan, J.F. Lee & B. VanPatten (Eds.) *Language and language use: Studies in Spanish* (pp. 241–259). Lanham, MD: University Press of America.

VanPatten, B. (1990). Theory and research in second language acquisition and foreign language learning: On producers and consumers. In B. VanPatten & J.F. Lee (Eds.) *Second language acquisition/Foreign language learning* (pp. 17–26). Clevedon, UK: Multilingual Matters.

VanPatten, B. & Cadierno, T. (1993). Explicit instruction and input processing. *Studies in Second Language Acquisition, 15,* 225–243.

VanPatten, B. & Lee, J. (Eds.) (1990). *Second language acquisition/Foreign language learning* (pp. 17–26). Clevedon, UK: Multilingual Matters.

Véronique, D. (1987). Reference to past events and actions in narratives in L2: Insights from North African Learners' French. In C.W. Pfaff (Ed.), *First and second language acquisition processes* (pp. 252-272). Cambridge, MA: Newbury House.

Wenden, A. & Rubin, J. (Eds.) (1987). *Learner strategies in language learning.* Englewood Cliffs, NJ: Prentice Hall.

White, L. (1991). Adverb placement in second language acquisition: Some effects of positive and negative evidence in the classroom. *Second Language Research, 7,* 133–161.

White, L. (1992). On triggering data in L2 acquisition: A reply to Schwartz and Gubala-Ryzak. *Second Language Research, 8,* 120–137.

White, L. & Trahey, M. (1993). Positive evidence and preemption in the second language classroom. *Studies in Second Language Acquisition, 15,* 181–204.

White, L., Spada, N., Lightbown, P.M., & Ranta, L. (1991). Input enhancement and L2 question formation. *Applied Linguistics, 12,* 416–432.

Williams, M. (1988). Language taught for meetings and language used in meetings: Is there anything in common? *Applied Linguistics, 9,* 45–58.

CHAPTER 3

Why Syntactic Theory?

Maria-Luise Beck
University of North Texas

INTRODUCTION

It goes without saying that graduate programs in second/foreign language (L2) acquisition should include a teaching methods course. Beyond such a basic course, however, the justification for other courses is somewhat less transparent. Indeed, the point of this chapter is to justify one or more courses in generative grammar and the concomitant study of acquisition. One could argue that students need this kind of training in syntax, if for no other reason than that it will enable them to evaluate some of the current research appearing in journals such as *Second Language Research* or *Language Acquisition.* However, this reason alone may not be sufficiently convincing. Thus, the purpose of this chapter is to attempt to provide more direct justification for such training by sketching in some detail what one might gain from the study of formal syntax. In effect, the goal of this chapter is not to provide a general overview of syntactic research in L2 acquisition, but rather to provide a rationale for including course work in generative syntax and acquisition in L2 graduate programs.

The general approach of this chapter involves a discussion of some of the expectations that one can have of grammars and the grammar-related concepts that graduate students should come to understand. The key term here is "expectations," which includes the notion of "minimum criteria." In formal linguistics, such expectations or criteria have been categorized into different "levels of adequacy": observational, descriptive, and explanatory (Chomsky 1964). The overall structure of this chapter follows these three levels of grammatical analysis, each of the sections providing both informal definitions and specific examples.

OBSERVATIONAL ADEQUACY

The first level of adequacy for grammars is observational adequacy. For a grammar to reach this level of adequacy, it must be able to produce some (usually selected) set of sentences. Using, say, a corpus of 50 sentences drawn from a given language, one may imagine attempting to construct a grammar that produces just these sentences. Note, however, that natural languages do not contain a finite number of sentences; rather, the number of sentences in natural languages appears to be infinite, or nearly so. For example, note that every speaker of English would be able to continue sentence (1) *ad infinitum:*

(1) John said that Mary said that Jane said that Walter said that Jean said that . . . Harry left.

What examples like (1) suggest is that speakers have the capacity, or "mental grammar," to produce an infinitely large number of sentences. And because human memory is believed to be finite, formal linguists assume that the mental grammar, whatever its ultimate form, is composed of a finite number of linguistic rulelike entities.[1]

An observationally adequate grammar should generate all the structurally possible sentences in a language; it should, of course, also exclude all of the structurally impossible sentences. Attaining this level of adequacy is certainly no easy task; indeed, the sheer heft of standard grammar-reference volumes like Quirk & Greenbaum (1978) for English or *Duden Grammatik* (1973) for German attests to the enormity of such work.[2] However, many grammars appear to meet, or at least attempt to meet, this level of adequacy, usually through a series of rules along with exceptions or similar restrictions.

One can justifiably ask why one would even want to consider other, more abstract grammars, such as the generative-transformational grammars in, for example, Baker (1978) for English or Huber & Kummer (1974) for German. Both the reference-type and the abstract generative-transformational grammars strive to attain observational adequacy, but the descriptions in reference-style grammars have the distinct advantage of being much more accessible to a wider audience. The point is that the particular form of the grammar, at least at first glance, appears to make little difference. Consider sentence (2):

(2) *Jane saw Harry.*

For such a sentence, one could imagine two treelike grammars, represented in (3) and (4), both of which divide the S(entence) into its constituent parts.

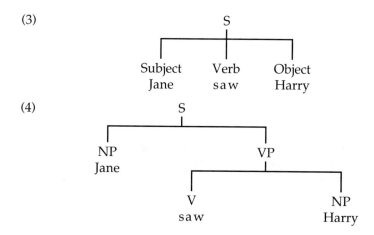

There are striking differences between the grammars in (3) and (4). First of all, the grammar in (3) has a linear structure in which Subject, Verb, and Object branch directly off of S(entence). The grammar in (4), by contrast, has a hierarchical "treelike" structure in which S is separated from *saw* and *Harry* by an additional phrase, the Verb Phrase (VP). In addition, the grammar in (3) includes a clearly designated Subject and Object, while the grammar in (4) indicates subjecthood and objecthood only by the relative positions of the Noun Phrases (NPs) under S and the VP. Finally, the grammar in (3) includes no specification as to the actual, internal makeup of the Subject or Object, while the grammar in (4) suggests that both are NPs (even though the two NPs are single, unmodified nouns). More generally, the grammars in (3) and (4) differ in that (4) is more abstract, positing phrasal levels that are not immediately visible in (3). Importantly, though, both grammars result in sentence (2) and are therefore both observationally adequate.

It was pointed out above that grammars are composed of a finite set of rules or rulelike entities. The treelike representations in (3) and (4) may not at first glance appear to embody this idea. However, such treelike representations can be and often are rewritten in the near-equivalent format of rules, technically known as phrase structure, or PS, rules. For the representations in (3) and (4), the associated PS rules would be like those shown in (5) and (6), respectively.

(5)   S → Subject Verb Object

(6)   S → NP VP

VP → V NP

To read such rules, one employs the term "expands into" for the arrow (→). Hence, the rule in (5) would be read as "S(entence) expands into Subject Verb Object," and the two rules in (6) would be read as "S expands into NP and VP" and "VP expands into V and NP." For expository purposes, however, treelike representations will be used instead of PS rules in the rest of this discussion.

Given that some grammars may be far more abstract than others, it seems that the simpler, more easily understood grammar (e.g., a grammar as represented in [3]) is a more accessible type. These considerations suggest a certain indisputable value to the study of grammars such as those found in standard grammar-reference volumes. Indeed, one can wholeheartedly support the proposal that students of second language acquisition should be encouraged to enroll in an advanced grammar course that treats the L2 of interest in observationally adequate ways.

Pause to consider . . .

what it means for a grammar to have "observational adequacy". How do teachers benefit from being familiar with observationally adequate grammars of the languages they teach? Is it sufficient to study only this level of grammar? Why or why not?

As noted, an observationally adequate grammar should generate all and only those of the sentences that are possible constructions in a language. A descriptively adequate grammar, however, must do all that and more: It must also capture the adult's intuitions about language structure.

What are "Intuitions About Language Structure"?

Before approaching the technical details of descriptively adequate grammars, it will be of value to explain what is meant by intuitions about language structure. Consider the meaning of *tear up* in example (7).

(7)   *The guy tore up Main Street.*

Native speakers readily note that sentence (7) has two possible interpretations. In one interpretation, the person is 'driving fast.' When the sentence conveys this meaning, the individual phrase *up Main Street* provides the direction in which this kind of driving is taking place; it contrasts, for example, with *tear across Main Street, tear down Main Street, tear past Main Street,* and so forth. The other possible interpretation is that the person is 'destroying' the street. When the interpretation involves 'destroy,' one interprets *tear up* as a "two-word verb." However, many readers interpret the word *up* in (7) as a preposition, even though such an interpretation is grammatically at odds with the meaning of 'destroy.' The fact that English two-word verbs permit a second position for the nonverbal element (i.e., *up*) will help us illustrate why this is so.

(8)   *The guy tore Main Street up.*

Let us now employ the native speaker's intuitions: If the meaning associated with sentence (8) is 'destroy,' then the sentence is a possible one in English. Importantly, however, if the meaning of (8) is 'drive fast,' with a preposition of direction located after its object, then the sentence is structurally impossible. This finding suggests that *up*, when used with *tear* to mean 'destroy,' is not a preposition at all; rather, it represents what is sometimes called a "particle," which is employed in the two-word verb *tear up.* More generally, the example shows that a native speaker can have very different intuitions about one and the same string of words. Furthermore, as shown by the impossibility of (8) to mean 'drive fast,' these intuitions involve more than a case of a single word having two meanings. Rather, the difference between intuitions is related to a difference in structure.[3]

Capturing Intuitions

The discussion above shows that a native speaker may have two different intuitions about the same sequential string of words. Crucially, a descriptively adequate grammar of such sentences would have to incorporate such differing intuitions; any grammar that does not distinguish between such intuitions would not be descriptively adequate. To see an example of how a descriptively adequate grammar represents such differing intuitions, consider again the ambiguous sentence (7). As noted, native speakers intuit that the person is either destroying the street or driving fast on it. Again, when *tear up* means 'destroy,' the verb includes both *tear* and the particle *up*. To incorporate this particular intuition in the grammar, we employ a representation in which *tear* and *up* are both part of a single verb. This is shown in the partial tree (9), in which both the verb *tore* and the particle *up* are under a single V(erb).

(9)

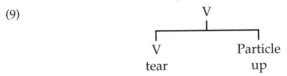

The other intuition, in which *tear up* means to 'drive fast in a particular direction,' involves the verb plus the directional preposition *up*. This intuition is shown in the partial tree (10), where the V(erb) P(hrase) divides into a V(erb) and a P(reposition).

(10)

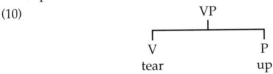

If we now employ the intuitions incorporated in (9) in a full representation of the sentence, we find (11).

(11)

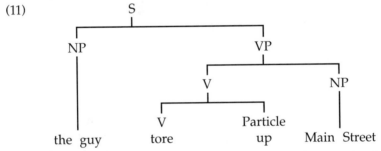

And if we employ the representation of the verb plus preposition in (10) as a full tree, we find (12), in which the preposition is now included as part of a full prepositional phrase (PP).

(12)

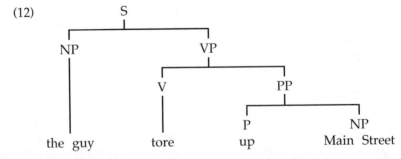

The grammars indicated in trees (11) and (12) directly incorporate the different intuitions that native speakers have about sentence (7). To make the descriptive adequacy of these trees more obvious, consider trees (13) and (14), which, like trees (11) and (12), represent the two-word verb and the verb-plus-particle constructions, but in a nonhierarchical (i.e., linear) way.

(13)

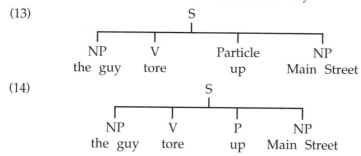

(14)

The important point to note about trees (13) and (14) is that they fail to capture the two intuitions, namely, that the two-word verb is a single verb and that the verb and prepositional phrase are separate entities.

As stated, descriptively adequate grammars are those that generate all of the structurally possible sentences and none of the impossible sentences of a language and that, in the ways illustrated above, directly incorporate the native speaker's intuitions about language structure. One of the goals of modern grammatical theory is, at a minimum, to attain descriptive adequacy.[4] Given the significant differences between the two types of grammars discussed so far, one can only urge that graduate second language programs include a course that focuses on the study of descriptively adequate grammar, for its main benefit to students is clear: They will attain a far deeper understanding of the language in question. An additional benefit, one perhaps even more germane to the present discussion, involves language acquisition.

An example from the acquisition of German may help to demonstrate the additional benefit of a descriptively adequate grammar. But before we can discuss acquisitional facts, it will be necessary to sketch some commonly held assumptions about German syntax.

P*ause to consider . . .*

the difference between a descriptively adequate grammar and an observationally adequate grammar. How would each account for the ambiguous sentence *The wind blew over the trees?*

An Excursion into the Syntax of German

Standard German has two-word particle verbs that are similar to those of English (see above), except that the particle never appears in the position next to the verb in sentences that have direct objects. Example (15), below, illustrates a typical German main clause with a particle verb. Note that the German particle occurs obligatorily at the end of the clause.

(15)   *Chimpsky ass gestern die Bananen auf*
       Chimpsky eat+PAST yesterday ART bananas PARTICLE
       'Chimpsky ate up the bananas yesterday'

To represent the structure of the particle verb construction in German, a number of modern generative linguists (e.g., Travis 1991; Zwart 1993) have proposed a representation similar to (16).

(16)

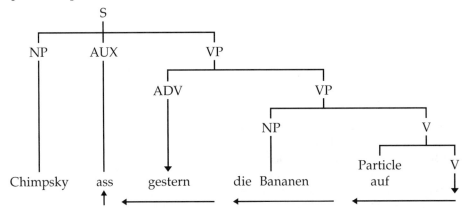

A number of details in (16) differ from the representations shown in (11) through (12). First of all, the VP appears to be "reversed"; that is, in the German VP, the verb appears on the right rather than on the left (cf. [11]). Furthermore, the representation in (16) seems to have a double VP, one above the adverb (ADV) and the other above the verb. This specific way of representing the position of the adverb is not particularly crucial to the analysis; suffice it to say that the adverb is ordered before the NP object, *die Bananen*. In addition, (16) includes a node with the label AUX. The AUX node represents syntactically important features, such as Tense, (Subject-Verb) Agreement, Aspect, and so forth. In fact, all clauses in German, as well as other languages, include such a node; it was omitted from the English representations above for expository purposes. Finally, what is also different about the representation of German in (16) is that the verb moves from its position inside the VP past the adverb to the AUX node, thereby placing the verb in second position between the subject and the adverb, but leaving the particle behind in final position.[5] This is shown in (16) by the arrowed line underneath.

Some readers, in particular those who have learned or taught German, may find it hard to accept the grammar represented in (16), especially the idea that the verb moves from final position to the second position in main clauses. After all, one could also imagine a grammar in which the particle moves from the second position to the final position. Indeed, early analyses like that in Huber & Kummer (1974) entertained just such a possibility. What is important to note here is that the grammar represented in (16) is based on the intuitions of native German speakers. One of these intuitions is that the German verb *aufessen* is a two-word verb similar to its English equivalent *eat up*. As a result, the verb and its associated particle are presented underlyingly as a single verb in tree (16), just as they were for *tear up* in English tree (11). Further intuitions involve those associated with both main clauses and embedded clauses. Consider sentences (17) through (23). (Following standard practice in linguistics, an asterisk indicates those sentences that are impossible in German.)

(17)   *Chimpsky ass gestern die Bananen auf.*
"Chimpsky ate yesterday the bananas up."

(18)   **Chimpsky ass auf gestern die Bananen.*
"Chimpsky ate up yesterday the bananas."

(19)   **Chimpsky aufass gestern die Bananen.*
"Chimpsky up-ate yesterday the bananas."

(20)   *Er schrieb, dass Chimpsky gestern die Bananen aufass.*
"He wrote that Chimpsky yesterday the bananas up-ate"

(21)   **Er schrieb, dass Chimpsky ass gestern die Bananen auf.*
"He wrote that Chimpsky ate yesterday the bananas up."

(22)   **Er schrieb, dass Chimpsky ass auf gestern die Bananen.*
"He wrote that Chimpsky ate up yesterday the bananas."

(23)   **Er schrieb, dass Chimpsky aufass gestern die Bananen.*
"He wrote that Chimpsky up-ate yesterday the bananas."

The common thread running through the intuitions in (17) through (23) is that the particle does not occur in any position other than the final one, and that the verb appears in second position in main clauses and in final position in embedded clauses. If the two-word verb *aufessen* is represented as a single verb in clause-final position, as the grammar in (16) has it, then it is only in the main clause that the verb moves to the second position.[6]

Descriptive Adequacy and Acquisition

General research on L2 acquisition (cf., Larsen-Freeman & Long 1991; Bardovi-Harlig 1995; Bardovi-Harlig, Ch. 2) has shown that learners both in and outside of the classroom traverse largely identical stages in their acquisition of syntax. For the acquisition of German by native speakers of Spanish, Italian, or English, Clahsen (1984) and Ellis (1989) have shown that the initial stages appear schematically, as in (24).

(24)   *Stage One: S V O*
Stage Two: S V$_{finite}$ ADV O V$_{nonfinite}$

Some comment on (24) may clarify what occurs here. Initially, L2 learners appear to begin with a subject-verb-object order, where verbs are not distinguished in terms of finiteness (i.e., whether they are inflected or not). At a later stage, learners acquire the particle-verb construction, indicated in (24) as the clause-final nonfinite verb. At the same stage, adverbs (ADV) begin to appear in the medial position between the finite verb and the object.

One could characterize the stages in (24) with a non-hierarchical (linear-type) grammar. Thus, the two stages could be represented by (25) and (26) for stages one and two, respectively.

(25)

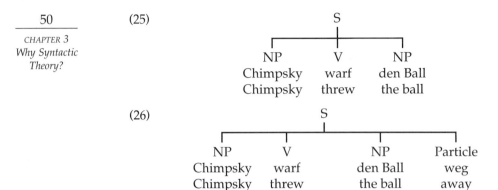

(26)

Trees (25) and (26) are acceptable means of representation, as long as one is interested only in schematically reproducing the data (in this case, acquisitional data). Conversely, these grammars make no attempt to represent intuitions of linguistic structure. In other words, they attain observational adequacy, but not descriptive adequacy.

As an alternative, one may conjecture that the two stages could be represented with hierarchical grammars, such as those represented in (27) and (28).

(27)

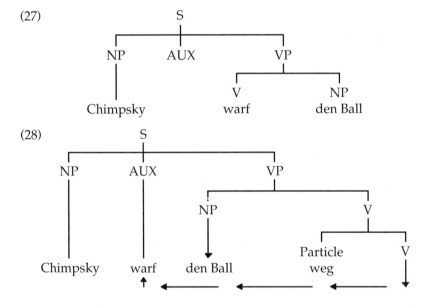

(28)

The grammars represented in (27) and (28) do attain observational adequacy, as readers may readily ascertain. However, the more important question is whether they attain descriptive adequacy. The mere fact that these two representations are hierarchical (rather than linear) does not automatically qualify them as descriptively adequate. The relevant criterion is whether they do, in fact, capture intuitions about syntactic structure. Consider the representation in (27) first. If the grammar represented in this tree were to qualify as descriptively adequate, then one would want to know more about stage-one learners' intuitions. In particular, one would want to know whether such learners find sentences like (29) to be structurally possible or not.[7]

(29)   *Ich weiss, dass Chimpsky warf den Ball.*
       "I know that Chimpsky threw the ball."

Of course, sentences like (29) are structurally impossible in standard German (cf. [21]). However, it is not the native speakers' grammar that one is attempting to represent here, but rather the interlanguage (IL) grammar of stage-one learners. In this regard, if the grammar described in (27) were a correct representation of the stage-one IL grammar, then sentences like (29) should be structurally possible in the intuitions of these learners.[8] In short, the grammar represented in (27) would only qualify as descriptively adequate if learners at this stage found sentences like (29) to be possible.

Now consider the representation in (28) for stage-two learners. Note that this representation is nearly identical to (16), which reflects native speakers' intuitions. As in the case of the stage-one representation, however, the interest here is not in the native speakers' grammar, but in the grammar of stage-two learners. In other words, one is interested in discovering the stage-two learners' intuitions of syntactic structure. On the other hand, because the representation in (28) is, in all relevant respects, identical to the native-speaker grammar in (16), learners' intuitions would have to be the same as well. In particular, stage-two learners would necessarily have to have the same intuitions as the native speaker about sentences (17) through (23). Only if stage-two learners were to have the intuitions illustrated in (17) through (23) could one say that the grammar represented in (28) is descriptively adequate. Otherwise, the representation in (28) can only be said to be observationally adequate.

Thus, descriptively adequate grammars not only generate the relevant linguistic data, but also represent intuitions of linguistic structure, both those of the native speaker as well as those of the second language learner. Again, the value of including course work on descriptively adequate grammatical theory is clear: Such work not only adds depth to students' understanding of the language they will be teaching, but also enhances the understanding of their students' language acquisition well beyond what is possible through grammars that attain only observational adequacy.

---

*P*ause *to consider . . .*

whether a grammar should capture a learner's intuition as well as the native speaker's. How does the notion of grammar as a theory of language differ from the notion of grammar as a system of prescriptive rules as found in reference or pedagogical grammars? Are learners' intuitions represented in the latter type of grammars?

EXPLANATORY ADEQUACY

As just shown, discerning descriptively adequate grammars for learners sheds a certain amount of light on acquisition. On the other hand, it is important to realize what descriptive adequacy does not do. For the acquisition of German syntax discussed above, for example, one might want to know how learners come up with representations such as those in (27) and (28) in the first place. In other words, what is missing is an *explanation* for acquisition, or non-acquisition, as the case may be. For this purpose, one turns to grammatical theory that strives for explanatory adequacy; that is, grammars that generate the relevant data, represent intuitions, and, at the same time, provide an explanation for the acquisition of structural knowledge.

The type of grammatical theory that attempts to attain explanatory adequacy involves certain important views about the nature of cognition and learning, as well as a number of reformulations in generative theory itself. The present section, therefore, begins with a cursory review of the informing ideas behind modern generative theory. Thereafter comes an illustration of the kind of technical reformulation that characterizes modern explanatory theory. The chapter then turns to how this reformulated theory makes an explanation of acquisition possible.

Views on Cognition and Learning

The starting point that underlies the modern generative view of cognition and learning is an almost trivial observation: All native speakers, regardless of educational preparation, possess uniform and implicit abstract structural knowledge of the language to which they are exposed in their local surroundings. For example, the intuitions of speakers whose ambient language comprises dialects of English from many parts of the United States uniformly indicate that sentences like (30) are structurally possible, while sentences like (31) are structurally impossible.

(30)   *Who did you say went to the store?*

(31)   **Who did you say that went to the store?*

By contrast, the intuitions of speakers whose ambient language comprises dialects of English from, for example, (rural) Texas uniformly indicate that sentences like (30) and (31) are both structurally possible.

A striking contrast then exists between the variation one observes in other areas of learning and the across-the-board and uniform nature of such implicit structural knowledge. This contrast, especially the uniformity of structural knowledge, begs for an explanation. Generative theory proposes that such knowledge derives from an independent, task-specific cognitive mechanism that is given antecedently as part of the innate endowment. The common understanding in generative linguistics is that the vast majority of one's structural knowledge is in place at birth; that is, prior to the onset of (native) language acquisition. Acquisition of those characteristics that are not given as part of the innate endowment (and that thus determine the structural differences among particular languages, regional varieties, and so forth) occurs automatically and without apparent conscious effort. Finally, such acquisition is thought to occur on the basis of mere exposure to the ambient language. Corrective or instructional efforts are not necessary.[9]

Since the late 1970s and continuing through the present day, the technical nature of generative theory has undergone dramatic changes that have made dealing with acquisition in an explanatory way much more feasible. It is not possible, in this chapter, to discuss all of the technical innovations that characterize modern theory; instead, the following provides an illustrative sketch of the kind of changes that have resulted in a theory capable of explaining acquisition. The example deals with further refinements on the hierarchical nature of basic phrase structure.

Consider the nature of a noun phrase followed by a prepositional phrase (PP), as in (32) and (33).

(32)   *the cup with stripes*

(33)   *the cup of tea*

One possible way to represent these phrases is found in the structurally identical trees in (34) and (35). (The term DET stands for "Determiner," which includes the articles *the, a, an.*)

(34)

(35)

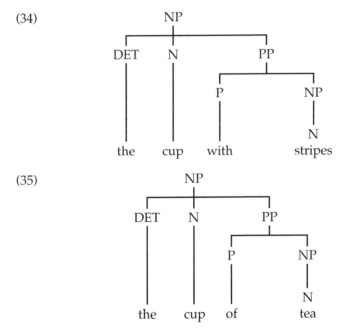

Trees (34) and (35) are somewhat more fully representative in that the NPs also include a node N to represent the single nouns *cup, stripes,* and *tea.* They attain descriptive adequacy in that they represent the intuition that *with stripes* and *of tea* are phrases that have their own identity (i.e., as PPs) apart from the rest of the NP.

Do trees (34) and (35) fully represent the intuitions of the native speaker? Perhaps not completely. To show that these representations, as they currently stand, do not fully reflect native speaker intuitions, we must employ one of the "tools of the trade" of syntactic analysis, the so-called "substitution test." Performing such a test involves, in effect, substituting one word for one or more other words. Hence, in (36) and (37), the pronoun *she* substitutes for the full NP *the chair of the department*.

(36)   *The chair of the department appointed an ad-hoc committee.*

(37)   *She appointed an ad-hoc committee.*

Performing such a test, one can draw specific conclusions about syntactic structure: when a replacement word successfully substitutes (i.e., does not create a sentence or phrase that is structurally impossible), then the word or words replaced must be exhaustively dominated by one and only one node. For example, in (36), since all of the words in the phrase *the chair of the department* would exhaustively be dominated by the single node NP in a phrase-structure tree, the substitution shown in (37) results in a structurally possible sentence.

Consider another substitution, this one employing the expression, *one* to replace parts of noun phrases. Consider sentences (38) and (39).

(38)   *He used a blue cup, and I had a white cup.*

(39)   *He used a blue cup, and I had a white one.*

The fact that we can replace the word *cup* with the word *one* in (39) demonstrates that the word *cup* alone must be dominated exhaustively by one and only one node. But what is this node? One may imagine that this node could be N itself, as trees (34) and (35) suggest. However, when one attempts *one*-substitution in (32) and (33), native speakers' intuitions indicate that the structure of such phrases is rather more complex. These intuitions are shown in (40) through (43).

(40)   *the cup with stripes*

(41)   *the one with stripes*

(42)   *the cup of tea*

(43)   **the one of tea*

Note that *one* substitutes successfully for *cup* in (41), but unsuccessfully for *cup* in (43). The conclusion that one can draw from these intuitions is that the phrase structure trees (34) and (35), which are identical, must be incorrect: There must be more to the structure of these phrases than is indicated by trees (34) and (35) and the structure associated with the NP, *the cup with stripes* in (32) must be different from the structure of the NP, *the cup of tea* in (33). In fact, the general conclusion among generative linguists has been that such trees must have intermediate branches (and nodes) for the subparts of phrases so that such subparts also have their own internal structure. Following this view, the NP in (32) would have the modified phrase structure representation shown in (44), while the NP in (33) would have the modified representation shown in (45). In these phrase structure representations, the new intermediate nodes are labeled as N' (read "N-bar").

(44)

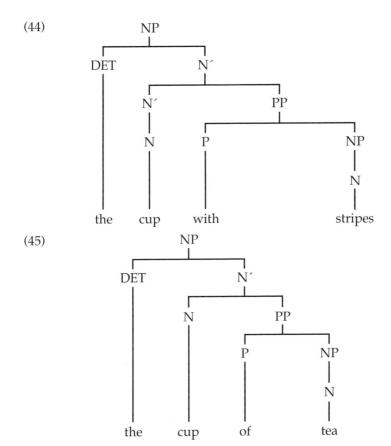

(45)

With the reformulated trees (44) and (45) we are in a position to make sense of the native speaker's intuitions about *one*-substitution shown in (40) through (43). Suppose that *one* substitutes not for a complete NP or just for N, but only for N'. Hence, when *one* substitutes, it would replace exhaustively all of the material that N' dominates. In tree (44), the lower N' dominates only *cup*, so the phrase *the one with stripes* is correctly predicted to be possible in the native speaker's intuitions (see [41]).[10] In tree (45), N' does not dominate only *cup*, and so the phrase, *the one of tea* is correctly predicted to be impossible (see [43]).

The discussion above provides the kind of evidence and rationale that has led to the postulation of intermediate nodes in the hierarchical structure of trees. The general conclusion of syntactic research, again based on the intuitions of native speakers, is that all phrases have such intermediate, single-bar nodes. Hence, (English) VPs and PPs have representations like those in (46a) and (46b).

(46a)

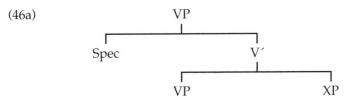

(46b)

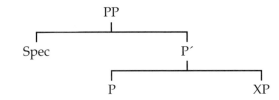

Both (46a) and (46b) have the element "Spec" (meaning "specifier") as a sister to the single-bar node, directly under the top-most node; the Spec node is assumed to appear as a catch-all (of a particular type) in representations with intermediate nodes.

Taking stock, one can now represent a sentence like (47) as tree (48).

(47)   *The woman with the hat worked on the car.*

(48)

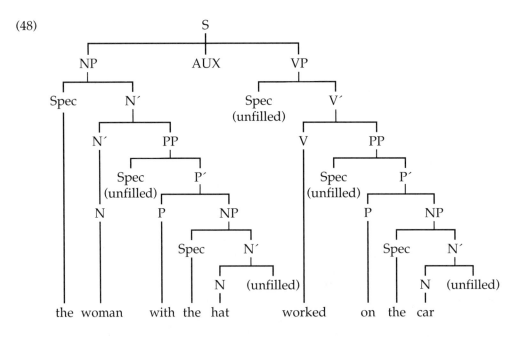

In (48) all nodes are represented, including those that are not filled (with words), in this particular sentence.

Tree (48) illustrates a significant generalization: All phrases have the same structure. This common structure can be represented in a kind of formula in which the terms "X" and "Y" stand for any members of the set {N, P, V}. The general schema is shown in (49).

(49)

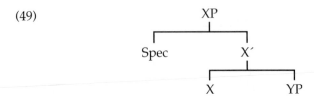

There is, however, an apparent exception to the general schema in (49), namely at the level of S itself, the structure of which is repeated in (50).

(50)

Research reported in Chomsky (1986) showed, however, that the S node also follows the general schema shown in (49). Hence, the structure of this level, now with the relabeling "IP" (Inflectional Phrase, for S) and INFL (Inflection, for AUX), is as shown in (51).

(51)

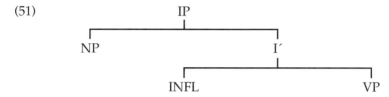

The significant generalization here is that all phrases have exactly the same internal, hierarchical structure.

The generalization in (49), however, represents only the underlying word order of English (or other languages with the same underlying word order).[11] The obvious question is how one would represent languages that have different underlying word orders. The general solution proposed in modern generative research (cf. Fanselow & Felix 1987) has been that the relative ordering of elements in (49) differs for languages with different word orders. Recall from the discussion of German syntax, for example, that the VP is "reversed," in comparison to English. The difference between English and German VPs can be represented in the partial trees (52) and (53), respectively.

(52)

(53)

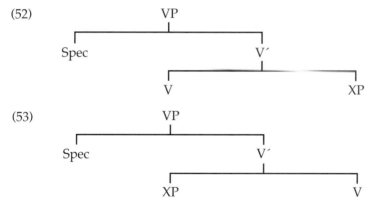

Examples (52) and (53) illustrate a concept that is far more general. In effect, the idea is that every phrase in all humanly possible languages has exactly the same internal, hierarchical structure as in (49), the only difference is the "headedness" of phrases: that is, the relative ordering of individual elements. In other words, every phrase in any language will necessarily conform to one of the four possibilities shown in (54a-d).

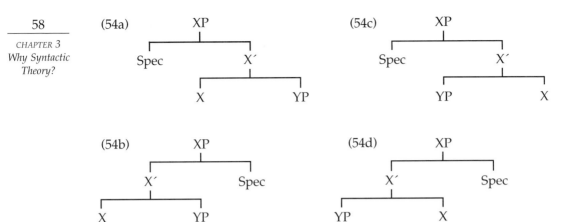

Hence the German VP conforms to (54c) while the English VP conforms to (54a); NPs in both English and German conform to (54a). The hierarchical possibilities illustrated in (54a-d) are known collectively as "X-bar Theory" and comprise what is known as a principle of "Universal Grammar" (UG). It is the (collective) principles of UG that are thought to comprise the innate (and implicit) knowledge of language that children are born with. X-bar Theory, like other principles of UG, has an associated "parameter," in that language-particular possibilities (here, underlying word order) can be determined by inspection of sentences of the ambient language. In other words, principles of UG have associated parameters, and the parameters comprise and delimit what the child must learn from experience.

---

*P*ause *to consider . . .*

how a generative grammar is different from a pedagogical grammar. What is the value of each as a resource for language teachers?

Explaining Acquisition

We are now ready to see how principles, such as X-bar Theory, make it possible to explain language acquisition. For this purpose, we return to the example on the second language acquisition of German discussed above. The particular question posed at the outset of that section was how learners may come up with representations, such as those in (27) and (28), in the first place.

To begin, let us reformulate the representations in (27) and (28) using the hierarchical terms of X-bar Theory. (Reformulating representations in this way simply means that learners have implicit knowledge of UG, including X-bar Theory.) For stage one of development, the representation in (27) is repeated here as (55a), and the X-bar reformulation is in (55b).[12]

(55a)

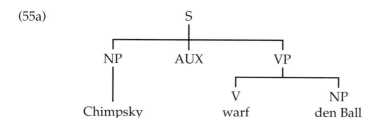

(55b)

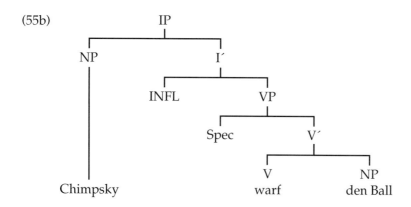

The explanation for how stage-one learners arrive at (55b) involves a UG-based theory of "parametric transfer" (duPlessis, Solin, Travis & White 1987; White 1989). This theory hypothesizes that (most of) what comprises the learner's native language representation makes up the initial representation of the second language.[13] The L2-German representation in (55b) is thus also the native language representation of the Romance- and English-speaking learners tabulated in Clahsen (1984) and Ellis (1989). In a significant sense, then, stage one involves not acquisition, but nonacquisition, because the representation is simply transferred from the native language.

For stage two of acquisition, the original formulation in (28) is shown here as (56a), and the X-bar theoretic version as (56b).

(56a)

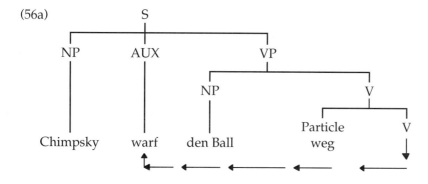

(56b)

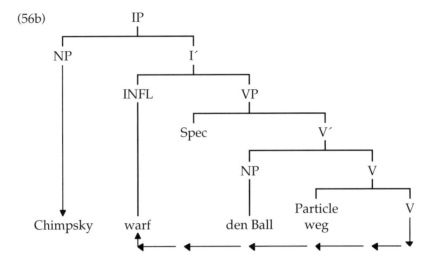

What must be explained here is the developmental transition from the stage-one representation in (55b) to the stage-two representation in (56b). Unlike the explanation for stage one, the explanation must involve acquisition itself; that is, a change in the underlying grammar.

The general view in generative research on acquisition is that such developmental change is driven by input sentences that do not match what the current (IL) grammar is able to generate. For example, given a grammar as represented in (55b) and given the strong constraints imposed by UG on what comprises a possible grammar (see discussion above), consider exposure to particle-verb sentences like (57) from the ambient language (here, standard German).

(57)   *Chimpsky macht seinen Mund auf,*
       "Chimpsky makes his   mouth open."
       '*Chimpsky opens his mouth.*'

What is important to understand about this situation is that there is a mismatch between input like (57) and what the stage-one grammar in (55b) is able to generate because such a grammar cannot position a particle in clause-final position.[14] Recall that an element cannot move to a position that does not already exist in the underlying structure (see Note 6). The result of such a mismatch is that the grammar, as it currently stands, requires change. To resolve the mismatch, the only possibility that UG allows is to create the grammar represented in (56b): (i) change the headedness of VP to order the verb and its complement from the verb-complement order to the complement-verb order, and (ii) move the verb from the VP to INFL. The explanation for the acquisition of the grammar in (56b) boils down to the constraints imposed by the principles of UG in combination with exposure to sentences in the ambient language.

Pause to consider . . .

what explanatory adequacy contributes to a grammar. Why are observational and descriptive adequacy together insufficient to account for L2 (and L1) grammatical competence?

Generative Research on L2 Acquisition

The goal of this chapter has been to sketch some of the nature of syntactic theory and how it might help to explain acquisition. From this discussion, it seems clear that knowledge of explanatory theory should form a basic complement to graduate preparation. At face value it may eventually shed some light on issues such as what kind of language input learners may need (simple exposure, correction, and so forth) and at what stage different kinds of input may be most effective.[15] There is, however, much more to modern generative research on L2 acquisition than suggested in this chapter. It has been argued that the principles of UG explain first language (L1) acquisition, but not L2 acquisition. In other words, the (adult) L2 learner does not have "access" to the very innate component that makes L1 acquisition possible in the first place (cf. Bley-Vroman 1990; Schachter 1996; White 1989, 1996a; and the contributions in Eubank 1991b). If further basic research into the fine structure of L2 knowledge were to show this proposal to hold true, the consequences— including those for L2 teaching—would be substantial.

Owing to the great amount of research that has been conducted, it is not possible to summarize here the corpus of basic generative research into L2 knowledge (for overviews of the field, however, see the suggested further readings). Because this particular research program is an ongoing international effort that has not found consensus among researchers on basic issues, it would be unwise to draw firm conclusions from it. Moreover, it is important to realize that an understanding of such research also presupposes the very kind of basic graduate-level course work being promoted here. In other words, including UG course work in graduate programs in second/foreign language acquisition will make it possible for students to evaluate and eventually to contribute to this body of research.

Pause to Consider . . .

how the principles of UG contribute to our understanding of second language acquisition.

CONCLUSION

Although it may now be apparent that grammatical theory should have a place in graduate programs in second/foreign language acquisition, it may still be difficult to determine which courses should be required in such programs. Three courses appear to be particularly beneficial: As noted in the first section of this chapter, students should take a well-designed course in advanced grammar in which they would study an observationally adequate grammar. Such courses may be offered under titles like "Pedagogical Grammar," "Traditional Grammar," or "Grammar for Teachers of English (French, German, etc.)." In addition, students should be encouraged to enroll in a course that presents a grammatical theory that strives for explanatory adequacy. These are often called "Syntax" courses, but sometimes have more specific titles, such as "Government and Binding Theory" or "Principles and Parameters Theory." Such courses will familiarize students with the nuts and bolts of modern generative theory. Given the complexity of the material to be covered, such courses are, however, unable to include studies of acquisition as well. Hence, a third course covering the ever-growing body of generative acquisitional research such as "Theory of Second Language Acquisition" or "Syntactic Studies in Second Language Acquisition," offers the ideal complement to a program of study in syntactic theory.

***P**ause to consider . . .*

what you consider to be the most important ways in which knowing more about syntactic theory will help you as a language teacher.

NOTES

[1]The circumlocution "rulelike entities" is used here instead of "rules" because, as we will note below, modern theory employs not "rules," but "principles."

[2]Pedagogical grammars in standard language-teaching texts are not included in this group because these grammars are, by design, generally not intended to attain observational adequacy if the corpus to be described is the infinite set of sentences and non-sentences.

[3]Sentences involving simple lexical ambiguity (as opposed to structural ambiguity) are generally easy to spot. Consider *Jumbo had a banana in his trunk.* Here *trunk* can mean either a wooden container used for travel, a storage compartment of a car, or an elephant's trunk.

[4]As we shall see in the next section, the goal of modern theory actually goes further.

[5]Such movement applies only in clauses in which the subject is in initial position. Although the details need not concern us here, clauses that have some other constituent in initial position involve a different kind of verb movement.

[6]In fact, other considerations of the type of sentences that one would examine in a course in syntactic theory suggest the essential correctness of the grammar repre-

sented in (16) as well. One such consideration concerns the nature of natural language grammars at large: They do not admit movement (e.g., of the verb) to positions that do not already exist in structural representations. Hence, movement of the verb to AUX in (16) is possible since AUX must exist anyway, but movement of the particle to a final position would necessitate the *ad-hoc* creation of a position that does not already exist.

[7]How one goes about eliciting such intuitions is a matter of research methodology and is thus beyond the scope of this paper. For a discussion, see Birdsong (1989), Nunan (1996), Sorace (1996), and White (1989).

[8]Recall that a grammar such as that represented in (27) does not permit the verb to appear in final position, as it would for native speakers.

[9]The linguistic and psycholinguistic evidence in support of these fundamental views of linguistic cognition is varied and fascinating, but providing this evidence is beyond the scope of this chapter. Interested readers are urged to turn, for language acquisition at large, to Gleitman & Newport (1995), Jackendoff (1994), Lightfoot (1982), Newmeyer (1983), or Pinker (1994, 1995), and for L2 acquisition in particular, to Eubank (1991a), Eubank & Beck (1993), Eubank & Gregg (1995), Eubank & Juffs (1995), Gregg (1996), White (1989, 1996a), and Schwartz (1993).

[10]In addition, of course, there is also an upper N' in (44), so *one*-substitution is predicted to be possible for this N' as well. This prediction is borne out by the possibility of phrases and substitutions with *one* as shown in the following: Let's drink our coffee out of *the cups with stripes*. You take this *one* (= *cup with stripes*), and I'll take that *one* (= *cup with stripes*).

[11]Underlying word order refers to the order of elements in a tree prior to, for example, verb movement. Hence, the underlying word order of German is SOV and the derived word order is SVO.

[12]Because the acquisitional data of interest concern the clausal level and do not hinge on the structure associated with individual NPs, the representations are simplified in that the full structure associated with NPs is not shown.

[13]In fact, the UG-based theory of parametric transfer is currently subject to intensive research. Schwartz & Sprouse (1994, 1996) argue, for example, that the entirety of the native language representation makes up the initial second language representation. At the opposite extreme, Vainikka & Young-Scholten (1994, 1996) propose that only the structure of VP, NP, and PP transfer into the initial representation; IP is initially absent. Taking a middle ground, Eubank (1993/1994, 1996) and Beck (1996) claim, though for very different theoretical reasons, that verb movement does not transfer.

[14]Saying that the grammar cannot deal with such input does not imply that learners cannot understand such sentences, since comprehension involves much more than just syntactic decoding and thus could be successful even in spite of syntactic difficulties.

[15]For an example of this, see Ch. 2.

KEY TERMS, CONCEPTS, AND ISSUES

generative grammar
formal linguistics
levels of adequacy
  observational
  descriptive
  explanatory

generative transformational grammars
reference grammars
pedagogical grammars
interlanguage grammar
Universal Grammar
tree

rule
PS rules
linear structure
hierarchical structure
intuitions
generate

structural knowledge
underlying
transfer
developmental transition
input
X-bar Theory

EXPLORING THE TOPICS FURTHER

1. *Introductory texts.* Goodluck (1991) treats first language acquisition from a generative perspective, while Haegeman (1994) gives a thorough introduction to syntactic theory and the Principles and Parameters Approach. White (1989) offers a thorough and easy-to-understand introduction to second language acquisition research and related issues in the Principles and Parameters Approach.
2. *General overviews of research questions and findings.* The following will provide good, solid overviews of research in the fields of second language acquisition and syntax-related issues: Eubank (1991a), Eubank & Beck (1993), Eubank & Juffs (1995), Flynn (1996), Gass (1996), Ritchie & Bhatia (1996), Schachter (1996), White (1996a, 1996b).
3. *Collections.* The following volumes contain numerous articles on syntax-related research in second language acquisition. The respective publication dates give a rough indication of older and more recent advances in the field: Flynn & O'Neill, eds. (1988); Gass & Schachter, eds. (1989); Eubank, ed. (1991); Hoekstra & Schwartz, eds. (1994).
4. *Journals.* Though articles in this area may appear from time to time in linguistic journals with a broader orientation, such as *Language,* the journals that specialize in formal language acquisition research are *Second Language Research, Studies in Second Language Acquisition,* and *Language Acquisition.* The latter journal publishes research on native language and second language acquisition.

REFERENCES

Baker, C.L. (1978). *Introduction to generative-transformational syntax.* Englewood Cliffs, NJ: Prentice-Hall.

Bardovi-Harlig, K. (1995). The interaction of pedagogy and natural sequences in the acquisition of tense and aspect. In F.R. Eckman, D. Highland, P.W. Lee, J.L. Mileham & R.R. Weber (Eds.) *Second language acquisition theory and pedagogy* (pp. 151–168). Hillside, NJ: Lawrence Erlbaum.

Beck, M.L. (1996). The status of verb-raising among English-speaking learners of German. *Toegepaste Taalwetenschap in Artikelen, 55,* 23–33.

Birdsong, D. (1989). *Metalinguistic performance and interlinguistic competence.* Berlin: Springer-Verlag.

Bley-Vroman, R. (1990). The logical problem of foreign language learning. *Linguistic Analysis, 20,* 3–49.

Clahsen, H. (1984). The acquisition of German word order: A test case for cognitive approaches to L2 development. In R.W. Andersen (Ed.), *Second languages. A cross-linguistic perspective,* (pp. 219–42). Rowley, MA: Newbury House.

Chomsky, N. (1964). *Current issues in linguistic theory.* The Hague: Mouton.

Chomsky, N. (1986). *Barriers.* Cambridge, MA: MIT Press.

Duden. *Grammatik der deutschen Gegenwartssprache* (third ed.). (1973). Mannheim, Germany: Bibliographisches Institut, Dudenverlag.

duPlessis, J., Solin, D. Travis. L. & White, L. (1987). UG or not UG, that is the question: A reply to Clahsen & Muysken. *Second Language Research, 3,* 56–75.

Ellis, R. (1989). Are classroom and naturalistic acquisition the same? A study of the classroom acquisition of German word order rules. *Studies in Second Language Acquisition, 11,* 305–28.

Eubank, L. (1991a). Introduction: Universal Grammar in the second language. In L. Eubank (Ed.), *Point counterpoint. Universal Grammar in the second language,* (pp. 1–48). Amsterdam: John Benjamins.

Eubank, L. (Ed.). (1991b). *Point Counterpoint. Universal Grammar in the second language.* Amsterdam: John Benjamins.

Eubank, L. (1993/1994). On the transfer of parametric values in L2 development. *Language Acquisition, 3,* 184–208.

Eubank, L. (1996). Negation in early German-English interlanguage: More valueless features in the L2 initial state. In L. Eubank & B. D. Schwartz (Eds.), What is the L2 initial state? *Second Language Research* [special issue], *12,* 73–106 .

Eubank, L. & Beck, M.L. (1993). Generative research on second-language acquisition. In A.O. Hadley (Ed.), *Research on language learning: Principles, processes, and prospects: The ACTFL foreign language education series,* (pp. 58–105). Lincolnwood, IL: National Textbook Company.

Eubank, L. & Gregg, K. (1995). "Et in amygdala ego"?: UG (S)LA and neurobiology. *Studies in Second Language Acquisition, 17,* 35–57.

Eubank, L. & Juffs, A. (1995). Morphosyntax and argument structure in L2 acquisition: A brief overview of research. *GLOT International, 1*(9/10), 3–6.

Fanselow, G. & Felix, S. (1987). *Sprachtheorie 2. Die Rektions- und Bindungstheorie.* Tübingen, Germany: Francke.

Flynn, S. (1996). A parameter-setting approach to second language acquisition. In W.C. Ritchie & T.K. Bhatia (Eds.), *Handbook of second language acquisition* (pp. 121–158). San Diego: Academic Press.

Flynn, S. & O'Neill, W. (Eds.). (1988). *Linguistic theory in second language acquisition.* Dordrecht: Kluwer.

Gass, S. (1996). Second language acquisition and linguistic theory: The role of language transfer. In W.C. Ritchie & T.K. Bhatia (Eds.), *Handbook of second language acquisition,* (pp. 317–345). San Diego: Academic Press.

Gass, S.M. & Schachter, J. (Eds.). (1989). *Linguistic perspectives on second language acquisition.* Cambridge: Cambridge University Press.

Gleitman, L.R. & Newport, E.L. (1995). The invention of language by children: Environmental and biological influences on the acquisition of language. In L.R. Gleitman & M. Liberman (Eds.), *Language: An invitation to cognitive science,* (second edition, Vol. 1), (pp. 1–24). Cambridge, MA: The MIT Press.

Gregg, K. (1996). The logical and developmental problems of second language acquisition. In W.C. Ritchie & T.K. Bhatia (Eds.), *Handbook of second language acquisition,* (pp. 49–81). San Diego: Academic Press.

Goodluck, H. (1991). *Language acquisition: A linguistic introduction.* Oxford, UK and Cambridge, MA: Blackwell.

Haegeman, L. (1994). *Introduction to government and binding theory* (second edition). Oxford, UK and Cambridge, MA: Blackwell.

Hoekstra, T. & Schwartz, B.D. (Eds.). (1994). *Acquisition studies in generative grammar.* Amsterdam: John Benjamins.

Huber, W. & Kummer, W. (1974). *Transformationelle Syntax des Deutschen* (Vol. 1). München, Germany: Wilhelm Fink.

Jackendoff, R. (1994). *Patterns in the mind.* New York: Basic Books.

Larsen-Freeman, D. & Long, M.H. (1991). *An introduction to second language acquisition research.* London: Longman.

Lightfoot, D. (1982). *The language lottery.* Cambridge, MA: MIT Press.

Newmeyer, F. (1983). *Grammatical theory.* Chicago, IL: University of Chicago Press.

Nunan, D. (1996). Issues in second language acquisition research: Examining substance and procedure. In W.C. Ritchie & T.K. Bhatia (Eds.), *Handbook of second language acquisition,* (pp. 349–374). San Diego, CA: Academic Press.

Pinker, S. (1994). *The language instinct.* New York: Morrow.

Pinker, S. (1995). Language acquisition. In L.R. Gleitman & M. Liberman (Eds.), *Language. An invitation to cognitive science* (second edition), (Vol. 1), (pp. 135–182). Cambridge, MA: The MIT Press.

Quirk, R. & Greenbaum, S. (1978). *A concise grammar of contemporary English.* New York, NY: Harcourt Brace Jovanovich.

Schachter, J. (1996). Maturation and the issue of Universal Grammar in second language acquisition. In W.C. Ritchie & T.K. Bhatia (Eds.), *Handbook of second language acquisition,* (pp. 159–193). San Diego: Academic Press.

Schwartz, B. D. (1993). On explicit and negative evidence effecting and affecting competence and linguistic behavior. *Studies in Second Language Acquisition, 15,* 147–63.

Schwartz, B.D. & Sprouse, R.A. (1994). Word order and nominative case in nonnative language acquisition: A longitudinal study of (L1 Turkish) German interlanguage. In T. Hoekstra & B.D. Schwartz (Eds.), *Acquisition studies in generative grammar,* (pp. 317–368). Amsterdam: John Benjamins.

Schwartz, B. D. & Sprouse, R. A. (1996). L2 cognitive states and the Full Transfer/Full Access model. In L. Eubank & B.D. Schwartz (Eds.), What is the L2 initial state? *Second Language Research* [special issue], *12,* 40–72.

Sorace, A. (1996). The use of acceptability judgments in second language acquisition research. In W.C. Ritchie & T.K. Bhatia (Eds.), *Handbook of second language acquisition,* (pp. 375–409). San Diego, CA: Academic Press.

Travis, L. (1991). Parameters of phrase structure and verb-second phenomena. In Robert Freidin (Ed.), *Principles and parameters in comparative grammar,* (pp. 339–64). Cambridge, MA: The MIT Press.

Vainikka, A. & Young-Scholten, M. (1994). Direct access to X-bar theory: Evidence from Korean and Turkish adults learning German. In T. Hoekstra & B.D. Schwartz (Eds.), *Acquisition studies in generative grammar,* (pp. 265–316). Amsterdam: John Benjamins.

Vainikka, A. & Young-Scholten, M. (1996). Gradual development of L2 phrase structure. In L. Eubank & B.D. Schwartz (Eds.), What is the L2 initial state? *Second Language Research* [special issue], *12,* 7–39.

White, L. (1989). *Universal Grammar and second language acquisition.* Amsterdam: John Benjamins.

White, L. (1996a). Universal Grammar and second language acquisition. In W.C. Ritchie & T.K. Bhatia (Eds.), *Handbook of second language acquisition,* (pp. 85–120). San Diego: Academic Press.

White, L. (1996b). The tale of the ugly duckling (or the coming of age of second language acquisition research). In A. Stringfellow, D. Cahana-Amitay, E. Hughes, & A. Zukowski (Eds.), *Proceedings of the 20th Annual Boston University Conference on Language Development,* (pp. 1–17). Somerville, MA: Cascadilla Press.

Zwart, C.J.W. (1993). Verb movement and complementizer agreement. In. J. Bobaljik & C. Phillips (Eds.), *Papers on Case and Agreement I,* (pp. 297–340). MIT Working Papers in Linguistics, Vol 18. Cambridge, MA: Department of Linguistics and Philosophy, MIT.

CHAPTER 4

Phonology in Language Teaching: Essentials of Theory and Practice

Martha C. Pennington
University of Luton, UK

INTRODUCTION

Historically, phonology has been a central aspect of mainstream approaches to language teaching such as Audiolingualism and the Direct Approach, as well as of non-mainstream approaches such as The Silent Way and Counseling-Learning. Yet in recent times, the teaching of phonology and, with it, pronunciation has fallen out of favor, owing in large part to the influence of a popular understanding of Communicative Language Teaching, Krashen's (1982) theory of unconscious "acquisition" vs. conscious "learning," and the related Natural Approach (Krashen & Terrell 1983), which advises against an explicit focus on accuracy. Recently, however, there are encouraging signs that attention to phonology in language instruction is reviving, based on a re-evaluation of learner needs and the communicative value of pronunciation (Morley 1991), with increased attention to research as well (Pennington 1994).

As in the field of reading, where exclusively top down, conceptual approaches are now complemented by bottom-up, analytical approaches (cf. Lee, Ch. 8), in the current orientation to phonology in language teaching, the traditional bottom-up, segment-based focus on accuracy is complemented by a top-down, trans-segmental approach. As part of this wider focus, recent discussions of phonology in second language acquisition also recognize the social and psychological aspects of pronunciation behavior (Morley 1991; Pennington 1989a; Pennington & Richards 1986). The teaching of pronunciation in a second or foreign language has also broadened its focus in the current generation to one which embraces learner-centered and communicative orientations to classroom activities (Celce-Murcia 1987; Pica 1984; Wong 1987).

Given that a teacher can reasonably be expected to have a knowledge base covering the substance of the area to be taught, it would seem important to ground language teachers in both the mechanics and the meaning of phonology in the target language as well as in the language(s) of the learners whom

67

they expect to teach. Where the learners represent a diverse group from different language backgrounds, as is common in ESL classes, a comparative orientation to the target language in relation to other languages is useful background for the language teacher. It would also seem important in preparing teachers for language instruction to link phonology with other aspects of theory and practice in language learning and education more generally. To these ends, the discussion of the present chapter begins with an introduction to the key concepts and terms of phonology, the nature of English pronunciation, and the types of difficulties which non-native speakers experience in learning a second language. Then, in the main body of the chapter, research on second language learning and phonology is reviewed, with implications drawn for teaching practice.

---

*P*ause to consider . . .

how pronunciation contributes to communication. Have you ever under- or overestimated a learner's grammatical or linguistic ability based on his/her pronunciation?

WHAT IS PHONOLOGY?

The term, "phonology" refers to the sound patterns of a language or the pronunciation patterns of speakers of a language. It can also refer to the study of these sound patterns or pronunciation patterns. In phonology (in the latter sense), sound patterns are analyzed at two levels: "segmental" and "trans-segmental," or "prosodic." At the segmental level, the consonants and vowels, that is, the "phonemes," of a language are identified, indicated by symbols between two slash marks, for example, /b/ or /p/. For each phoneme, a pronunciation target is specified in terms of the "place of articulation," "manner of articulation," and "voicing" of the individual consonant or vowel.

Examples of places of articulation are "bilabial" (articulated with the two lips, as in the pronunciation of /p/ (*pie*), /b/ (*buy*), /m/ (*my*), /w/ (*why*); "labiodental" (articulated with the bottom lip and upper front teeth, as in the pronunciation of /f/ (*fee*) and /v/ (*vee*)); and "alveolar" (articulated with the tongue tip touching the gum ridge behind the upper front teeth, as in /t/ (*too*), /d/ (*do*), /s/ (*sou*), /z/ (*zoo*), and /n/ (*noon*)). Examples of manners of articulation are "nasal" (produced with air flowing out of the nose, as in /m/ (*mow*) and /n/ (*know*)); "stop" (produced with a complete closure of two articulators, as in /b/ (*by*), /p/ (*pie*), /t/ (*tie*), and /d/ (*dye*)); and "fricative" (produced with audible friction, as in /f/ (*feel*), /v/ (*veal*), /s/ (*seal*), and /z/ (*zeal*)). In the dimension of voicing, sounds are also classified as either "voiceless" (i.e. produced without vocal cord vibration), as in /h/ (*hi*), /p/ (*pie*), /t/ (*Thai*), /f/ (*fie*), and /s/ (*sigh*), or "voiced" (i.e. produced with vocal cord vibration), as in /m/ (*me*), /b/ (*be*), /w/ (*we*), /d/ (*dee*), /n/ (*knee*), /v/ (*vee*),

/z/ *(zee)*, and all vowels. Vowels are further classified according to tongue position in two dimensions as High/Mid/Low and Front/Central/ Back. For example, /i/ *(he)* is a high front vowel, /u/ *(who)* is a high back vowel, and /a/ *(ha)* is a low central vowel.

Languages differ in the number of vowels and consonants in their phonological systems and in the specific characteristics of these. As a consequence, a language learner will often have to learn to recognize and to produce different types of phonemes as well as different types of distinctions among the phonemes of the second language phonological system. For example, whereas English has two phonemes produced with a relatively high and front tongue position, /i/ *(bean)* and /ɪ/ *(bin)*, Spanish has only one, /i/ *(si* 'yes'). The tongue position for Spanish /i/ is close but not identical to English /i/. Thus, a Spanish speaker learning English must not only learn to articulate a new phoneme and to distinguish it carefully from the native language phoneme, but must also learn to differentiate it from another similar phoneme in the second language.

Such cases are very common in learning a second language. As another example, a Japanese speaker learning English must learn to differentiate the /l/ and /r/ phonemes from the native language phoneme /r/ *(ryokan* 'inn'). The Japanese phoneme shares the properties of both English /r/ and /l/, as well as having its own unique characteristics. Like all phonemes in all languages, the pronunciation of Japanese /r/ varies depending on the context of neighboring sounds. Part of the difficulty in learning English is that the range of contextual variation for the one Japanese phoneme overlaps two different phonemes in English. Consequently, the Japanese learner of English must learn to separate distinctions which are "subphonemic (allophonic)" in the native language into two phonemes in the second language and then to "fine-tune" pronunciation to the exact targets for /r/ and /l/ in English.

The Japanese learner of English must, moreover, acquire not only the basic distinction between the /r/ and /l/ phonemes but also the fine distinctions within each of these phonemes—their "allophones," as they are pronounced in different contexts. This will include, for instance, somewhat different pronunciations for each phoneme in the contrasting contexts illustrated below:

- Beginning of a word vs. following another consonant (e.g., *lay/play, ray/gray*);
- Between vowels vs. at the end of a word (e.g., *belly/bell, berry/bear*)
- Before a high front vowel vs. before a high back vowel (e.g., *leak/look, reak/rook*).

These are only some of the articulatory distinctions a language learner must acquire at the segmental level, the level of phonemes and their allophones or positional variants.

At the trans-segmental or prosodic level, the phonologist seeks to characterize properties of stretches of speech, or utterances. The "prosody" of a language, that is, its prosodic properties, includes "voice setting," "intonation," "tone," and "rhythm." The voice setting is the overall posture of the vocal organs for speech, including such features as the following:

- How tight ("tense") or loose ("lax") the setting of the vocal cords is for voicing;
- How open the jaw is in general for pronunciation;
- Whether the tip of the tongue is used to articulate sounds;
- Whether the tip of the tongue, if active in pronunciation, is curled ("retroflexed");
- Whether the back of the tongue is generally raised or lowered during articulation;
- The degree to which the lips are used in articulation

Differences among languages in any or all of these voice-setting features produce differences in overall "voice quality" as well as in the articulation of individual sounds.

Intonation refers to the pattern of "pitches" (how high or low the voice is) that occur over an utterance. Different patterns of pitches, or "intonation contours," are associated with different linguistic functions and meanings. It is common across languages for high or high-rising pitch to indicate a question and for falling pitch to indicate a statement. It is also common for non-falling (level or low-rising) pitch to be employed by speakers to indicate unfinished units such as non-final clauses or non-final items of a list. Thus, the initial clause (1) in the example below, ends in non-falling pitch, signifying that the message is not yet finished, whereas the final clause (2) ends in a pitch fall, signifying completion of the message. Similarly, the final item of the list in (2) ends on a pitch fall, whereas the items preceding it end with non-falling pitch, signifying that the list is not yet complete:

(1)   *You must not have gotten home until very late last night.*

(2)   *because I called you at 10:00 pm, 11:00 pm, and midnight.*

At a general level, the characteristics of intonation contours and the relationships of intonation to meaning are similar across languages. However, the details of intonation contours vary substantially from language to language. In addition to these differences in the physical nature of intonation, there are differences in the degree and the way in which intonation is exploited in languages.

Some languages, such as Chinese and many African languages, also have "tones," which are set pitch patterns for the pronunciation of individual words. Intonation languages, such as English, seem to exploit the possibilities for varying pitch patterns across whole utterances to a greater extent than tone languages, in which the pitch patterns of utterances are largely determined by the tone patterns of individual words. In such languages, intonation is often focused on final particles, which express questioning as well as various types of attitudinal meaning. As a consequence, speakers of tone languages who are learning English will have to learn to notice and to exploit utterance-level pitch patterns to indicate grammatical, as well as attitudinal, meanings to a far greater extent than they would in their native languages.

The rhythm of an utterance is made up of a pattern of "accents," or "stresses." An accent or stress refers to a point in a stretch of speech which is more prominent than the surrounding context. This prominence results when the speaker adds extra energy to the production of a unit of speech, thereby accentuating it. The unit to which extra energy is added may be a phrase, a word, or a part of a word—a syllable (a vowel plus its surrounding consonants, if any). When a speaker adds extra energy to the production of a unit of speech, the unit becomes louder, longer, and/or higher in pitch. These properties, individually or in combination, amount to phonological prominence. The rhythm of an utterance is then the pattern of "accented" or "stressed" units alternating with "unaccented" or "unstressed" units (those which are softer, shorter, and/or lower in pitch).

The example below shows how the rhythm of utterances is built by an alternating pattern of accented and unaccented syllables. The accented syllables (preceded by stress marks, ') are made more prominent by being pronounced longer, louder, and/or higher in pitch than the unaccented syllables:

'Rose is	'in a
'coming	'minute
'over	'in a 'minute
'coming 'over	or 'two
'Rose is 'coming 'over	'in a 'minute or 'two
'Rose is 'coming 'over 'in a 'minute or 'two.	

The unit of timing that is relevant for the rhythm of languages varies from small units comprising individual segments (e.g., Japanese), to larger units comprising individual syllables (e.g., Spanish), to even larger units consisting of one stressed syllable and its accompanying unstressed syllables (e.g., English). Thus, a non-native speaker of English must learn to perceive and produce stressed and unstressed syllables, as well as combinations of these, composing larger units of speech in the proper rhythm.

For English, the target for rhythm is equal spacing between stresses, which requires compressing the unstressed syllables in between, resulting in much reduction, in addition to overlapping and compression of individual segments. These effects of "co-articulation," which result in contractions (e.g., *I've, it's, won't*) and various weak or blended forms in colloquial pronunciation (e.g., *yer* for *your*, *gonna* for *going to*, and *jever* for *Did you ever*), are more extreme for English than for some other languages. As a result, the learner of English must learn to rely more on ear (how words are actually pronounced in context) than eye (how words are spelled).

---

*P*ause to consider . . .

the phenomena of stress and co-articulation in English. What complications in the learning of the phonology of English might these represent for the learner? What effect might variable pronunciation of syntactic strings like *did you, what did you,* and *did you ever* have on the clarity of input for learners, both for the development of the L2 phonology itself and in helping learners establish sound-structure-meaning correspondences? (cf. VanPatten, Ch. 1, for a discussion of input.)

THEORETICAL FOUNDATIONS OF TEACHING PRACTICE

As in all other aspects of teaching, instructional approaches for second language phonology should be based at a general level on learning theory and, more specifically, on what is known about how people learn languages, particularly in their phonological aspect. From an examination of the literature in learning theory, second language acquisition, and the teaching and learning of pronunciation, it emerges that instruction geared to improving second language phonology should take into account universal principles of learning as well as speech perception and production processes. It should also take into account the individual factors which can affect the development of phonology in a second language. These include age, first language influence, prior educational experiences, psychological readiness and motivation, and socio-cultural motivation. These topics are addressed below to form a perspective on phonology that places it in the larger context of second language acquisition theory and language teaching practice. The chapter concludes with suggestions for classroom practice.

Learning Processes in Phonology

Universal Principles of Learning

As in other aspects of language learning, general, or universal, principles of human learning guide the acquisition of a second language and its phonology. First of all, people learn what is most salient in terms of perception or in terms of their own needs or interests. For example, learners of English attend to stressed items (content words), since these are perceptually highlighted, more than unstressed items (function words such as articles and grammatical endings). Because they command more attention, items which are commonly stressed are likely to be learned before those which are generally unstressed. In addition, some learners attend to certain areas of vocabulary more than others because of a particular interest in the field in which that vocabulary is used. Because of their special interest, these individuals may attend more to the pronunciation of that set of words than will other learners, thus possibly gaining an advantage for learning their pronunciation. People learn what they need most for communication, spending less time on those aspects of language which are for them of low utility. From this perspective, they also learn content words before function words and grammatical endings, in addition to certain areas of vocabulary most useful to them.

It is also a natural phenomenon of learning that people acquire general patterns before details and in fact tend to overgeneralize the most common patterns to cover the less usual or exceptional cases. In phonology, this means that learners naturally acquire basic patterns for constructing utterances, such as falling intonation for statements and rising intonation for questions—often including *wh-* questions, by overgeneralizing on the pattern for *yes/no* questions—before learning the details of usage and the ways in which these contours can be varied for particular purposes. Another natural learning principle is comparison and contrast. Learners will compare and contrast instances of language to help them sort through the information they receive and on this basis classify sounds into categories and patterns of words, phrases, and longer utterances. Through comparison and contrast, the learner overgeneralizes some cases and undergeneralizes or misclassifies others, assuming sameness or similarity where there is difference and assuming difference where forms are in fact equivalent.

As another principle of learning that is relevant to second language acquisition, learners tend to simplify the learning task and the content of learning to accommodate to their limited ability in interpretation and production of language. As a consequence of the tendency towards simplification, syllable-initial consonant clusters such as /pr/, /pl/, /tr/, /kr/, /spr/, /str/, /skr/, as well as syllable-final ones such as /sp/, /st/, /sk/, /sps/, /sts/, and /sks/, may undergo cluster-reduction processes whereby the second and/or third member of the cluster will be lost. As a complementary type of simplification process, an "epenthetic", or linking, vowel may be added as a means of simplifying the production of two neighboring consonants, so that a word such as *blue* is pronounced as /bilu/ or /bulu/, or *stay* becomes /sitei/ or /istei/. Also as a consequence of the tendency to simplify, the minor aspects of phonology, such as the production of unstressed syllables or words and the details of pronunciation of individual sounds, will not be developed in the early stages of acquiring a second language. The direction of second language simplifications, which are often the same as or similar to those made by children learning the phonology of their first language, may help to identify the most unmarked or universal aspects of language as against the more marked and language-particular aspects.

In speaking a second language, the natural phonological processes of strengthening of articulation in salient contexts and weakening of articulation in non-salient contexts are operative, as they are in first-language production. This means that information which is the focus of a message will also be produced in such a way as to become the focus of attention, that is, it will be accentuated by such devices as raising the voice, in terms of pitch and/or loudness, and articulating slowly and carefully. Each of these devices draws a listener's attention to the elements, that is, the particular words or parts of utterances, which are pronounced in this way. While the important elements of a message are naturally foregrounded, the elements of lesser importance are naturally backgrounded by such devices as low pitch, soft voice, and rapid articulation. The elements which are pronounced in a de-accentuated way are thereby de-emphasized for the listener.

The contrast of accentuated (strong) and de-accentuated (weak) pronunciation helps a listener to parse an utterance and to interpret the relative significance of its individual components and the overall significance of the message. It is also an aspect of pronunciation which comes naturally in that the contrast between strong and weak features of pronunciation is similar in all languages, particularly in its trans-segmental manifestations of raising vs. lowering the pitch or loudness of the voice, slowing down vs. speeding up the speaking rate, and articulating in an emphatic vs. a non-emphatic manner. This contrast is therefore a useful feature of phonology for language learners to attend to in speaking as well as in listening, especially in the early stages of acquiring a second language, when other aspects of the second language are not well-developed.

The implication of the foregoing discussion for teaching is that the more salient and general aspects of phonology such as the rhythmic patterns of sentences, the intonation of basic communicative patterns such as set types of questions and answers, understandable pronunciation of key words, and basic pronunciation of phonemes should be addressed to help the learner develop intelligibility and overall information-structuring and message coherence before minor points of articulation are introduced (Gilbert 1993; Rogerson-Revell 1990). Another implication is that it might be valuable to simplify the learner's task to some extent by focusing on key words in listening and pronunciation activities, under the assumption that function words and the details of articulation are more likely to be learned both gradually and in context. It might also be of value to focus the learner's attention on the contrast of the native language with the second language, to point out aspects of the phonology that could mistakenly be viewed as the same in form or function but which are not.

Speech Perception and Production Processes

Although much of the information presented to the senses is apprehended by human beings on an unconscious level, it seems that new knowledge in second language acquisition is gained at least in part through noticing and conscious attention (Schmidt 1990). Thus, the salience of phonological input is related to its accessibility for the language learner. Research shows that some aspects of phonology (e.g., the American English retroflex /r/) are more salient than others to learners in general and in relation to specific first-language and second-language backgrounds (Cunningham-Andersson 1990; Zuengler 1988). In addition, phonological input can be made more accessible by increasing its salience, for example, by presenting it in a particularly memorable way, to ensure that it will be noticed and processed by the language learner. It may also be necessary to raise the learner's level of attention to a more conscious awareness in order for phonological learning to progress beyond a certain point of reasonable communicative success. Research reviewed by Harley (1986) suggests that accuracy in second language performance may not develop outside of explicit attention to form, and this may be as true for phonology as it is for grammar. As language learners become more conscious of their own and others' phonological performance, they develop their monitoring capability for self-assessment and self-correction.

Leather's (1990) work on acquisition of Chinese tone demonstrates a strong interrelationship between perception and production in learning the phonology of a second language. In Leather's study, which made use of visually enhanced lessons presented on computer, training in one modality (production or perception) proved to be sufficient for enhancing learning in the other modality as well. This important result suggests that listening-oriented work—at least in a highly focused and salient mode of presentation—will be of value for spoken production and also, perhaps somewhat surprisingly, that practice in oral production will result in improved auditory perception. Thus, it seems that phonological production and perception exist in a mutually reinforcing relationship in which improvement in either area can effect improvement in the other mode. Other work in second language phonology shows that the interrelationship of production and perception is not a stable one during the course of language acquisition (Boatman 1990). At an early stage of acquisition, learners can hear distinctions in the second language which they cannot consistently make, while intermediate-stage learners can sometimes produce phonemic distinctions which they cannot consistently discriminate in perception (Sheldon & Strange 1982). Thus, it seems that perceptual ability might develop ahead of productive ability at first, but that this early advantage for perception may no longer hold at a later stage—though perception may match or surpass production again as acquisition progresses to an advanced level. Taken together, the implication of these findings is that the two modalities of perception and production should both be addressed and interrelated in instruction which is aimed at improving second language phonology.

The salience of the phonological aspect of speech or of specific aspects of the phonology of a second language can be increased by instructional activities designed to focus the learner's attention preparatory to other activities or retrospectively through reflection and feedback on performance. Such activities are usefully focused contrastively, to encourage the learner to notice the difference between one phonological feature and another or the effect that one style of pronunciation or another has on the meaning and communicative force of a message. Salience and memorability can also be increased by interrelating oral, aural, and visual modalities in instruction. For example, matching of spoken performance and listening discrimination to visual displays of pitch contours has proved beneficial for pronunciation in several studies (e.g., de Bot & Mailfert 1982; Champagne-Muzar, Schneiderman & Bourdages 1993; Leather 1990). Such matching may be accomplished in a traditional language laboratory or a computer-assisted environment (Chun 1989; Pennington 1989b), or it might be accomplished in home study using a workbook which is keyed to an audiotape and which includes visualizations of pitch contours or other aspects of phonology in graphic form, such as plots of vowel productions in phonetic space (Rochet 1990).

In building phonological targets for perception, not only the salience of input but also the breadth of input is important. As part of this breadth of input, language teachers can—through use of recorded material, conversation partners, or guest speakers—expose learners to a wide range of speakers and contexts in the second language. Esling (1987) suggests that expanding learners' exposure to different voices in the second language may be more valuable for performance than articulatory drilling, on the pedagogical principle of "collection not correction" (p. 469). Along with plentiful input, learners need opportunities to practice and to receive feedback on their performance, in order to trigger and maintain the creative construction process which continually adjusts perceptual targets and performance in the acquisition of a second language.

Pause to consider . . .

how perception is different from comprehension. How does perception contribute to comprehension? Compare aural perception and comprehension to perception and comprehension of written input (cf. Lee, Ch. 8).

The Factors Affecting Phonology in a Second Language

Age

With adolescent and adult learners, who have passed the "critical period" for language acquisition (Long 1990; Scovel 1988), both the process and the outcome of learning are different from those of children. As compared to the child, adults learn in a much more deliberate, conscious, and self-conscious manner. Also, as compared to children, adults learn in a less holistic, more analytic manner, segmenting the stream of speech into units of words and sounds and attending much less to the larger context of communication than the child does.

Although the child in a sense learns in a more natural way, the older learner in several senses possesses much more advanced learning skills than the child (Singleton 1989). The adolescent or adult, for example, has a much more advanced capability for analyzing the stream of speech and for generalizing on experiences to extract regularities. Also with age comes the ability to focus attention and to direct behavior to accomplish certain goals. Thus, an older learner can learn language systematically, in a pre-planned program. An older learner can also monitor and regulate behavior more effectively than a younger learner, and make changes to adjust performance as needed.

Language teachers can try to exploit adult capabilities, such as their more analytical ability and their superior self-evaluative and self-monitoring skills. The language teacher can capitalize on these adult capabilities by designing the autonomous pronunciation class or the speaking skills curriculum to incorporate analytic, reflective, and self-directed approaches to learning pronunciation. These approaches might incorporate pre-production work involving articulatory training and consciousness-raising to build awareness of the important attributes of the second language phonological system. Such training and consciousness-raising might include comparison of native language to second language phonemes and trans-segmental properties or to pronunciation of individual words where one of the languages includes many loan words from the other, as for Japanese vis-à-vis English. The adult pronunciation curriculum might also make use of the approaches of "oral dialogue journals" and self-study using computerized training systems such as Visi-Pitch (Kay Elemetrics, Pine Brook, New Jersey) or Video Voice Speech Training System (Micro Video, Ann Arbor, Michigan). For the adult learner, a combination of (1) *pre-production* instruction and consciousness-raising, (2) *in-production* meaning-oriented input arising through language use and negotiation in communicative tasks, and (3) *post-production* feedback on intelligibility and overall communicative success is likely to achieve the best results.

*P*ause to consider . . .

what advantages children have over adults when it comes to acquiring the phonology of a second or foreign language. How can adults use age to their advantage in learning L2 phonology in an instructional setting?

First Language Influence

Whereas children approach the learning of their mother tongue in the most naive and untutored way, adolescent and adult learners may draw on their previously acquired knowledge. In the learning of a second language, the influence of the first language is known as "language transfer." In the case of pronunciation, this may result in a recognizable accent in the second language based on the phonological system of the native language.

The pronunciation of the mother tongue may transfer at both the segmental and the trans-segmental levels. At the level of individual phonemes, learners tend to identify the phonemes of the second language with those of their mother tongue, which are usually not in fact identical. This tendency to "equivalence classification" (Flege 1987) means that in the early stages of language acquisition, the phonological system of the second language is built to a large extent directly on the sound system of the native language. In particular, sounds in the second language which are close but not identical to those in the native language tend to be equated in production as well as in perception. Only gradually does the learner become able to make distinctions between the sounds and the phonemic categories of the native language and those of the second language.

Transfer may be wholesale, affecting all items with the same phonological form (e.g., all words containing a certain vowel or consonant), or piecemeal, affecting only certain lexical items. In the more usual case, the effects of transfer are not categorical, but rather occur to a greater or lesser extent in certain contexts. The research of Hammarberg (1990) shows that some aspects of phonology transfer easily from the first language, while other aspects are more variable. In the more variable cases, the forms produced by the language learner often represent a combination of transfer effects and unique language learning—that is, "interlanguage" (Selinker 1992)—effects resulting from natural phonological processes and the learning processes of simplification and overgeneralization.

According to Major (1987), transfer effects will be most in evidence in the early stages of learning a second language and in the most informal communicative situations: that is, those where the learner is least focused on form and correctness. The natural developmental effects of phonological processes and general learning processes will, in contrast, be most in evidence in the middle stages of language learning and in intermediate communicative situations, that is, those which are neither highly informal nor highly formal.

Not only the learner's level of proficiency and the general context and level of formality of communication, but also the context of neighboring phonemes (Dickerson 1976) and the familiarity of individual lexical items (e.g., from cognates or loan words in the native language [Hammarberg 1984]) will affect the extent of transfer and the course of development in individual cases. The way in which individual lexical items are produced by second language learners and their course of development from the early to the late stages of acquisition show many different patterns (Wieden 1990). At the same time, on a general level, the course of second language acquisition can be described as one in which the phonological targets are progressively refined away from those of the native language and towards those of the second, or "target," language. Although production varies depending on context, and although each segmental phoneme or trans-segmental feature follows a different course of development, the general course of second language development seems to be one involving cycles of broadening and narrowing the phonological targets and the range of variation towards a closer match to the targets and range of variation which represent the phonological system of the second language (Baptista 1990).

The foregoing discussion suggests that it is normal—and in fact essential—for language learners to have variable and errorful performance over the course of language acquisition, as they work to expand and focus their phonological system towards the second language targets. One implication for teaching is that pronunciation "errors" are often a sign of language acquisition processes at work. Another implication is that learners need considerable time and communicative opportunities to work through the process of focusing and refocusing their phonological system towards the system of the target language. In this process of elaborating and refining the phonological system, it may be of value to expose learners through listening material to a wide range of speakers' voices and types of discourse, as input to help shape their developing phonological targets.

---

*P*ause to consider . . .

an example of first language influence in L2 phonology. How can educational experiences affect the phonological acquisition of a second or foreign language? Why might it be important for a teacher to identify the source of a pronunciation problem as being developmental or transfer?

Prior Educational Experiences

Along with the processes of first-language transfer and natural development, language learners' educational experiences may directly or indirectly affect their phonological acquisition. When learning a second language, adults will generally make use of their previously acquired skills and experiences of learning through explicit teaching, in both language and other subjects. In addition, there may be a certain learning style or approach which has been encouraged by previous education and which affects the way older learners approach the second language and its phonology.

For example, students in many Asian countries are often taught English based on a phonemic system of long and short vowels (/iː/ vs. /i/, /eː/ vs. /e/, /uː/ vs. /u/, /oː/ vs. /o/, and sometimes also /aː/ vs. /a/), which may be derived from the system of the native language but which does not fit the pronunciation of most varieties of English very well. Such prior training no doubt influences pronunciation in the second language by encouraging simplification of the English vowel system or equivalence classification between the vowel phonemes of the mother tongue and the second language (Pennington 1994). Equivalence classification and inaccurate or simplified production of phonological targets may also be encouraged by the focus on the written language which is common in many educational systems. The implication for teaching is that pronunciation instruction cannot be based on the written language or on the sound-symbol correspondences of orthography. Rather, symbols representing pronunciation which are to be used with second language learners should be carefully chosen: (1) to reflect the actual pronunciation of individual phonemes and the contrasts of the phonological system of the second language, and (2) to be maximally distinctive in relation to the first language(s) of the learners.

In general, the older learner should be guided to learn the phonology of the second language as a separate system distinct from that of the native language and encouraged to experiment with new forms of pronunciation which can be refined over time. The learner's attention can also be drawn to the specific context effects of the second language in speaking and listening and their relationship to fluency and message content. Most importantly, the learner needs to be encouraged and motivated to speak frequently and over extended periods. In this way, both the natural and the experienced learning processes of adult learners will be activated to develop the phonological system of the second language on its own terms.

Psychological Readiness and Motivation

A speaker's native language pronunciation patterns become cognitively and articulatorily routinized at an early age. As a stable part of cognitive structure and motor performance, a speaker's pronunciation patterns are a component of self-expression and thus of personality structure and representation of self. Pronunciation is part of a person's presentation of self also in that one's voice quality, style of speaking, and manner of pronouncing individual sounds symbolically represents personality as well as attitudes and momentary moods. Because of this relationship to personality and presentation of self, it is inherently ego-threatening to change one's pronunciation (Guiora et al. 1972), and speakers of a second language tend to hold on to their native language accent as a way to maintain a secure identity. In the worst case, the change in identity represented by changing pronunciation in a substantial way brings on an "identity crisis"; in the best case, it helps learners expand their repertoire of roles and identities to meet an expanding range of communication situations.

For success in acquiring the pronunciation patterns of a second language, language learners must be in a favorable psychological state: that is, ready to learn, in a mood to learn, and not threatened by intimidating or impossible tasks. By creating a comfortable and secure learning environment to lower the learner's "affective filter" (Krashen 1982), the language teacher can develop psychological conditions in the classroom which are favorable to language learning and help avoid an "identity crisis" in adult learners. For this purpose, a climate of security and helpfulness needs to be established whereby learners are willing to risk trying new things and making mistakes. Drawing on Krashen's (1982) notion of the "i + 1" level and Swain's (1985) notion of "comprehensible output," in order to make progress in acquiring the phonological patterns of a second language and their meaningful correlates, learners must be open to new experiences and be stimulated to go beyond the self and its present state. They must also be motivated enough to engage in frequent and sustained periods of use of the second language.

The learner motivation and involvement that are crucial for success in second language phonology can be developed through use of stimulating lesson material, that is, material which has a high level of interest and which incorporates such elements as humor, challenge, goal-setting, and feedback, to encourage continued attention and work towards a high level of performance. To stimulate a high level of experimentation, risk-taking, and commitment, the language teacher can incorporate the learner's own motivations into learning tasks, emphasizing those aspects of learning pronunciation which are self-directed and which are pursued for self-generated purposes. In this way, the pronunciation or speaking lesson, rather than being based on a structural syllabus, is aimed at fulfilling learners' needs. One example of this sort of approach is that of Acton (1984), whose pronunciation learning program attempted to increase adult learners' self-investment in pronunciation improvement by "contract learning" and pronunciation activities directly related to communicative needs in the workplace.

The pronunciation or speaking class can also be established as a safe environment to practice new roles and identities in simulations of the kinds of communicative tasks learners will need to perform outside of class. Classroom work can also encourage learners to view the pronunciation features of the second language as offering them new communicative resources by (1) exposing them to a variety of speakers communicating in different social roles and tasks, and (2) raising their consciousness of the part played by pronunciation in establishing roles and ensuring communicative success.

Socio-Cultural Motivation

Pronunciation is part of a person's presentation not only of the individual self, but also of the collective self: that is, the self as a member of various socially and culturally defined groups (see Hartford, Ch. 5). Thus, males and females have somewhat different targets and rules for phonology, as do members of different social classes and ethnic and cultural groups. Before nonnative speakers will accommodate (Zuengler 1991) to the pronunciation of the speakers of a particular cultural and linguistic group, they must have a desire to do so and feel that their own personal and group identity is secure.

If language learners hold negative views of the target language culture and/or its speakers, they will be unlikely to accommodate to their pronunciation patterns. It is not uncommon for language learners to hold negative stereotypes of the target language as sounding unpleasant, having (undesirable) connotations of formality, or being very difficult to learn. They may also find that certain sounds seem particularly unpleasant or have an uncomfortably strong symbolic association with the target language and its people. In such cases, which are generally based on stereotypes, learners may retreat into the native language phonological patterns as a way to avoid a close association, both symbolic and actual, with the target language group and its culture.

Perhaps the easiest situation is one in which the speaker has a desire to integrate into the second language group and live as a member of the culture. At the very least, the non-native speaker who wishes to speak the second language well must have a desire to communicate with those who speak the second language and to be well-thought of by them. Where language learning is for strictly opportunistic, instrumental purposes, or is extrinsically motivated or coerced, rather than being based on integrative or intrinsic motivations, the attention given by the language learner to phonology is likely to be less than the attention given to other language features less closely associated with the individual's personality and socio-cultural value set.

To address the fact of the social and cultural component of phonological performance, the language teacher can try to build social motivation for pronunciation, for example, by simulations of social experiences where pronunciation may make the difference between a successful and an unsuccessful performance. The language teacher can also attempt to create intrinsic motivation by seeking to build knowledge of and a positive view of the target language, its culture, and the people who speak the language. The language teacher can work on these knowledge and attitudinal goals while also modeling a variety of phonological targets by use of tape-recordings of popular figures or songs, or by use of radio or television broadcasts related to cultural heritage or linguistic history. It might also be of value to build awareness of stereotyping of languages, cultures, and groups, as well as of stereotyped pronunciation features (Cunningham-Andersson 1990; Zuengler 1988) in both the native and the target language and of how these stereotypes impede learning and communication. Additionally, attention can be given to key features of accent and phonological style shifts, as a way to model and to motivate shifts in accent and style on the part of the non-native speaker.

---

*P*ause to consider . . .

what motivational factors may help or hinder learners in the acquisition of a target-language pronunciation. Can you think of specific examples from your own language-learning experience?

Classroom Application

The Need for Practice, Contextualization, and Feedback

As the physical manifestation of language (i.e., through the movements of the articulators), phonology is an aspect of language where, even more than in the learning of words and grammatical rules, practice and feedback are crucial. In the early stages of learning, phonology can be treated in pre-production or post-production activities as a deliberate form of linguistic processing, under the conscious control and attention of the learner. The goal of such activities is for the phonological patterns of the second language to be eventually stored in memory through practice and so to become ingrained—unconscious and automatized—i.e., under automatic processing and no longer requiring deliberate control. As the shift from deliberate (conscious) to non-deliberate (automatic) control occurs, the learner's attention can be freed from the concerns of articulation and directed more towards matters of meaning and interaction in managing the communication process.

Practice in pronunciation is essential for learning at both a cognitive and a physiological (i.e., articulatory) level, so that the behavior can become routinized and automatic. Also, the nature of phonological learning is such that reinforcement is essential for making the memory connections needed for quick recognition or recall of the phonological representations (for perception) and the motor programs (for production) of lexical items for use in spontaneous performance. A useful progression for reinforcing phonological patterns in adult learners is from mechanical to meaningful to communicative practice in phonology, as described in Pennington (1996, ch. 6). Reinforcement of learning can be promoted by focused repetition, followed by progressive contextualization of phonological features or contrasts in more and more environments, beginning with a small number of limited lexical and phrasal contexts and moving gradually to a larger number of discourse-level contexts.

In progressively wider contextualization of an aspect of phonology, if the contexts provided are realistic, meaning will automatically be attended to. In this way, learners refine their production and perception of the second language on a mechanical, physiological level as the associations of sound and meaning become increasingly unconscious and automatic. If, in addition to meaning, communication is attended to, through speaking and listening tasks which have a phonological focus and a communicative purpose (as in the types of exercises illustrated in Celce-Murcia [1987] or Pica [1984]), a further level of contextualization is added in which the learner gains experience applying aspects of the phonology of the second language to fulfill communicative needs.

In addition to practice and contextualization, feedback on performance is important for building accurate production and perception in a second language. Moreover, research has demonstrated that feedback on some types of errors aids acquisition in communicative learning situations (Lightbown & Spada 1990). One reason may be that attention formerly devoted by the learner to problems or errors can, after feedback has been given to alter performance, be devoted to other aspects of communication. Another reason may be that explicit attention to errors in instructional contexts improves the learner's ability to consciously regulate performance. In either case, it would appear that feedback on problem areas in phonology may be able to increase the efficiency of learning and the effectiveness of communication.

Without feedback, learning will be slow and errors can become ingrained, resulting in "fossilized" phonological performance that can have a negative effect on communication. In order to affect phonological performance, feedback need not necessarily be of the articulatory-corrective type, but may rather be focused on clarification of meaning or on phonological requirements for successful communication. Or, the feedback may attempt to connect visual models of pronunciation such as intonation contours with auditory models or motor programs, as in the research of de Bot and Mailfert (1982); Champagne-Muzar, Schneiderman, and Bourdages (1993); and Leather (1990), among others.

General Guidelines

Based on the discussion provided in this chapter, the following recommendations can be made for classroom work on pronunciation:

- focus on the trans-segmental before the segmental level;
- increase salience of pronunciation features;
- integrate work on perception and production;
- provide plenty of practice in mechanical and meaningful aspects;
- tie features of pronunciation to communicative functions;
- relate pronunciation work to learner needs;
- teach phonology of key words and areas of vocabulary of particular use or interest to the learners;
- contrast the target language with the native language sound system;
- offer multiple models of the phonology of the second language;
- create a relaxed and stimulated classroom environment that encourages experimentation and risk-taking;
- encourage intrinsic motivation such as interest in language, language learning, the target language, speakers of the target language, and the target culture.

These recommendations can serve as general guidelines for planning or evaluating a pronunciation course or component of a larger speaking curriculum. In addition, the findings reviewed in this chapter suggest that instruction in second/foreign language phonology will be most successful when it takes into account the need to develop language in a communicatively rich environment, accepts that errors are part of the natural learning process, and enlists the adult's own special abilities to promote meaningful input and comprehensible output through in-production feedback on performance arising as part of the communicative task, supplemented by pre-production instruction and post-production feedback.

CONCLUSION

This overview of second language phonology has been built on the assumption that phonology is central to other aspects of communicative competence and language development, with the implication that pronunciation is an important aspect of language instruction. It has reviewed the findings of second language acquisition research in relation to phonology as giving direction for teaching practice. When a theoretical base is combined with a knowledge of the segmental and trans-segmental phonology of the target language in relation to the students' mother tongue, the language teacher is then in a good position to assess and prioritize learners' oral language problems and to effectively respond to these, either through an autonomous pronunciation class or through input and feedback on pronunciation which can be tied in with other classroom or out-of-class activities. In this way, a grounded form of pronunciation instruction is built on a foundation of knowledge and theory about phonology and the nature of language learning, bringing phonology in from the sidelines of applied language study and to a more central position where it rightfully belongs.

---

*P*ause to consider . . .

what you consider to be the most important ways in which knowing more about phonology will help you as a language teacher.

KEY TERMS, CONCEPTS, AND ISSUES

phonetics
phonology
pronunciation
segmental
phonemes
  allophones
description of sounds
  place of articulation
  manner of articulation
  voicing
trans-segmental/prosodic
  stress
  intonation

pitch
rhythm
voice quality
perception
production
competence
  discourse competence
  phonological competence
  grammatical competence
loudness
speaking rate
salience
affective filter

EXPLORING THE TOPICS FURTHER

1. *Classic articles on the teaching of pronunciation.* Readers might be interested in a number of articles focusing on pedagogy, each with some theoreti-

cal interest as well. A comprehensive overview of the field of pronunciation instruction and its evolution into the 1990s is provided by Morley (1991). Pennington and Richards (1986) presents a broad-based, communicative view of pronunciation in place of a narrow, segmental view. Also worth exploring are Acton (1984) on changing fossilized pronunciation, de Bot & Mailfert (1982) on the teaching of intonation, and Stevick (1978) on learner pronunciation and the presentation of self.

2. *Practical books.* There are several books written for language teachers that provide a foundation in phonology with a focus on curriculum and pedagogical concerns in the teaching of English as a second or foreign language. See, for example, Bowen & Marks (1992), Kenworthy (1987), and Pennington (1996). Edited volumes with multiple perspectives include Avery & Ehrlich (1992) and Morley (1987, 1995). Wong (1987) and Brazil, Coulthard & Johns (1980) are resources for the teaching of American and British English intonation, respectively.

3. *Research and theory.* The following books present key research in second language phonology: Ioup & Weinberger (1987) and James & Leather (1987) are collections of research by American applied linguists, and European linguists and applied linguists, respectively; Scovel (1988) offers a highly readable discussion of the physiological basis of accented speech.

4. *Journals of interest. ELT Journal* is a very good source of papers on the teaching of pronunciation; *TESOL Quarterly* occasionally has papers on this topic, too, which are accessible although often more theoretical than the papers in *ELT. Language Learning* is the best source for research on second and foreign language phonology, closely followed by *Studies in Second Language Acquisition.*

REFERENCES

Acton, W. (1984) Changing fossilized pronunciation. *TESOL Quarterly, 18,* 71–85.

Avery, P., & Ehrlich, S. (Eds.). (1992). *Teaching American English pronunciation.* Oxford: Oxford University Press.

Baptista, B. O. (1990). The acquisition of English vowels by Brazilian learners. In H. Burmeister & P. L. Rounds, (Eds.), *Variability in second language acquisition, Proceedings of the Tenth Meeting of the Second Language Research Forum* (pp. 187–204). Eugene, OR: University of Oregon.

Boatman, D. (1990). The perception and production of a second-language contrast by adult learners of French. In Leather & James (Eds.), *New Sounds 90. Proceedings of the 1990 Amsterdam Symposium on the Acquisition of Second-Language Speech* (pp. 57–71). University of Amsterdam.

Bowen, T. & Marks, J. (1992). *The pronunciation book.* London: Pilgrims/Longman.

Brazil, D., Coulthard, M., & Johns, C. (1980). *Discourse intonation and language teaching.* Harlow: Longman.

Celce-Murcia, M. (1987). Teaching pronunciation as communication. In J. Morley (Ed.), *Current perspectives on pronunciation* (pp. 1–12). Washington, DC: TESOL.

Champagne-Muzar, C., Schneiderman, E. I., & Bourdages, J. S. (1993). Second language accent: The role of the pedagogical environment. *IRAL: International Review of Applied Linguistics in Language Teaching, 31,* 143–160.

Chun, D. M. (1989). Teaching tone and intonation with microcomputers. *CALICO Journal,* September, 21–46.

Cunningham-Andersson, U. (1990). Native speaker reactions to non-native speech. In J. Leather & A. James (Eds.), *New Sounds 90. Proceedings of the 1990 Amsterdam Symposium on the Acquisition of Second-Language Speech* (pp. 1–13). University of Amsterdam.

de Bot, K., & Mailfert, K. (1982). The teaching of intonation: Fundamental research and classroom applications. *TESOL Quarterly, 16*, 71–77.

Dickerson, W. (1976). The psycholinguistic unity of language learning and language change. *Language Learning, 26*, 215–231.

Esling, J. H. (1987). Methodology for voice setting awareness in language classes. *Revue de Phonétique Appliquée, 85*, 449–473.

Flege, J. (1987). A critical period for learning to pronounce foreign languages? *Applied Linguistics, 8*, 162–177.

Gilbert, J. A. (1993). *Clear speech.* (Second Edition). Cambridge: Cambridge University Press.

Guiora, A., Ben-Hallahmi, B., Brannon, R., Dull, C., & Scovel, T. (1972). The effects of experimentally induced changes in ego states on pronunciation ability in a second language: An exploratory study. *Comprehensive Psychiatry 13*, 421–428.

Hammarberg, B. (1984). Learnability and learner strategies in second language syntax and phonology. In A. Davies, C. Criper, & A. Howatt (Eds.), *Interlanguage* (pp. 153–175). Edinburgh: University of Edinburgh Press.

Hammarberg, B. (1990). Conditions on transfer in phonology. In J. Leather & A. James (Eds.), *New Sounds 90. Proceedings of the 1990 Amsterdam Symposium on the Acquisition of Second-Language Speech* (pp. 198–215). University of Amsterdam.

Harley, B. (1986). *Age in second language acquisition.* San Diego, CA: College-Hill Press.

James, A., & Leather, J. (Eds.). (1987). *Sound patterns in second language acquisition.* Dordrecht: Foris.

Ioup, G., & Weinberger, S. (Eds.). (1987). *Interlanguage phonology: The acquisition of a second language sound system.* New York: Newbury House/Harper & Row.

Kenworthy, J. (1987). *Teaching English pronunciation.* London: Longman.

Krashen, S. D. (1982). *Principles and practice in second language learning.* Oxford: Pergamon Press.

Krashen, S. D., & Terrell, T. D. (1983). *The natural approach: Language acquisition in the classroom.* Oxford: Pergamon Press.

Leather, J. H. (1990). Perceptual and productive learning of Chinese lexical tone by Dutch and English speakers. In J. Leather & A. James (Eds.), *New Sounds 90. Proceedings of the 1990 Amsterdam Symposium on the Acquisition of Second-Language Speech* (pp. 72–97). University of Amsterdam.

Lightbown, P., & Spada, N. (1990). Focus-on-form and corrective feedback in language teaching: Effects on second language learning. *Studies in Second Language Acquisition, 12*, 429–46.

Long, M. H. (1990). Maturational constraints on language development. *Studies in Second Language Acquisition, 12*, 251–285.

Major, R. (1987). A model of interlanguage phonology. In G. Ioup & S. Weinberger (Eds.), *Interlanguage phonology: The acquisition of a second language sound system* (pp. 101–124). New York: Newbury House/Harper & Row.

Morley, J. (Ed.) (1987). *Current perspectives on pronunciation.* Washington, DC: Teachers of English to Speakers of Other Languages.

Morley, J. (1991). The pronunciation component in teaching English to speakers of other languages. *TESOL Quarterly, 25*, 481–520.

Morley, J. (Ed.) (1995). *Perspectives on pronunciation learning and teaching.* Alexandria, VA: Teachers of English to Speakers of Other Languages.

Pennington, M. C. (1989a). Teaching pronunciation from the top down. *RELC Journal, 20*, 20–38.

Pennington, M. C. (1989b). Applications of computers in the development of speaking/listening proficiency. In M. C. Pennington (Ed.), *Teaching languages with computers: The state of the art* (pp. 99–121). La Jolla, CA: Athelstan.

Pennington, M. C. (1990). The context of L2 phonology. In H. Burmeister & P. L. Rounds, *Variability in second language acquisition, Proceedings of the Tenth Meeting of the Second Language Research Forum* (pp. 541–564). Eugene, OR: University of Oregon.

Pennington, M. C. (1994). Recent research in second language phonology: Implications for practice. In J. Morley (Ed.), *Perspectives on pronunciation learning and teaching* (pp. 94–108). Alexandria, VA: TESOL.

Pennington, M. C. (1996). *Phonology in English language teaching: An international approach.* London: Longman.

Pennington, M. C., & Richards, J. C. (1986). Pronunciation revisited. *TESOL Quarterly, 20,* 207–225.

Pica, T. (1984). Pronunciation activities with an accent on communication. *English Teaching Forum,* July, 2–6.

Rochet, B. (1990). Training non-native speech contrasts on the Macintosh. In M.-L. Craven, R. Sinyor, & D. Paramskas (Eds.), *CALL: Papers and Reports* (pp. 119–126). La Jolla, CA: Athelstan.

Rogerson-Revell, P. (1990). *Speaking clearly.* Cambridge: Cambridge University Press.

Schmidt, R. W. (1990). The role of consciousness in second language acquisition. *Applied Linguistics, 11,* 129–158.

Scovel, T. (1988). *A time to speak: A psycholinguistic inquiry into the critical period for human speech.* Cambridge, MA: Newbury House.

Selinker, L. (1992). *Rediscovering interlanguage.* London: Longman.

Sheldon, A., & Strange, W. (1982). The acquisition of /r/ and /l/ by Japanese learners of English: Evidence that speech production can precede speech perception. *Applied Psycholinguistics, 3,* 243–261.

Singleton, D. (1989). *Language acquisition: The age factor.* Clevedon, England: Multilingual Matters.

Stevik, E. W. (1978). Toward a practical philosophy of pronunciation: Another view. *TESOL Quarterly, 12,* 145–150.

Swain, M. (1985). Communicative competence: Some roles of comprehensible input and comprehensible output in its development. In S. M. Gass & C. G. Madden (Eds.), *Input in second language acquisition* (pp. 235–253). Cambridge, MA: Newbury House.

Wieden, W. (1990). Some remarks on developing phonological representations. In J. Leather & A. James (Eds.), *New Sounds 90. Proceedings of the 1990 Amsterdam Symposium on the Acquisition of Second-Language Speech* (pp. 189–197). University of Amsterdam.

Wong, R. (1987). *Teaching pronunciation: Focus on English rhythm and intonation.* Englewood Cliffs, NJ: Prentice-Hall.

Zuengler, J. (1988). Identity markers and L2 pronunciation. *Studies in Second Language Acquisition, 10,* 33–49.

Zuengler, J. (1991). Accommodation in native-nonnative interactions: Going beyond the "what" to the "why" in second-language research. In H. Giles, J. Coupland, & N. Coupland (Eds.), *Contexts of accommodation: Developments in applied sociolinguistics* (pp. 223–244). Cambridge: Cambridge University Press.

CHAPTER 5

Sociolinguistics in Language Teacher Preparation Programs

Beverly S. Hartford
Indiana University

INTRODUCTION

When second/foreign language teachers are asked by their students why the native speakers they have heard do not all sound alike, they may be asking those teachers a sociolinguistic question. When teachers report that their students don't seem to be "motivated," they may be making a sociolinguistic comment. When they are asked to participate in textbook selection, materials preparation, and curriculum planning, teachers also are involved in sociolinguistics issues.

Sociolinguistics is a vast field whose primary concern is with language in use. It is comprised of a number of recognized subfields, only some of which will be discussed in this chapter. One major subfield, pragmatics, is discussed in Chapter 6 by Kasper, and one other related field, the growth of World Languages, is discussed in Chapter 7 by Brown. The present chapter is concerned primarily with "speech communities," "language contact and change," "language variation," "language attitudes," and "language planning." Some of these topics have direct applicability to the language learner and, therefore, the language teacher, and some contribute to our understanding of the second language acquisition process in a more theoretical way. In Chapter 2, Bardovi-Harlig argues that the language teacher needs to understand the theory of second language acquisition. The contributions of the study of sociolinguistics are important for that understanding.

SPEECH COMMUNITIES

In contrast to most work in second language acquisition, whose focus is primarily on the individual learner, most work in sociolinguistics has been concerned with the "speech community." Individuals (the concern of second language acquisition) belong to and are shaped by various communities (the concern of sociolinguistics); moreover, communities are made up of individuals. Thus, the interface between second language acquisition and sociolinguistics is important to applied linguists. Classroom learners belong to speech communities, as do teachers. The learners are likely to reflect behaviors and attitudes partially shaped by their memberships in these communities, while at the same time they—by the very nature of the language classroom—aim towards joining yet another speech community. For these reasons, among others, it is important that teachers understand the nature of speech communities.

Although it may appear to be relatively simple to identify a speech community, sociolinguists have shown that the concept of "speech community" is actually highly complex, especially when language variation is taken into account. One might assume, for instance, that all speakers of language X comprise a speech community, and for some purposes this may be adequate. However, two problems can arise from this assumption: For linguists, popular names for linguistic systems (or what sociolinguists call "lects") do not necessarily coincide with a linguistic description of the language. That is, sometimes a designation, such as "Language X," comprises quite different linguistic systems. The classic example is "Chinese," which actually consists of a wide variety of lects, many of which may have little in common linguistically and are even mutually unintelligible. In this case we might say that "Chinese" speakers do not constitute a speech community.

Conversely, sometimes two or more lects with different names, such as "Language Y" and "Language Z," may be regarded in linguistic description as the "same" language, yet their speakers do not regard themselves as members of the same speech community. Such is the case with Hindi and Urdu, spoken in India and Pakistan. Although they use different orthographies—and Urdu has more words of Arabic origin than Hindi—they are, from the point of view of linguistic description, essentially the same. However, speakers of the respective varieties do not consider themselves to be members of the same speech community.

A contrasting definition of "speech community" is a "group of speakers who are mutually intelligible." This definition, too, is problematic, for the extent of mutual intelligibility must be taken into consideration: Spanish and Portuguese are said to be mutually intelligible to a great degree, but their speakers are generally regarded as belonging to different speech communities. The same is true of many languages, such as Serbian and Croatian, Swedish and Norwegian, and Nepali and Hindi.

Finally, sociolinguists note that in most of the world, multilingual communities are more common than monolingual communities. How are such communities to be designated? Does a speaker belong to more than one speech community in such a context, or may the community be seen as a complex network of interactions and language usage? The concern for determining what constitutes a speech community and a language brings up another basic consideration, important for applied linguistics: If the determination of what is or is not a language and what is or is not a speech community is fuzzy, then how are we to understand the notion of "native speaker," which is generally used as a reference point for both grammatical description (cf. Beck, Ch. 3), and target language materials design (cf. Kasper, Ch. 6)? Is the "native speaker" the idealized Chomskyan speaker/hearer or is the notion somewhat messier and more variable? How can we decide what the target for language acquisition should be, especially in our materials design and selection? To understand the relevance of sociolinguistics to language teaching, we must understand the sociolinguistic approach to these considerations.

> ### *P*ause to consider . . .
>
> some of the definitions proposed for "speech community." What would you consider your own speech community? Who are the other members? What are some of the criteria you use to define membership? Is it possible to belong to more than one speech community?

LANGUAGE CONTACT AND CHANGE

In the discussion above, I mentioned that the majority of communities in the world are not monolingual, but rather, multilingual. Sociolinguists have long been interested in what the effect of such contact is on the speakers and their lects in such communities. Some of the things they have learned are of direct relevance to second language acquisition and thus to the language teacher. Multilingual communities will contain some multilingual individuals (although not all members of such communities need be multilingual). When languages exist together in such communities, over a period of time they may undergo changes that reflect the long-term contact. Most obviously, they may borrow lexical items from one another that may become so integral a part of the borrowing language that monolingual speakers would not recognize their origins, but rather think of them as a part of their own language which, of course, they are. Many examples of such cases exist. In American English, for example, large numbers of words of Spanish origin have become a part of the monolingual speaker's lexicon, words such as *patio, rodeo,* and *lasso*. While bilingual Spanish-English speakers may realize the linguistic origins of these words, most monolingual English speakers do not and consider them to be full-fledged English words. Other words of Spanish origin are also widely used by monolinguals, although their origin may be recognized. Such words would include concepts that reflect recent, widespread cultural borrowings, such as food items like *taco, burrito,* and the like.

Less obviously, syntax and semantics may change as a result of contact between speech communities. Clearly, it is the multilingual individuals who originate these changes, but frequently they are adopted by the community of speakers as a whole, so that both multilinguals and monolinguals employ them. When studying language variation (see discussion below), sociolinguists attempt to document changes that may be taking place within a lect and to determine what factors may be involved in those changes. Of interest to second language acquisition and applied linguists is the nature of these changes.

If, as one might suppose, the changes occur as a result of interlanguage structures, then the fact that these are not idiosyncrasies of individual learners, but instead, represent a community of speakers, may lead us to better understand the factors involved in second language acquisition.

English provides some excellent examples of how its semantics and syntax may be undergoing changes in language contact situations. These situations occur not only in multilingual communities, but are also emerging in communities where it is used extensively as a foreign or second language. For example, Hartford (1993) found a change in the semantics of the past perfect in English as used in a South Asian English-as-a-Foreign-Language community. She discovered that although Nepali/English bilinguals use the past perfect to signal an event which has preceded another past event, as do native speakers of English, its primary meaning is one of "remoteness": When an event is conceived by the Nepali English speaker as being relatively temporally remote, he/she may use the past perfect even if there are no intervening events between the event reported and the time of speaking. Furthermore, this meaning has been extended to "psychological remoteness": Events which are seen as relatively unimportant may be reported with the past perfect.

Furthermore, Hartford (1995) shows that syntactic reflexes of discourse have also undergone a change. In this community, given certain features of discourse such as recoverability and previous mention, verb objects may be omitted. Thus, a speaker of this lect may say, "This is the first time I saw your magazine. I saw it previously, but did not get" (p. 246). This particular structure has not been documented in studies of second language acquisition of English that concentrate primarily on heterogeneous groups of learners studying in the host environment. The fact that it emerges in a homogeneous community of learners with limited native-lect input provides a challenge to those researchers interested in the roles of input and transfer. For example, researchers would need to look not to only psycholinguistic and language theory for explanation, but would also need to consider sociolinguistic questions such as: What roles do size and homogeneity of learner groups play in second language acquisition? How does foreign language acquisition differ from second language acquisition? How do conditions such as geographical or socioeconomic isolation affect the acquisition of a foreign language that will be used extensively in the learners' community among themselves?

These changes have come about as a result of non-native speakers whose interlanguage may be regarded as a community phenomenon, not an individual one. Although the changes are unlikely to spread to native speakers, they do exemplify how a lect may show a change at the syntactic/semantic level in even a limited contact situation. The very real existence of variability must be understood by language teachers and materials designers. A language teacher in this circumstance would need to realize this is a widespread usage among Nepali/English bilinguals and understand that classroom learners may be receiving this as input from other Nepali English speakers. When the teacher is a speaker of this lect, then he/she will understand the meaning. However, both the native English teacher and the Nepali teacher will have to decide what policy they will have regarding which target to utilize: the local "changed" norm or some other target.

Pidgins and Creoles

One kind of speech community that sociolinguists have studied is of special interest to second language acquisition and so of help to teachers in their understanding of the second language acquisition process. These speech communities seem to provide further evidence for the existence of an innate language acquisition device. They also reveal how much learners may bring to learning situations, even under the most difficult of circumstances. These are speech communities that use lects known as pidgins and creoles. Although this is an oversimplification, generally, **pidgins** may be defined as those lects which arise in a context where interaction is among speakers who have different L1s. This interaction is usually confined to short periods of time and to highly limited functions, such as trade and commerce. The speakers do not make any sustained attempt to learn each others' language, but rather they develop a pidgin or *lingua franca*. They do not live together and they return to their own speech communities after such interactions. Thus, a pidgin is created among these speakers. Though it serves highly limited purposes, it is said not to be anyone's native language. In fact, teachers with students from a variety of first languages may even notice a type of "pidgin" developing in the classroom, allowing learners to communicate with one another![1]

Pidgins, which are regarded as highly simplified languages, share many features with one another, even though the contacting languages may be different and their geographical location highly varied. Although some linguists disagree about particulars, the following characteristics have been reported as common among pidgins (Mühlhäusler 1986, pp. 155–156).

1. Drastically reduced inflectional morphology;
2. SVO word order;
3. invariant word order for questions, commands, and statements;
4. lack of number distinctions in nouns;
5. minimal contrast in pronouns: person and number, but often not case;
6. minimal number of prepositions, which may have other grammatical functions, such as genitive marking; and,
7. one *wh*-question word for all functions.

Sometimes in a situation like that described for the inception of pidgins, circumstances bring about the creation of a language which actually becomes the native language of the speech communities in contact. This new language is generally known as a "creole." Although sociolinguists disagree about the exact nature of such circumstances, most agree that the original community was made up of individuals who spoke different languages and who lived together and intermarried over a period of time. Most also agree that at some time the community lost contact (usually quite abruptly) with the communities of speakers of the various languages who were originally in contact. Thus, the newly isolated speech community was forced to develop a lect that could fully function for its communicative needs. Creoles generally have a lexicon that is derived predominantly from one language (the lexifying language), but a syntax, semantics, and phonology that differ from their originating languages. Often these newly developed lects are called by the language that contributes the lexicon, so that we have, for example, "English Creoles" and "French Creoles," even though their respective grammars cannot be said to be English or French.

Present-day creole-speaking communities, such as those in Jamaica, show a great range of variability, usually referred to as a "continuum." Three areas along this continuum are the "basilect," "mesolect," and "acrolect." The basilect represents those varieties which are syntactically and semantically most remote from the lexifying language, while the meso- and acrolects are closer. Members of creole speech communities may be able to use lects along the entire continuum or within a smaller range. Often the lects are correlated with sociolinguistic factors, such as rural/urban, level of education, age, and socioeconomic status. In Haiti, for example, the speakers of acrolectal Haitian Creole tend to be well-educated urban dwellers. These speakers may also be bilingual in French and Creole, which are distinct languages. In Jamaica, the sociolinguistic factors are similar to Haiti, but acrolectal Jamaican English may be thought of as a true variety of English, while the mesolectal and basilectal varieties share fewer syntactic features with English.

From a first and second language acquisition point view, the nature of these languages and their creation poses some interesting questions. Pidgins throughout the world share many characteristics, as do creoles, even though the contacting languages may be quite different. This apparent similarity among such geographically diverse lects has led to speculation as to whether they may represent, at least in their earliest stages, the basic processes employed by a language acquisition device. Both types of lects arise under circumstances of radically reduced input. Although pidgins are generated by adults, creoles are believed to be generated primarily by children as they are born into a speech community that has no one language that fulfills all the necessary functions and that provides limited input from the languages used by the speech community. As we investigate these languages and their origins, we would expect to see some similarity to the processes of acquisition of first and second languages. We should also expect to learn more about the roles of input and positive/negative evidence. In light of these concerns, two important hypotheses have emerged from linguists who are interested in these interfaces.

Schumann (1978) suggests that the same factors that are involved in the creation of pidgins may also be found in second language acquisition. His *Pidginization Hypothesis* claims that in early second language learning, especially in untutored learners, the linguistic systems look similar to those of pidgin languages. That is, he notes, both are "simplified" in the following senses:

- They tend to rely on word order rather than inflectional morphology. For example, possession may be shown by the juxtaposition of two nouns without a preposition or possessive marker, as in (1).

  (1) *You need change **the face the girl*** [the girl's face]. (p. 33)

- Function words and prepositions are used only minimally or are lacking entirely, as in (1).
- Verb auxiliaries tend to be absent as in (2).

(2) *They skiing.* (p. 60)

• Word-order inversions, such as in questions, are avoided, as in (3).

(3) *You no like the beer?* (p. 30)

These and other characteristics that Schumann discusses leads him to claim that:

> . . . pidginization may characterize all early second language acquisition . . . .. [It] would be characterized by the temporary use of a non-marked simple code resembling a pidgin . . . .. The code may reflect a regression to a set of universal primitive linguistic categories that were realized in early first language acquisition (pp. 110, 112).

The basic appeal of the Pidginization Hypothesis is that it attributes the similarities in quite different learning circumstances to the presence of some universal properties of language acquisition. Schumann suggests further that the reasons that second language learners may develop interlanguages that become more targetlike and less pidginlike are largely a result of socio-cultural circumstances. This aspect of the hypothesis is discussed later in this chapter in the section on language attitudes.

Bickerton (1981, 1984), who has investigated creole languages, has developed the *Bioprogram Hypothesis*. In looking at the linguistic and sociohistorical circumstances of the origins of creole languages, Bickerton concludes that humans are born with a quite specific grammar that is evident in early first language acquisition, in early creole grammars, which are so similar to one another, and in early second language systems. Specifically, he claims, this grammar makes some of the following primary distinctions. First, the grammars divide events into punctual/non-punctual categories (rather than by temporality). That is, rather than focusing on *when* an event takes place, they focus on the (non)endurance of the event. Second, they divide entities, such as noun phrases, into specific/nonspecific and known/unknown (to the hearer).

Some second language acquisition studies have been conducted to test the two hypotheses (Andersen 1983; Huebner 1983; Stauble 1978; Romaine 1988). Although the results vary, the resemblance among the three types of learners appears to hold in non-tutored learning situations.

---

*P*ause to consider . . .
_____

the characteristics of pidgins and early second language acquisition. How do the Pidginization Hypothesis and Bioprogram Hypothesis account for similarities across learning contexts?

LANGUAGE VARIATION

Essentially all speech communities, no matter how many "languages" are said to be present, show inherent linguistic variation. There is no such thing as a monolithic speech community. Rather, speech communities are made up of webs and tiers of relationships and interactions, and the speakers vary their language use as they wend their way through them. This variation is meaningful and principled to a large extent and is used to symbolize a speaker's various identities in the speech community. Factors like gender, education, social status, and interactional status[2] all contribute to the principles of variation. Language learners bring all of this to the classrooms and, as we will see below, it has an influence on their language learning in a variety of ways. If teachers understand that language variation is normal, both in fluent native speakers and learners, and if they have some knowledge of what factors contribute to variation, then they will be better equipped to assess their learners and to design appropriate classroom materials and activities.

Speakers choose linguistic forms that they believe to be best suited to a particular speech event. They may control a range of styles and registers, from very formal to very informal, from basilectal to acrolectal, and if they use forms usually associated with a different register than that required by the given speech event, their interlocutors will often notice. For example, we don't generally expect college professors to use slang in a lecture, but we also don't expect them to use technical language in a casual conversation. Similarly, students may notice that their speech is probably a bit more "careful" when talking to professors than when talking to their roommates. And roommates would probably notice if their fellow roommates spoke to them in a register more appropriate for addressing a professor.

The work of Labov (1966, 1972a, 1972b) has been instrumental in establishing the manner in which speech community members vary their language, as well as in discovering the primary factors that seem to be involved. In his work, Labov was able to show that aspects of language such as phonological and syntactic variation could be correlated with linguistic environment and social context. He demonstrated that what had been assumed by most linguists as nonessential "performance" features were to a large degree rule-governed, if one were to write a grammar whose rules were based on statistical predictability rather than on a dichotomous "obligatory/optional" basis, as are most present-day generative grammars.[3] The degree of predictability of a particular realization (variant) of a feature (variable) could be determined taking both linguistic and sociolinguistic parameters into account.

For example, Labov (1972b) examined the variation in final consonant clusters among members of several different New York City speech communities. He was able to show that linguistic environments, such as the nature of the following segment—whether or not the cluster was a separate morpheme (e.g., past tense, as in *walked*, or plural, as in *books*) or part of the root (as in *desk*)—made a difference as to the possibility that the consonant cluster would be maintained or reduced. He found that the final consonant cluster in *fist* was more likely to be reduced than the final consonant cluster in *missed*. The position (or environment) in the sentence also makes a difference. When they occurred before vowels in utterances, such as *He put his fist in my face* or *He missed a pitch,* the clusters were less likely to be reduced than if they were in utterances like *Her fist touched my chin* or *She missed my party*, where they are followed by consonants (pp. 15, 26).

Interacting with linguistic environment were sociolinguistic factors. Members of the working class were more likely than middle class speakers to reduce the clusters, and women were less likely than men. Members of African-American teenage groups (Black English Vernacular speakers) showed a somewhat different pattern than did non-members, or Anglo teenage boys. In addition, the style of the speech event made a difference: whether it was more formal, as in reading a passage, or more casual, as in conversation. Taking these and other such factors into account, Labov was able to show that much language variation is principled and fairly predictable.

Gumperz (1972, 1982) and Hymes (1972) contribute further to our understanding of language variation by taking into account notions of the speech event and interactive relationships (cf. Kasper, Ch. 6, for a discussion of Hymes). These studies provide us with a strong foundation for the understanding of language variation. However, the early studies generally look only at monolingual speakers or at fully developed multilinguals. Among those interested in second language acquisition, the question arose as to whether the principles would extend to the highly variable interlanguages of second language learners.

Ellis (1989) suggests two types of interlanguage variability: horizontal and vertical. The first refers to "synchronic variability": that is, variability within any interlanguage "stage"; the second refers to diachronic or "developmental variability." Most research in second language acquisition has looked at the latter, but for now I will be concerned with the former.[4] Several studies have shown that linguistic context affects interlanguage variation. I will not discuss these studies here, because they are described in some depth in the chapters by Bardovi-Harlig and Pennington. Second language acquisition studies have also shown, although with some contradictory results, that non-linguistic factors may also be involved in interlanguage variation. One of the more frequently investigated factors is the role of stylistic variation. Generally studies have shown that interlanguages tend to be more targetlike in contexts that require a more formal style, such as essay writing. Tarone (1983, 1985), in a series of classic studies, showed that learners' interlanguages varied according to task and to the differing degrees of attention required by such tasks. Her learners used the morphemes under investigation more accurately in tasks such as essay writing than in tasks such as oral interviews. Tarone (1988, 1989) provides a good overview of these types of studies.

Another area related to variation is discourse domain, which is a topic or area of particular importance to a speaker. Selinker & Douglas (1985) suggest that interlanguage varies according to contexts where learners have more or less experience and therefore more or less knowledge schemata. They claim that interlanguages will vary as learners shift from one domain to another. Woken & Swales (1989) and Zuengler (1989) also investigate the role of discourse domain on variation. Whyte (1992, 1995) showed that discourse domain alone was not enough to account for interlanguage variability, but also the degree of "investment" and the recentness of experience with a domain influenced the variation in accuracy. Discourse form, interlocutors, and type of speech event have been shown to correlate with interlanguage variability.

One general area in the study of variation involving interlocutors that is particularly relevant to applied linguistics is "speech accommodation theory." This theory, primarily developed by the social psychologist Giles (Giles & Smith 1979), posits that speakers may vary their language in ways that symbolize the relationship that the speakers wish to obtain with their interlocutor(s), especially with regard to group membership. Thus, in order to show group solidarity, speakers will "converge" their speech patterns, that is, choose language varieties that accommodate to the other speakers. Conversely, speakers may choose to show their lack of solidarity with other speakers and choose linguistic patterns that "diverge" from those speakers and that usually symbolize membership in another group. Accommodation is of course a process: convergence and divergence may occur in the same conversation with the same interlocutors when speakers feel it necessary to express these relationships.

Accommodation theory is important to language teachers in at least two ways. The first relates to input. Ferguson (1971) suggests that when native speakers of a target language interact with either first or second learners of that language, they often accommodate their speech to the learner. In the case of the first language learner, this input has traditionally been called "baby talk" (referred to as "motherese" or "caretaker talk" by linguists), the simplified variety that adults frequently use when talking to young children. Ferguson suggests that, in a similar fashion, native speakers adjust to non-native speakers, that is, they converge their speech patterns to suggest a solidarity with the learner. Several studies (Gaies 1977; Long 1981; Gass & Varonis 1985; Wesche & Ready 1985, among others) have shown that this convergence may indeed take place with non-native learners,[5] so that they receive an accommodated, converged, and somewhat simplified input. Moreover, as Gaies (1977), among others, has shown, classroom teachers also converge to their students, using what is called "teacher-talk," whose complexity varies according to the perceived proficiency level of the learner. Although it is not clear that this accommodation provides the precise sort of comprehensible input discussed by Krashen (1982), it does seem to be the case that this sort of language variation occurs naturally in speech communities.

The second way in which accommodation theory may be useful for language teachers is that it may explain some of the behaviors of their students. Some studies have shown that learners (not just native speakers) practice convergence and divergence in their interlanguage production. For example, Beebe & Zeungler (1983) showed that young Puerto Rican second language speakers of English varied their use of complex sentences according to whether their interlocutors were monolingual English speakers, bilingual Spanish/English with no noticeable accent, or bilingual Spanish/English with an accent. Young (1989, 1991) showed that Chinese second language speakers of English varied their use of the plural marker according to traits that they shared with their interlocutors.

Some interesting questions are raised for teachers and language assessors if, in fact, learners do show competence in linguistic accommodation. For example, consider the observation that students may produce certain structures with a great deal of accuracy when talking to their teachers, yet may produce these same structures with much less accuracy when talking with one another or with fellow native-speaking students. This kind of variation may very well reflect *greater* rather than *less* linguistic competence. When assessment is at stake, issues, such as not only what target language should be tested, but also how much sociolinguistic competence should be assessed, need to be addressed.

P*ause to consider . . .*

language variability. What are some situations where you change how you speak?

LANGUAGE ATTITUDES

Learner Attitudes and Motivation

As mentioned by other authors in this book (Bardovi-Harlig, Ch. 2; Pennington, Ch. 4; Kasper, Ch. 6), it is not always necessarily the case that learners wish to become identified as members of the target language group. Thus, they may opt for speech varieties that symbolize such non-membership and diverge in some way from the target community. Bardovi-Harlig and Pennington mention this phenomenon in regard to the acquisition of syntax and phonology, and Kasper in regard to pragmatic competence. Teachers may mistakenly view such learners as not "motivated."

In a model that shares some of the underlying principles of "accommodation theory," Schumann (1978, 1986), as part of his pidginization hypothesis, suggests some socio-cultural explanations for why learners may not become native-like. In his "acculturation model," Schumann hypothesizes a construct known as "social distance." The model, designed mainly to account for the language acquisition of immigrant groups, in what could be designated as "good" and "bad" language learning situations, takes into account the following factors that may affect various patterns of group solidarity:

1. Dominance: In the spheres of economics, politics, technology, and culture, is the L2 (learner) group dominant, non-dominant, or subordinate?
2. Integration patterns: Is the L2 group pattern one of assimilation, acculturation, or preservation?
3. Enclosure: How separate are the L1 and L2 groups geographically and institutionally?
4. Cohesiveness: How cohesive is the L2 group?
5. Congruence: Are the L1 and L2 groups culturally congruent?

6. Attitudes: What are the attitudes of the L1 and L2 groups towards each other?

7. Intended length of residence: How long does the L2 group intend to stay in the L1 community? (1978, p. 77)

9

Language Attitudes

Schumann discusses the various constellations of these factors and how they may promote or deter the acquisition of the target language by members of the L2 community. For example, if the L2 group is economically and politically dominant, as was the case in many colonial settings, then its members may feel no urgent need to learn the host community's language. Moreover, if that group has no desire to change and integrate, further reason then exists for minimal L2 acquisition. Conversely, if the immigrant group has come to the host community with the intention of integrating or assimilating into an economically dominant culture and, therefore, also intending long residence, then the likelihood of maximal L2 acquisition is enhanced. Thus, the model offers us a socio-cultural explanation for learner "motivation."

Although Schumann (1986) says that this model applies only to languages in contact, others have used it to investigate language learning in university classrooms, where it may be relevant when such classrooms mirror outside language contact. Certainly in elementary and secondary classrooms where language students may actually belong to an immigrant group, teachers may find that the students' attitudes towards the language are to some degree molded by their speech communities.

An alternative model also may explain learner motivation. Lambert (1967), Lambert et al. (1960), and Gardner (1985) developed an instrument to measure the degree of motivation that a learner might have for acquiring the target language. This instrument, which essentially assesses sociocultural attitudes, was used in the following study: Subjects were asked to complete a number of attitude scales about the target language, the target culture, their reasons for studying the target language, and their own socio-cultural profiles. The last point included measures of tolerance for ambiguity and for strength and flexibility of cultural identification.

The investigators identified two main motivations, or "orientations," among learners. Certain learners were studying the language for "instrumental" reasons, that is, because it was a requirement or because they needed it to accomplish some other goal, such as to get into college or to get a particular type of job. The other type of learner was studying for "integrative" reasons, that is, for interest in the target culture itself or with the intention of becoming closer to the target culture. These two orientations were loosely correlated with the socio-cultural profiles of the learners: The integratively oriented learners tended to show greater tolerance for ambiguity and to have flexible cultural boundaries. Lambert et al. (1960) then showed that the two orientations predicted different kinds of language acquisition success. Among their subjects, the integratively oriented learners tended to be better at communicative activities, while the instrumentally oriented were better at satisfying course and teacher requirements.

However, when other subjects from other populations were given the same instrument, much less clear-cut results were found. Most importantly, English as a second/foreign language subjects tended to report instrumental orientations more frequently than integrative, yet they were successful with communicative language. Therefore, it seems that intended integration with the target culture need not be a primary factor in successful language learning.

The constructs of integrative and instrumental orientations have been problematic, as it is very difficult to identify and measure them. Furthermore, most studies have utilized only a one-time administration of the tests, overlooking the fact that a learner's orientation may change over time, especially with continued contact with the target language and with factors such as changes in proficiency levels.

---

*P*ause to consider . . .

whether students with instrumental motivation are likely to have different language-learning profiles than students with integrative motivation. Would you expect these students to be good at different skills?

Other investigators have been interested in the relations between the learner as a member of a socio-cultural group and language acquisition success. Acton (1979) for example, suggests that it is not necessarily *actual* social distance that is a factor for the individual learner (vs. a community of learners), but rather *perceived* social distance. Attempting to allow the individual learner to place him/herself in relationship to the two cultures involved, Acton asked learners to quantify what they perceived to be the distances between themselves and the target culture, themselves and their own culture, and between the two cultures: therefore, not having to portray themselves as being like either of the cultures if they chose not to. They were asked about certain cultural institutions or events, such as marriage, divorce and so forth. Those learners who were neither too close to nor too distant from either culture did better on standard tests of proficiency. He called this the "optimal" distance.

What we learn from these studies is that there is a general belief among second language acquisition researchers and others in the field that individual learners are affected by the communities to which they belong and that, in turn, their ultimate language learning outcome may be influenced by their perceptions of this membership.

---

*P*ause to consider . . .

the concepts of social distance and instrumental and integrative motivation. How do these concepts relate to learners as members of speech communities and as individuals?

Communities generally develop an ethos regarding their communication systems that designates some variations as desirable and "good," and some others as undesirable and "bad." Often this becomes codified into a belief system about what is a "standard" (i.e. "good") form of the language(s) and what is "nonstandard" (i.e. "bad"). Sociolinguists refer to the lects that are encoded in these belief systems as "prestige" and "nonprestige" varieties. Linguistic features that are identified with the nonstandard lect become stigmatized, and so may the users of those features. A simple example can illustrate this.

It is common in many languages to employ two morphological markers of negation. For example, French generally requires the presence of both *ne* and *pas* for verb negation. These markers are regarded by their speakers as standard. In English, however, using more than one negative morpheme is stigmatized by the standard sector of speakers. A sentence like *He doesn't have no gas* is regarded as nonstandard and the users of the "double negative" (and there are many such users) may be also socially stigmatized, seen as "stupid," "low class," or "uneducated." Clearly, it isn't the linguistic form itself that is problematic, in spite of the arguments that two negatives logically result in a positive. Languages are not necessarily "logical," and if they were, we would not expect to find other languages with multiple negation. Sociolinguists are able to show that it is the communities' attitudes towards many such variations that determine their acceptability.

Just as these attitudes may develop among monolingual speakers in a community, so may attitudes develop towards varieties that are regarded as arising from non-native speakers or from multilinguals. The attitudes may even pervade the subcommunity towards its own variety. It may be judged as nonstandard, and the speakers may consequently be socially stigmatized. In a series of well-known experiments, Lambert (1967, 1972), Lambert et al. (1960), Gardner (1985), Giles & Ryan (1982), Ryan et al. (1982), and Sebastian & Ryan (1983) explored such attitudes. Employing a method known as the matched-guise technique, they asked subjects to make a series of judgments about speakers whose lects were varied.

The classic work (Lambert et al. 1960) used a stimulus audiotape upon which randomly distributed Canadian French/English bilingual speakers were recorded speaking in each language. The Anglo- and Franco-Canadian judges, who were unaware that they were hearing a single speaker twice (once in each language guise), were asked to rank each speaker on a series of descriptors ("semantic differential"). Generally, both groups of judges ranked the English guise speakers higher in traits that might be regarded as important for socio-economic success, such as intelligence and education. These have become known as "status-stressing" traits. For the other set of traits, "solidarity-stressing," speakers were ranked more in accord with the judges' own group membership; that is, the Franco-Canadian judges ranked the French guise speakers higher on these traits, and the Anglo-Canadians ranked the English-guise speakers higher on the same traits. These results represent community stereotypes regarding speakers and their language varieties. In particular, the investigators believe that the Franco-Canadians exhibit some "linguistic insecurity," by regarding speakers in their own group's language guise as being of a lower socio-economical status than that of speakers from the other group. Linguistic insecurity is believed to contribute further to language variation found in speech communities, where individuals may adopt the "prestige" variant in order to obtain identity with the group that is perceived to be socially and economically more powerful.

These early studies prompted later investigations into attitudes towards varieties of the "same" language, that is, dialects, bilingual, and non-native varieties (the latter two sometimes referred to as "accented" speech). Some of the studies employed the matched guise approach, some used modifications of it. The studies that looked at non-native speakers have shown that native speakers make judgments about non-natives based on several factors, some of which may be quite complex. Obviously, one factor is the perceived intelligibility of the non-native speaker. Those who are perceived to be less intelligible tend to be downgraded by native speakers. Furthermore, various aspects of the interlanguages that differ from the prestige target have been judged according to "gravity," or how irritating the difference is to the native speaker. Thus, native speakers make language-based judgments about non-native speakers, based on linguistic differences.

The picture becomes somewhat more complex, however, than a straightforward one-to-one relationship between interlanguage forms and judgment of speakers. Ryan (1983) and Sebastian & Ryan (1983) demonstrate that judges often evaluate a speaker on his/her presumed group membership. That is, people may, upon hearing a non-native speaker, place the speaker as a member of a particular language community, either as specific as a language itself, such as "Spanish speaker," or more generally, such as "Asian language speaker." Once evaluators have made this categorization, they then attribute to the speaker any stereotypical traits that these evaluators may hold for that language community. These would include fairly general stereotypes, such as "hard-working" or "lazy," "serious" or "fun-loving," but they often also include more specific attributions, such as class membership. If Asians were to be perceived as belonging to the working class, and a speaker were classified as "Asian," then that speaker might also be attributed all the stereotypes and beliefs associated with the working class. Although positive attributions certainly are possible, the likelihood of negative evaluation is great. Such non-native speakers may find themselves at a disadvantage in such activities as seeking employment in the target community or in being judged the intellectual equal of prestige lect native-speaking fellow students in a classroom.[6]

In selecting the target lect and in determining which learner variations require more classroom attention, the teacher will need to take these attitudinal factors into consideration. In the second language classroom in the target language environment, teachers ordinarily select the prestige lect(s) as the target. However, in the foreign language classroom, where, as was discussed earlier, another, perhaps more local, variety may be available in the immediate environment, the teacher must decide which variety will be the target and understand the social and attitudinal repercussions of that choice. In fact, selecting a native prestige variety might very well result in learners being negatively stereotyped by the local community. In a number of communities, a "been-to," someone who has been abroad to the target language native community and who returns using a native prestige variety, is regarded by the local community as "showing off" or as believing himself/herself to be "better" than the members of his/her community.[6]

Pause to consider . . .

that part of a learner's journey from beginning to advanced proficiency is also a journey towards becoming a member of the target speech community. How would you decide whether and when a learner becomes part of the target speech community? Does this identification rest with the teacher? the learner? the target speech community?

LANGUAGE PLANNING

Second/Foreign language teachers may find themselves involved in activities that would fall under the sociolinguistic rubric of "language planning." In general, language planning involves designing and implementing national language policy and/or "instrumentalizing" a language, that is, preparing a language for uses beyond its present scope. These activities can take place at several levels, most of which are not in the classroom (although they may have repercussions for that environment). It is common for language teachers to be included in language planning, since, in much of the world, they are regarded as the experts on language.

Language Policy

In many developing countries, as well as in a number of developed nations, public concern exists about which language(s) should receive what kinds of official sanction. Particularly in multilingual communities, attempts to establish which language(s) will be used for governmental and other official functions have involved sociolinguists and language teachers—often the same people. A wide range of considerations regarding language selection are involved, and the weight given to each consideration varies from situation to situation. Sometimes official languages are determined by the relative numbers of speakers of each, with the language(s) of the larger group(s) eventually being selected. Sometimes the language(s) of the group(s) with the most political power are selected. And sometimes, especially in post-colonial countries as may be found in Africa and Asia, the language of the colonizer is selected in order to avoid elevating one indigenous group over another. Other considerations may have to do with religion, with world recognition, or with the historical literacy of the language(s). This may often involve highly emotionally charged debates regarding the language choice. Sociolinguists are expected to be neutral participants in the process of selection: They are not supposed to be unduly influenced by their own speech community memberships, but rather to behave like objective social scientists in helping make the decisions. It is in this capacity that language teachers may be asked to be a part of the process.

The language policy decisions will usually have a direct impact on the language teacher. If the teacher teaches a world language, such as English, French, or Spanish, then the selection of that language as (one of) the official state language(s) will undoubtedly affect classroom policy and procedure, as well as teacher-training. Even if the language selected were not one of the world languages, but a more local one, the educational systems will usually be charged with teaching that/those language(s), often starting as early as in the elementary years. If the teachers are lucky, special language instruction classes will be arranged to help the students for whom the chosen language is not a first language. Teachers will also need to know the differences and similarities between younger second language learners and older ones, as well as to understand the expected breadth and depth of acquisition of the chosen official language in contrast to expectations in other classrooms where the foreign/second language is not state sanctioned. Finally, teachers must be able to organize classroom activities and design classroom materials accordingly.

In some cases, the young learners will be learning more than one second language in their early school years. This may come about because more than one official language has been selected and the students are not native speakers of any of them. This has happened, for example, in India, where the schools must teach both the language of the local state and one of the national languages, such as Hindi. The children may speak a smaller tribal language as their first language and so have to become fluent in at least two more languages, just to be successful in their school work. Teachers will need to understand the additional burdens such children face, both as classroom language learners and language community members.

Another very common scenario these days in which children are faced with learning more than one second language is the case where they must learn the official national language (usually most of their schooling will take place in this language), as well as one of the world languages. For example, in Nepal, all school children must learn the official national language, Nepali, which is Indo-Aryan, because all schooling takes place in this language. In fact, there are over one hundred mother-tongues in this country, many of which do not even belong to this language family, but rather to the Tibeto-Burman family, such as Tibetan. No official schooling is offered in these community languages. In addition to learning Nepali, children must also start to learn English in their 4th year, and this continues for however long they remain in school. The use of both of these languages, Nepali and English, is a result of language policy, and English as a foreign language teachers participated in the design of the policy.

In turn, teachers are trained at the university level to teach English as a foreign language at either the elementary level or the secondary (or higher) level. They may or may not be trained to teach Nepali as a second language, because such classes at the elementary level are scarce. Most teachers responsible for Nepali language training are responsible for the entire education of the children and are not language teaching specialists. Nepali as a second language is learned by the "submersion approach." This situation is not at all uncommon around the world, with untrained teachers having to carry out second language teaching tasks. The trained language teacher, even if not a teacher-trainer, will often be called upon for advice in these situations, asked to give workshops, or answer questions about materials and activities.

---

*P**ause to consider . . .*

that some countries have laws against using borrowings, such as *weekend*, *pizza*, or *jazz*, in a public speech. What does this suggest about a government's policy on language regarding change and variation?

Language Instrumentalization

A second (but not necessarily separate) area of language planning in which language teachers are frequently involved is the task of instrumentalizing (and often, standardizing) a language. In the modern world, many speech communities have come to realize the importance of their languages and the threat of extinction that some of them face. Many of these languages, for various historical reasons, have not developed, especially lexically, to handle modern technology and other functions. Moreover, many have not developed a standardized writing system. In language planning situations, more and more of these communities are choosing to develop their languages as official languages to be used for educational, technical, and governmental purposes. When this happens, the languages have to be "instrumentalized," that is, a writing system, a lexicon, and sometimes a more complex morphology and syntax must be developed in order to handle all of the functions that will be expected of it. Instrumentalization usually includes developing teaching materials as well, both for first language users (to develop literacy) and for second language learners (to learn an important state language).

Language teachers may be involved in the instrumentalization process at two levels: in the development of the language itself and in the design and implementation of classroom materials. At the first level, as with language planning, language teachers, who will be considered linguists and sociolinguists, may be involved in activities such as deciding which symbols to utilize in developing the official orthography. For example, it has to be decided at what level of linguistic variation the language should be represented. As was mentioned earlier in this chapter, we know that not all speakers of a language use it in exactly the same ways, especially pronunciation, and so, to develop a writing system, decisions about which pronunciation(s) to represent and how to do so become extremely important. If the linguist chooses a symbolic system that is very close to pronunciation, then only one subgroup's pronunciation is likely to be represented. If a more abstract system is chosen, so that a symbol could stand for a variety of pronunciations (such as the letter *a* in English, which is pronounced differently in the words *calf, car,* and *cater*), the orthography may be more difficult for all to acquire. Language teachers should know about these concerns to help make the best possible decisions.

In addition to the writing system, an instrumentalizing language has to develop means for adding new words. Some communities are happy to let this take place through normal borrowing (from other languages) processes, but others prefer to invent new morphemes consistent with the language's existent system for representing new concepts. Determining the best way for a language to add these new concepts is part of the work of the linguists involved in its instrumentalization.

At the second level of instrumentalization, many language teachers will be directly involved in the development of materials suitable for the classroom environment. This will not only involve L1-teachers, but also, in light of the multilingual nature of the world, L2-teachers. In this scenario, the students will be learning a language that is itself undergoing development, and their own input into this process may influence the direction of its path.

A case of successful instrumentalization of a language, in which language teachers (especially English as a second/foreign language teachers) were intimately involved can be found in Malaysia, a former British colony, where education had been almost exclusively in English. In the 1960s, the local language, Bhasa Malay, was declared the official language and the language of education. Bhasa Malay at that time had not been used in such a wide array of functions. In order for it to replace English in the schools and elsewhere, a concerted effort was made to develop the language so that both students and teachers of all subjects would be able to use it fully. English teachers, along with other experts, were called upon to work on the instrumentalization of Bhasa Malay. It was so successful that English truly became a foreign or second language and Bhasa Malay the working language of the country. Part of that success is due to the knowledge that the language teachers were able to bring regarding linguistic systems, linguistic variation, and language teaching to bear on that situation.

CONCLUSION

Sociolinguistics has been able to account for a great deal of language variation and has provided important insights for the applied linguist and language teacher. Some of the following principles are particularly relevant:

- Speech communities do not show a one-to-one correlation with language names: sometimes a language includes more than one speech community; sometimes a speech community contains more than one language;
- Speech communities are better thought of as "clines" along which speakers control a number of varieties. Language variation is a natural part of linguistic competence;

- Speakers will employ a particular variety because of the type of speech event they are engaged in. They will also choose a variety, depending on whom they are interacting with, and they will choose varieties that reflect the group(s) they wish to be identified with (or, sometimes, disassociated from). These choices may change from speech event to speech event;
- Language attitudes, both those of learners towards the target language and their own language and those of the speech communities towards learners, may play a large role in how successfully the language is acquired. They also play a part in linguistic variation.

The classroom teacher, knowing that much language variation is principled and natural, even among native speakers, can help the learners to understand the same. The fact that learners notice variation among the target language speakers can be utilized to promote awareness of how language is used to get things done and to make subtle statements about who one is in the speech community. Understanding that variation is normal can also help the teacher in better understanding the variation produced by the learners. Especially important is the realization that learners often demonstrate variability not only because of a developing interlanguage, but also because different language events may produce different types of linguistic behaviors, just as is the case with native speakers. This should be taken into account not only for the day-to-day classroom interactions, but also in regard to the types of activities, including assessment and measurement activities, that are a part of most classrooms. The teacher, knowing that a more formal event, such as a written essay, may produce more formal language than a casual event, such as group discussion, should not be surprised to see the students' language reflect those differences.

For the language teacher who is charged with the selection or development of materials, consideration of what variety is regarded positively by the target community must be made. In that case, determination of the target speech community is necessary. English, for example, has not only three main communities of speakers (i.e. North America, Great Britain, and Australia), but also other speech communities whose English may well be the target (cf. Brown, Ch. 7). This leads to yet another sociolinguistic layer: Communities not only develop attitudes towards their own linguistic variation, they also develop attitudes towards that of others. In the case of English, some non-English communities prefer British English to North American or Australian English, while others prefer North American or Australian English; still others prefer variants such as Indian or Singapore English. The teacher involved in curriculum development will have to be aware of the general attitudes of the native culture to the target varieties, as well as of the attitudes of the target community towards its own variations.

Finally, in many countries, the language teacher is more than a classroom resource. Language teachers may become involved in shaping social policy through participation in activities such as language planning and instrumentalization. The more knowledge that language teachers have of the social nature of language, the more effective they can be in all of their roles.

Pause to consider . . .

what you consider to be the most important ways in which knowing more about sociolinguistics will help you as a language teacher.

NOTES

[1]It should be noted that some lects used as native languages are sometimes called by the name "pidgin." This may reflect their origins, but linguists regard them as "creoles" rather than pidgins.

[2]Interactional status is the role relationship that each speaker has in any particular interaction, such as student and teacher, expert and novice, store clerk and customer.

[3]Most linguists involved with writing grammars of linguistic competence are not concerned with the social circumstances under which a rule might apply. Thus, for example, their grammars would tell us how we make passives, but would not indicate under what social circumstances. Because they cannot predict when we would actually use a passive, linguists call such a rule "optional." This is in contrast with "obligatory" rules, such as the rule governing the inversion of subject and verb in questions (e.g., *Are you ready?*).

[4]In some ways, this is an artificial distinction, because both may be happening at once and may even be influencing one another. Sociolinguists may focus on one type or the other, but they generally agree that "horizontal" variation may represent a reflex of language change, either at the speech community level or at the individual level.

[5]Other studies have not confirmed that native speakers show any marked accommodation to non-native speakers. The differences in the findings may be partly due to what linguistic features are investigated. See Larsen-Freeman & Long (1991) for a fuller discussion.

[6]Eisenstein (1983) provides a good overview of these types of studies.

[7]See also Brown's discussion in Chapter 7 on choosing a target lect.

KEY TERMS, CONCEPTS, AND ISSUES

World Languages
mutual intelligibility
input
language variation
language contact
   contact situation
pidgin
creole
lingua franca
Pidginization Hypothesis
Bioprogram Hypothesis

speech accommodation theory
   convergence
   divergence
speech community
   multilingual
   monolingual
sociolinguistics
language simplification
continuum/cline
acrolect
mesolect

basilect	lect
borrowing	standard/nonstandard
interlanguage	prestige/nonprestige
motivation	linguistic insecurity
instrumental	language planning
integrative	language policy
social distance	language instrumentalization
actual social distance	standardization
perceived social distance	
optimal social distance	

EXPLORING THE TOPICS FURTHER

1. General overviews. For an excellent overview of the relationship between second language acquisition and sociolinguistics, see Preston (1989), Bayley & Preston (1996), and McKay & Hornberger (1996). For general overviews of sociolinguistics, see Fasold (1984, 1990), Wardhaugh (1986), and Hudson (1980). These all discuss the major areas of sociolinguistics and provide accessible introductions to the field.

2. Language Variation. Two volumes directly concerned with second language acquisition and language variation are Gass et al. (1989a, 1989b). For discussions of language variation, especially regarding dialects, see Labov (1972a) and Trudgill (1983).

3. Language Contact. For multilingualism and multilingual communities, Romaine (1995) provides a thorough and readable discussion of the sociolinguistic and psycholinguistic characteristics of multilingualism. A classic in the area, to which most other work refers, is Weinreich (1968). A more detailed account of language contact and change can be found in Thomason & Kaufman (1988). For overviews of pidgins and creoles, see Romaine (1988) and Mühlhäusler (1986). For specific discussions of the relationship of second language acquisition to pidgins and creoles, see Andersen (1983).

4. Language Attitudes. *Studies in Second Language Acquisition, 5* (1983), d'Anglejan (Ed.), is devoted to the relationships among language attitudes, language variation, and second language acquisition. In particular, the articles by Ryan and Eisenstein provide good summaries of work in this area. Also of interest regarding language attitudes are Crookes & Schmidt (1991), Edwards (1985), Ryan & Giles (1982), and Gardner (1985).

5. Language Planning. Edwards (1985) looks at language planning, and policy in particular, from the point of view of the problems of survival and maintenance of minority ethnic languages. He provides a concise overview of the language situation in a large number of countries. Hartford et al. (1983) looks at a number of case studies involving problems related to language instrumentalization and minority languages in education. See also Kasper, Ch. 6.

6. Journals of Special Interest. *Language in Society* contains a wide range of sociolinguistic studies. It publishes both quantitative and qualitative research on most of the areas mentioned in this chapter. It is not primarily

concerned with language acquisition, but does include work on the language of second language speakers.

Studies in Second Language Acquisition is the leading journal in the field of second language acquisition. Although most of the articles do not treat the sociolinguistics of language acquisition, the journal does include studies on language attitudes.

Language Problems and Language Planning includes studies on issues such as language socialization, language instrumentalization, language and attitudes, and other topics related to community languages.

Journal of Pidgin and Creole Languages is the leading journal on this topic. For the language teacher, the most important material is that treating pidgin and creole languages and their overlap with language acquisition.

Language Variation and Change is primarily dedicated to quantitative studies of language variation. Its major focus is on the variation of linguistic features and their relationship to social parameters.

Research on Language and Social Interaction addresses questions of language and community membership. It is concerned with social identity and interactive language. For the language teacher, articles on community membership may be useful.

REFERENCES

Acton, W. (1979). *Second language learning and perception of difference in attitude.* Unpublished doctoral dissertation. Ann Arbor: University of Michigan.

Andersen, R. (1983). A language acquisition interpretation of pidginization and creolization. In R. Andersen (Ed.), *Pidginization and creolization as language acquisition* (pp. 1–56). Rowley, MA: Newbury House.

d'Anglejan, A. (Ed.) (1983). Native speaker reactions to approximate systems. [Special issue]. *Studies in Second Language Acquisition*, 5.

Andersen, R. (Ed.). (1983). *Pidginization and creolization as language acquisition.* Rowley, MA: Newbury House.

Beebe, L. & Zeungler, J. (1983). Accommodation theory: An explanation for style shifting in second language dialects. In N. Wolfson & E. Judd (Eds.). *Sociolinguistics and language acquisition* (pp. 195–213). Rowley, MA: Newbury House.

Bickerton, D. (1981) *Roots of language.* Ann Arbor: Karoma.

Bickerton, D. (1984) The language bioprogram hypothesis and second language acquisition. In W. Rutherford (Ed.). *Language universals and second language acquisition* (pp. 141–161). Amsterdam: John Benjamins.

Edwards, J. (1985). *Language, society and identity.* Oxford: Blackwell.

Eisenstein, M. (1983). Native reactions to non-native speech: A review of empirical research. *Studies in Second Language Acquisition, 5,* 161–176.

Ellis, R. (1989). Sources of intra-learner variability in language use and their relationship to second language acquisition. In S. Gass, et al. (Eds.). *Variation in second language acquisition: Psycholinguistic issues* (pp. 22–45). Clevedon: Multilingual Matters.

Fasold, R. (1984). *The sociolinguistics of society.* Oxford: Blackwell.

Fasold, R. (1990). *Sociolinguistics of language.* Oxford: Blackwell.

Ferguson, C. (1971). Absence of copula and the notion of simplicity: A study of normal speech, baby talk, foreigner talk, and pidgins. In D. Hymes (Ed.). *Pidginization and creolization of languages* (pp. 141–50). Cambridge: Cambridge University Press.

Gaies, S. (1977). The nature of linguistic input in formal second language learning: Linguistic and communicative strategies in ESL teachers' classroom language. In H. Brown, C. Yorio, & R. Crymes (Eds.). *On TESOL '77* (pp. 204–212). Washington, D.C.: TESOL.

Gardner, R. (1985). *Social psychology and second language learning.* Rowley, MA: Newbury House.

Gass, S. & Varonis, E. (1985). Variation in native speaker speech modification to non-native speakers. *Studies in Second Language Acquisition, 7,* 37–58.

Gass, S., Madden, C., Preston, D. & Selinker, L. (Eds.). (1989a). *Variation in second language acquisition: Discourse and pragmatics.* Clevedon: Multilingual Matters.

Gass, S., Madden, C., Preston, D. & Selinker, L. (Eds.). (1989b.) *Variation in second language acquisition: Psycholinguistic issues.* Clevedon: Multilingual Matters.

Giles, H. & Ryan, E. (1982). Prolegomena for developing a social psychological theory of language attitudes. In E. Ryan & H. Giles, (Eds.). *Attitudes towards language variation* (pp. 208–223). London: Edward Arnold.

Giles, H. & Smith, P. (1979). Accommodation theory: Optimal levels of convergence. In H. Giles, & R. St. Clair, (Eds.). *Language and social psychology* (pp. 45–65). Oxford: Blackwell.

Gumperz, J. (1972). Introduction. In J. Gumperz & D. Hymes (Eds). *Directions in sociolinguistics: An ethnographic approach* (pp. 1–15). New York: Holt, Rinehart, & Winston.

Gumperz, J. (1982). *Discourse strategies.* Cambridge: Cambridge University Press.

Hartford, B. (1993). Tense and aspect in the news discourse of Nepali English. *World Englishes, 12,* 1–13.

Hartford, B. (1995). Zero anaphora in nonnative texts: Null-object anaphora in Nepali English. *Studies in Second Language Acquisition, 17,* 245–61.

Hartford, B., Valdman, A. & Foster, C. (Eds.). (1983). *Issues in international bilingual education.* New York: Plenum.

Hudson, R. (1980). *Sociolinguistics.* Cambridge: Cambridge University Press.

Huebner T. (1983). A longitudinal analysis of the acquisition of English. Ann Arbor, MI: Karoma.

Hymes, D. (1972). Models of the interaction of language and social life. In J. Gumperz & D. Hymes (Eds.). *Directions in sociolinguistics: An ethnographic approach* (pp. 35–71). New York: Holt, Rinehart, & Winston.

Krashen, S. (1982). *Principles and practice in second language acquisition.* Oxford: Pergamon.

Labov, W. (1966). *The social stratification of English in New York City.* Washington, D.C.: Center for Applied Linguistics.

Labov, W. (1972a). *Sociolinguistic patterns.* Philadelphia: University of Pennsylvania.

Labov, W. (1972b). *Language in the inner city.* Philadelphia: University of Pennsylvania.

Lambert, W.E. (1967). A social psychology of bilingualism. *Journal of Social Issues, 23,* 91–109.

Lambert, W. (1972). *Language, psychology, and culture.* Stanford: Stanford University Press.

Lambert, W.E., Hodgson, R., Gardner, R. & Fillenbaum, S. (1960). Evaluational reactions to spoken language. *Journal of Abnormal Social Psychology, 60,* 44–51.

Larsen-Freeman, D. & Long, M. (1991). *An Introduction to second language acquisition.* New York: Longman.

Long, M. (1981). Questions in foreigner talk discourse. *Language Learning, 31,* 135–158.

Mühlhäusler, P. (1986). *Pidgin and creole linguistics.* Oxford: Blackwell.

Preston, D. (1989). *Sociolinguistics and second language acquisition.* Clevedon: Blackwell.

Romaine, S. (1988). *Pidgin and creole languages.* London: Longman.

Romaine, S. (1995). *Bilingualism* (2nd ed.). Clevedon: Blackwell.

Ryan, E. (1983). Social psychological mechanisms underlying native speaker evaluations of non-native speech. *Studies in Second Language Acquisition, 5,* 149–159.

Ryan. E. & Giles, H. (Eds.). (1982). *Attitudes towards language variation.* London: Edward Arnold.

Ryan, E., Giles, H. & Sebastian, R. (1982). An integrative perspective for the study of attitudes toward language variation. In E. Ryan & H. Giles (Eds.). *Attitudes towards language variation* (pp. 1–19). London: Edward Arnold.

Schumann, J. (1978). *The pidginization process.* Rowley, MA: Newbury House.

Schumann, J. (1986). Research on the Acculturation Model for second language acquisition. *Journal of Multilingual and Multicultural Development, 7,* 379–392.

Sebastian, R. & Ryan, E. (1983) Speech cues and social evaluation: Markers of ethnicity, social class, and age. In: H. Giles & R. N. St. Clair (Eds.). Recent advances in language, communication, and social psychology. London: Lawrence Erlbaum.

Selinker, L. & Douglas, D. (1985). Wrestling with 'context' in interlanguage theory. *Applied Linguistics, 10,* 190–204.

Stauble, A. (1978). Decreolization: A model for second language development. *Language Learning, 28,* 29–54.

Tarone, E. (1983). On the variability of interlanguage systems. *Applied Linguistics, 4,* 142–53.

Tarone, E. (1985). Variability in interlanguage use: A study of style-shifting in morphology and syntax. *Language Learning, 35,* 373–403.

Tarone, E. (1988). *Variation in interlanguage.* London: Edward Arnold.

Tarone, E. (1989). Accounting for style-shifting in interlanguage. In S. Gass, C. Madden, D. Preston, & L. Selinker (Eds.). *Variation in second language acquisition: Psycholinguistic issues* (pp. 13–21). Clevedon: Multilingual Matters.

Thomason, S. & Kaufman, T. (1988). *Language contact, creolization, and genetic linguistics.* Berkeley: University of California.

Trudgill, P. (1983). *On dialect.* New York: New York University Press.

Wardhaugh, R. (1986). *An introduction to sociolinguistics.* Oxford: Blackwell.

Weinreich, U. (1968). *Languages in contact.* The Hague: Mouton.

Wesche, M. & Ready, D. (1985). Foreigner talk in the university classroom. In S. Gass & C. Madden (Eds.). *Input in second language acquisition* (pp. 89–114). Rowley, MA: Newbury House.

Woken, M. & Swales, J. (1989). Expertise and authority in native-non-native conversations: The need for a variable account. In S. Gass, C. Madden, D. Preston, & L. Selinker (Eds.). *Variation in second language acquisition: Discourse and pragmatics* (pp. 211–227). Clevedon: Multilingual Matters.

Whyte, S. (1992). Discourse domains revisited: Expertise and investment in conversation. In L. Bouton & Y. Kachru (Eds.). *Pragmatics and Language Learning, Vol. 3* (pp. 81–102). Urbana, IL: University of Illinois Press.

Whyte, S. (1995). Specialist knowledge and interlanguage development: A discourse domain approach to text construction. *Studies in Second Language Acquisition, 17,* 153–184.

Young, R. (1989). Ends and means: Methods for the study of interlanguage development. In S. Gass, C. Madden, D. Preston, & L. Selinker (Eds.). *Variation in second language acquisition: Psycholinguistic issues* (pp. 65–92). Clevedon: Multilingual Matters.

Young, R. (1991). *Variation in interlanguage morphology.* New York: Peter Lang.

Zuengler, J. (1989). Performance variation in NS-NNS interactions: Ethnolinguistic difference, or discourse domain? In S. Gass, C. Madden, D. Preston, & L. Selinker (Eds.). *Variation in second language acquisition: Discourse and pragmatics* (pp. 228–244). Clevedon: Multilingual Matters.

The Role of Pragmatics in Language Teacher Education

Gabriele Kasper
University of Hawaii at Manoa

INTRODUCTION

In this chapter, I discuss two important ways in which teachers should be informed about the relationship of pragmatics to language instruction. First, and perhaps most obvious, is that such information enables teachers to identify the pragmatic abilities in the L2 that second language learners need, incorporate pragmatic goals and objectives in curricula and syllabuses, and design appropriate activities to implement instructional plans. I shall argue that in order to identify learning tasks, it is not sufficient to know only how members of the target community act and interact linguistically in various contexts; it is also necessary to know how second language (L2) learners go about acquiring pragmatic competence, what kinds of L2 pragmatic information are easy or difficult to learn, to what extent learners rely on their L1 pragmatic knowledge to help them acquire pragmatic competence in the L2, how successful pragmatic transfer can be in terms of communicative outcomes, and what developmental paths learners go through in their acquisition of pragmatic competence. Information about these questions is crucial in order for teachers to make informed pedagogical decisions.

The second reason for including pragmatics in a teacher education program may be less obvious, but is nonetheless significant, not only for language teaching, but especially for language instruction. This is the function and organization of the teaching process itself, the roles of learners and teachers in it, their interaction practices, and their (mostly implicit) theories of (language) learning and teaching. Raising teachers' awareness of cross-culturally diverse patterns of linguistic action, including those performed under the institutional constraints of language classrooms, must play an essential role in the education and development of language teaching professionals.

114

CHAPTER 6
*The Role of
Pragmatics in
Language Teacher
Education*

PRAGMATIC KNOWLEDGE AS A COMPONENT
OF COMMUNICATIVE COMPETENCE

Communicative competence, a notion proposed by Habermas (1971) from a social-philosophical perspective and by Hymes (1971) from an anthropological viewpoint, was adopted by applied linguists and adapted as a target construct for language teaching in the Anglo-American context (cf. Savignon [1991]). An influential model, developed for language teaching and testing, was offered by Canale & Swain (1980); ten years later, Bachman (1990) revised and elaborated the original proposal.

In Bachman's (1990, p. 87) model, pragmatic competence constitutes one of two components of "language competence." The other component, "organizational competence," comprises knowledge of linguistic units and the rules of joining them together at the levels of sentence ("grammatical competence") and discourse ("textual competence"). Pragmatic competence is subdivided into "illocutionary competence" and "sociolinguistic competence." Illocutionary competence is the ability to match the semantic sense and meaning of an utterance with its "pragmatic force." For instance, the utterance *purple makes you look a little pale* can serve as an act (or have the "force") to dissuade the hearer from buying a garment of a particular color. A listener or reader must be able to interpret utterances, or longer stretches of discourse, by assigning them a pragmatic force; a speaker or writer needs to be able to express, through a particular utterance or text segment, the communicative intent he/she wishes to convey. Searle (1976) proposes a classification of illocutionary acts which includes five main categories:

- "Representatives," by means of which the speaker makes an assertion about some state of affairs in the world. Representatives can be assessed as true or false; such acts include claiming, arguing, proposing, explaining, and so forth;
- "Directives," by means of which the speaker gets the hearer to do something, such as requesting, instructing, pleading, advising, and so forth;
- "Commissives," by means of which the speaker commits himself/herself to a certain course of action (e.g., promising, vowing, pledging);
- "Expressives," by means of which the speaker expresses a particular feeling or attitude (e.g., thanking, apologizing, complimenting, congratulating); and,
- "Declaration," by means of which the speaker brings about some change in the world (e.g., appointing, hiring, or firing someone; naming things; defining terms).

In addition to the ability to produce and understand linguistic acts in speech and writing, Bachman includes under illocutionary competence the ability to perform a variety of language functions (1990). Although a distinction between speech acts and language functions is not always observed in language pedagogy, a distinct difference exists between these constructs; one of the strengths of Bachman's model is that it clearly distinguishes between the two notions.

> *Pause to consider . . .*
>
> Searle's speech act categories. Are all speech acts equally important for language learners? Consider different learner populations, instructional objectives, and receptive versus productive language use.

Hymes's (1964) model of language functions details the components of communicative events and assigns a particular function to each of them. The components include:

1. Addressor (sender);
2. Addressee (receiver);
3. Channel (contact medium);
4. Code (linguistic, paralinguistic, nonlinguistic);
5. Setting (linguistic and situational context);
6. Message-form (used linguistic and other conventions, genres, styles);
7. Topic (referential information, what is talked about [topic], and what is said about it [comment]); and,
8. The event itself (e.g., giving and responding to compliments; explaining a grammatical rule in a language class).

In carrying out a linguistic act, speakers or writers can focus on one or more of these components. This focusing-upon, or making salient of, a particular component in a communicative event is called a language function. By pairing off the eight components with their respective functions, the following list is obtained:

1. Focus on addressor–expressive (emotive) function;
2. Focus on addressee–directive (conative) function;
3. Focus on channel–contact (phatic) function;
4. Focus on code–metalinguistic function;
5. Focus on setting–contextual function;
6. Focus on message-form–poetic (imaginative, aesthetic) function;
7. Focus on topic–referential function; and,
8. Focus on the event itself–metacommunicative function.

In language learning and teaching, the metalinguistic and metacommunicative functions are particularly important; in fact, French applied linguists (e.g., Grandcolas & Soulé-Susbielles 1986) view the whole activity of language teaching as a metalinguistic event. Learners interacting with other learners or native speakers, whether inside or outside the classroom, often have to "negotiate" their intended meanings with the other participant(s). The input modifications in foreigner and teacher talk and the interactional modifications of learners' and their interlocutors' utterances through clarification requests and confirmation and comprehension checks (cf. Larsen-Freeman & Long [1991]; Ellis [1994]) are prime examples of metalinguistic activity. Likewise, learners' (and native speakers') use of "communication strategies" to compensate for

116

CHAPTER 6
The Role of
Pragmatics in
Language Teacher
Education

linguistic deficits or for the temporary inaccessibility of L2 words or structures has a metalinguistic function (cf. Kasper & Kellerman, 1997). Finally, error correction in the classroom is metalinguistic when it focuses on aspects of utterance form, such as grammatical or pronunciation errors. Other types of repair, however, may have a metacommunicative rather than a metalinguistic focus. For instance, clarification of speaker's intent—that is, clarifying the relationship between what the speaker said and what he/she meant—is a metacommunicative activity (cf. *That's not what I meant*).

The other main subcomponent of pragmatic competence in Bachman's model is "sociolinguistic competence." This construct subsumes a variety of abilities, all of which comprise different aspects of using language appropriately according to context (sensitivity to differences in dialect, variety, or register) and observing linguistic and cultural conventions that cannot be gleaned from the grammar, such as lexical phrases (Nattinger & DeCarrico 1992), metaphor, and cultural allusions. Sociolinguistic competence, thus, entails the ability to choose between linguistic alternatives dependent on contextual factors (cf. Hartford, Ch. 5).

GOALS AND PROCESS IN THE DEVELOPMENT OF PRAGMATIC COMPETENCE

Bachman's model of communicative competence specifies the subcomponents of pragmatic competence, but does not answer the question of how to determine the substance of these components (1990). In order to do this, one must decide whose illocutionary competence, for instance, should be modeled. The obvious answer to this question appears to be that of a "native speaker" of the target language. This is the approach usually taken in studies examining L2 learners' pragmatic knowledge. In a field of study called "interlanguage pragmatics," learners' and native speakers' comprehension and production of a particular speech act are compared, with the native speaker data serving as a baseline (cf. Kasper & Blum-Kulka 1993a). This approach has been useful in identifying where learners' and native speakers' linguistic action patterns are the same or different, and it is tempting to conclude that the identified differences are the "stuff" that should go into the pragmatic component of a language teaching curriculum. However, such a conclusion has a number of problems.

First, the "native speaker" is not a homogeneous entity. As captured in Bachman's component of "sociolinguistic knowledge," social, geographic, and situational variation occurs in any speech community. For example, it has been shown that native speakers of American English from the East Coast and West Coast favor different conversational styles (Tannen, 1981), and that native speakers of British, American, and Australian English opt for different levels of directness when making requests (Michaelis 1992). Which is the "right" variety to choose as a goal for language teaching? In an ESL situation, the answer may seem straightforward: the "national standard," or "local variety." For example, in Hawaii most local ESL teachers speak Hawaiian standard American English in class, teachers from the mainland speak their variety of stan-

117

*Goals and Process in
the Development of
Pragmatic
Competence*

dard American English, and teaching materials typically use some nondescript form of American standard. In an EFL situation, decisions about which varieties of English to teach are more difficult to make. EFL students all over the world use English at least as much as a *lingua franca*—that is, a shared means of communication with other nonnative speakers—as they do for communicating with native speakers. Choosing a variety of English for communication with native speakers on a principled basis is nearly impossible because it is hardly predictable where and with whom EFL students will need to communicate in English.

Second, a native speaker model, even if it were desirable, may not be a feasible goal for adult learners (cf. Brown, Ch. 7.) Research on critical/sensitive periods in second language learning has shown that the acquisition of phonology and syntax is constrained by maturational factors (Long 1992). Although little evidence for or against maturational constraints on the acquisition of pragmatic knowledge exists, it is possible that adult second language learners may not usually attain full native speaker proficiency. In fact, the interlanguage pragmatics studies examining advanced learners' linguistic action patterns document differences between such learners and native speakers (cf. Bardovi-Harlig & Hartford 1990, 1993). In the case of foreign language learners, native speaker pragmatic competence is a particularly unrealistic goal because these learners lack the quality and quantity of contact with the L2 that would provide them with the necessary input and occasions for using the L2 productively.

Third, emulating a native speaker model may not always be the most functional and desirable way of communicating in the L2. From the non-native speaker's perspective, there may be sociopragmatic aspects of the target culture that conflict with his/her beliefs and values and which he/she does not desire to accommodate (Clyne 1979; Thomas 1983). For example, we found in interviews with American learners of Mandarin that a female student objected to the common address terms for adult women because they were offensive according to the student's world view (Kasper & Zhang 1995). In studies of United States immigrants to Israel, these highly proficient speakers of English and Hebrew were found to exhibit an "intercultural style" when performing requests in either of their two languages. Intercultural styles allow bilingual speakers to set themselves apart from both their original and target culture (Blum-Kulka 1991; Blum-Kulka & Sheffer 1993).

From the perspective of the target community, nativelike pragmatic behavior exhibited by non-native speakers may not be entirely desirable either, just as diverging behavior may be seen as unproblematic or even particularly likable. For instance, Wetzel (1994) found in a recent matched guise study involving native speakers of Japanese that speakers who did not use the required polite forms *(keigo)* were rated more negatively than speakers who used *keigo*, no matter whether the used forms were correct or incorrect. Speakers using polite forms incorrectly were rated even more positively than the correct users. This study suggests that, for nonnative speakers, an attempt to conform with politeness norms, combined with clear markers of non-membership, may be particularly appreciated by community members. On similar lines, Aston (1993) describes how "foreignness" can function as a means to establish friendly relationships ("comity") between strangers.

118

CHAPTER 6
The Role of
Pragmatics in
Language Teacher
Education

A further concern is that what functions well for native speakers may not be that efficient for non-natives. Because participants have less shared knowledge on which to rely, communication involving non-native speakers may require more metalinguistic and metacommunicative activity to ensure mutual comprehension and help both parties express what they want to say (cf. previous section). Repairs, communication strategies, and other kinds of conversational adjustments have a prime function not just in ensuring understanding but in providing input for learning by extending the learner's current L2 knowledge.

For the learner's production of linguistic action in the L2, then, a native speaker model is not always the best option. Just how much convergence to the pragmatic behavior of native speakers seems desirable is highly context-dependent and, therefore, cannot be pinned down in a simple recipe. It depends on such factors as the non-native speaker's personal goals. For example, is it his/her ambition to become a member of the target community or to remain a recognizable outsider? It also depends on the ability to adopt L2 pragmatic behaviors, exposure to relevant input and occasion for use, and the contexts in which he/she interacts. As suggested by Hymes's (1964) "etic grid," the last factor is especially important because expectations of particular behaviors and accepted variation are highly context-dependent—for any participant, native or non-native. Language teaching should make learners aware of such sociolinguistic variation. Whether and to what extent the learner wishes to conform to native speaker expectations must remain his/her choice (Thomas 1983).

> ## *P*ause to consider . . .
>
> in what ways "nativelike pragmatic behavior exhibited by non-native speakers may not be entirely desirable." Give some examples. Would you expect native speakers to respond in the same way in cases where non-native speakers exhibit native speaker pragmatic behavior and where they don't?

The type of discourse where deviance from native speaker expectations has often undesired consequences is in institutional encounters with a "gate-keeping" function, such as in job interviews (Gumperz 1982), counseling sessions (Erickson & Shultz 1982; Fiksdal 1990), academic advising sessions (Bardovi-Harlig & Hartford 1990, 1993; Gumperz 1992), medical interviews (Rehbein 1986), pretrial interviews (Scollon & Scollon 1983), or language proficiency interviews (Ross 1995). In such situations, the non-native speaker is typically at the powerless end of an unequal power encounter. Hence, opportunities to control the discourse and initiate repair when something goes wrong are rare. At the same time, pragmatic failure in such encounters can be consequential for the client's personal and professional life. It is, therefore, particu-

119

*Goals and Process in
the Development of
Pragmatic
Competence*

larly important that teachers prepare students for the kinds of gatekeeping situations they are likely to encounter. The studies cited above document interactions between native "gate-keepers" and non-native clients, identify instances of pragmatic failure, and offer explanations why the participants miscommunicated. Importantly, some studies also report what kinds of behaviors may contribute to clients' successes in institutional encounters (e.g., Erickson & Shultz 1982; Fiksdal 1990). Studies of native and non-native speaker interaction in institutional settings are, thus, especially useful because they inform teachers as to how their students can cope successfully with institutional encounters.

Although convergent or divergent production of linguistic action may have different communicative effects in different contexts—and the ultimate decision as to how much or little to accommodate remains the learner's—such control is absent in listening and reading. It is clearly to the learner's advantage to understand as many native and non-native varieties and communicative styles as he/she can be expected to have contact with, and to develop efficient strategies of pragmatic comprehension in order to understand unfamiliar spoken or written text. Studies of pragmatic comprehension show that even advanced non-native listeners can have difficulties in assigning pragmatic meaning to speakers' utterances (cf. Takahashi & Roitblat 1994). One factor that facilitates or complicates pragmatic comprehension is the student's cultural background, as Bouton (1988) reports in a large study of non-native listeners' understanding of indirect responses. More recently, Bouton (1994) demonstrates that the student's ability to understand indirect responses can be greatly enhanced, and accelerated, through language teaching.

A large body of literature on non-native speakers' production of linguistic action (Kasper & Blum-Kulka 1993b) shows that adult non-native speakers make use of their pragmalinguistic and sociopragmatic ability: That is, they know that linguistic means can have different illocutionary and politeness functions and that social context factors influence which strategies and forms to choose. But the learner's range of pragmalinguistic options is often more limited compared to native speakers,' their form-function mappings may be different, and they use the same speech act realization strategies in different contexts.

One factor that can explain native and non-native speaker differences in speech act production is pragmatic transfer, that is, nonnative speakers' use of L1 pragmatic knowledge to understand or carry out linguistic action in the L2 (cf. Kasper 1992). Just as in grammar, vocabulary, or pronunciation, pragmatic transfer is often positive, that is, nonnative speakers base their choice of a speech act realization pattern in the L2 on what they would say in a corresponding L1 context, and this usage happens to be appropriate in the L2 as well. For instance, learners were shown to transfer some routines for requesting, such as *why don't you* and *do you mind,* from English to Hebrew (Blum-Kulka, 1982), or past-tense modal forms from Danish and German to English (House & Kasper 1987; Faerch & Kasper 1989). Because in these cases, the form-function mappings in the L1 match those in the L2, the transfer is positive.

Often, however, learners' tacit assumption of parallel form-function mappings in the L1 and the L2 do not correspond. Literal translations of L1 rou-

120

CHAPTER 6
The Role of
Pragmatics in
Language Teacher
Education

tines frequently do not work in the L2. For example, in order to express grati-tude in English, Japanese learners used apologetic formulae, and Middle East-ern students used proverbial expressions (Eisenstein & Bodman 1993). Both strategies would have been effective in Japanese and Arabic, respectively, but misfired in English. In addition to such cases of negative pragmalinguistic transfer, negative sociopragmatic transfer can also be observed. Studies by Beebe and collaborators show that learners may perceive L2 contexts in the same way as L1 contexts, for instance, by transferring their perception of the social status relationship between student and professor from Japanese to Eng-lish (Takahashi & Beebe 1993).

Whether positive or negative in outcome, transfer in pragmatics and else-where is always based on the assumption that things are "the same" in the L1 and the L2. Learners, however, do not always make such an assumption. They often have their own implicit theories about differences between their own and the target culture and language, and their linguistic action in the L2 may be guided by such theories.[1] For example, it has frequently been observed that Japanese non-native speakers of English are more direct in requesting or refus-ing than are native speakers. As some learners commented in one study, this is because they have the idea that Americans are very direct (Robinson 1992). Because of such stereotypical perceptions, the reverse stereotype of "Japanese politeness" is sometimes belied when Japanese speakers use English. A good way to reveal and counteract stereotypical perceptions is to explore in class what such stereotypes are, for instance, by role-playing refusal or request situ-ations. Students' ways of handling such speech acts can then be compared with native speaker conversations in similar situations, which can be brought into the classroom through audiovisual media or perhaps through a live per-formance by invited native speakers.

Positive pragmatic transfer is less salient than negative transfer and, per-haps, therefore not much commented on in the literature. From a language teaching perspective, however, it is important to know where learners transfer positively and, in fact, to encourage such transfer, because what students get "for free" from fundamental principles of communication and their specific L1 experience does not require much time in class. For example, just as little class time needs to be spent on the basic functions of English articles for students with a Germanic language background, it would not be necessary to explain to such students the use of *can you* and *could you* as request formulae because they intuitively transfer the equivalent modals from their native languages (cf. Faerch & Kasper 1989; House & Kasper 1987).

Negative pragmatic transfer is more salient than positive transfer because it is often a source of miscommunication. To continue the example of the Ger-manic language students, using *must* in directives (*you must park your car some-where else*) may sound rude in English, whereas its German equivalent is per-fectly polite if the speaker is in a position of authority (House & Kasper 1987). It is obviously useful to identify areas of pragmalinguistic and sociopragmatic negative transfer that are likely to result in pragmatic failure and to provide students with alternative means of expression. But it is problematic to put an equation mark between "negative pragmatic transfer" and "pragmatic fail-ure." As I argued earlier in this section, differences in linguistic action patterns do not necessarily result in miscommunication. Research examining native and non-native speaker interaction is the best source to inform teachers about successful and unsuccessful non-native speaker strategies.[2]

121

*Goals and Process in
the Development of
Pragmatic
Competence*

---

*P*ause to consider . . .

why negative pragmatic transfer may be more salient to the teacher or other listeners than positive pragmatic transfer. Give examples from your own language-teaching or learning experience where negative pragmatic transfer does not result in pragmatic failure.

We have examined how non-native speakers use their L2 pragmatic competence, but have not explored much how their pragmatic knowledge develops. For reasons discussed elsewhere (Kasper & Schmidt 1996), interlanguage pragmatics research has had a stronger focus on the structure of L2 learners' action patterns than on their acquisition. But the available studies offer some useful information to language teachers. One convergent outcome of different studies shows that beginning learners use short, packaged formulae which are gradually "unpacked,": that is, individual elements and structures become apparent over time and can be modified in various ways (Ellis 1992; Sawyer 1992; Scarcella 1979; Schmidt 1983). For example, Ellis (1992, p. 16f.) identifies the following sequence in the acquisition of request strategies in a British ESL classroom:

me no (blue)

give me (a paper)

can I have a rubber?

you got a rubber?

miss I want (i.e., the stapler)

Tasleem, have you got glue?

can I take book with me

can you pass me my pencil

can I borrow your pen sir

As this sequence suggests, there appears to be an important role for prefabricated speech in pragmatic development. But formulaic speech does not represent only an initial learning stage, a stepping stone towards the higher realms of creative language use. Routine formulae constitute a substantial part of adult native speakers' pragmatic competence. Learners need to acquire a sizable repertoire of routines in order to cope efficiently with recurrent social situations and discourse requirements (Coulmas 1981). Therefore, how pragmatic routines are acquired has to be addressed as a research issue in its own right (Wildner-Bassett 1984).

122

CHAPTER 6
The Role of
Pragmatics in
Language Teacher
Education

Of particular interest to language teachers is the question of whether and how pragmatic development can be enhanced through language instruction. Little research on the "teachability" of pragmatic competence has been done yet, but the few existing studies are encouraging. A clear advantage was found for ESL students who were instructed in complimenting and responding to compliments (Billmyer 1990) and in understanding different types of indirect responses (Bouton 1994). While some features of complimenting and implicature were more easily taught than others, focusing on aspects of pragmatic knowledge through consciousness-raising activities and communicative practice seems highly facilitative. In a classroom (pseudo-)experiment, Wildner-Bassett (1984) examined whether EFL learners' acquisition of gambits (routines for conversational management and modification of illocutionary force) was influenced by the instructional approach. She found that learners' use of gambits improved significantly, qualitatively and quantitatively, regardless of teaching approach. However, learners taught according to an eclectic approach were even more successful than their colleagues who had been exposed to a version of suggestopedia.

Other teaching proposals have not yet been empirically tested but are based on research on different linguistic acts. Olshtain and Cohen (1991) propose a sequence of activities in order to develop students' ability to apologize in the L2. Rose (1994) suggests using feature films in both the L1 and the L2 to help students perform requests in a foreign language. Bardovi-Harlig et al. (1991) examine how conversational closings are represented in teaching materials and suggest activities to support students' skills in closing conversations in a second language.

A PRAGMATIC VIEW OF LANGUAGE TEACHING

A look at the proposals for developing the aspects of pragmatic competence cited earlier reveals that they include two main types of classroom activities: activities aimed at raising the students' awareness about the pragmatic feature and activities offering various opportunities for communicative practice. Awareness-raising activities partly provide students directly with sociopragmatic and pragmalinguistic information, for instance, the function of complimenting in American culture, appropriate topics for complimenting, and typical formulae by which compliments are given and received. Such information can be conveyed through lecturing, group or pair work, or a combination of teacher- and student-centered activities. Sources of "data" from which students can observe particular pragmatic features range from native speaker "classroom guests" (Bardovi-Harlig et al. 1991) to videos of authentic interaction or feature films (Rose 1994). A second language context, furthermore, affords the opportunity to give students observation assignments outside the classroom. Such observation tasks can focus on sociopragmatic or pragmalinguistic features.

A sociopragmatic task would be, for example, to observe under what conditions native speakers of American English express gratitude (when, for what kinds of goods or services, to whom; cf. Eisenstein & Bodman 1993). Depending on the student population and available time, such observations may be open or structured. Open observations allow students to detect the important context factors. For structured observations, students are provided with an observation sheet which specifies the categories to explore (e.g., speaker's and hearer's status and familiarity, cost of the goods or service to the giver, degree to which the giver is obliged to provide the goods or service). A useful model for such an observation sheet is the one proposed by Rose (1994) for requests.

A pragmalinguistic task focuses on the strategies and linguistic means by which thanking is accomplished, what formulas are used, and what additional means of expressing appreciation are employed, such as expressing pleasure about the giver's thoughtfulness or the received gift, asking questions about it, and so forth. Finally, by examining in which contexts the various ways of expressing gratitude are used, sociopragmatic and pragmalinguistic aspects are combined. By focusing students' attention on relevant features of the input, such observation tasks help students make connections between linguistic forms, pragmatic functions, and their social distribution. Students are thus guided to notice the information they need in order to develop pragmatic competence in the L2 (Schmidt 1993). The observations made outside the classroom are reported to the class, compared with those of other students, and evaluated by the teacher. These discussion sessions can take on any kind of student- or teacher-centered format.

---

*P*ause to consider . . .

this quotation from Thomas's (1983) much-cited paper:
> Correcting pragmatic failure stemming from sociopragmatic miscalculation is a far more delicate matter for the language teacher than correcting pragmalinguistic failure. Sociopragmatic decisions are social before they are linguistic, and while foreign learners are fairly amenable to corrections which they regard as linguistic, they are justifiably sensitive about having their social (or even political, religious, or moral) judgment called into question (p. 104).

What are the implications of Thomas's position for pragmatic norms in second language teaching and the assessment of students' pragmatic competence? Do you concur with Thomas's point of view?

Although awareness-raising activities can be conducted in different forms of classroom organization, practicing linguistic acts and discourse functions requires student-to-student activities that allow for some kind of conversational exchange. Familiar activities based on conversational interaction are role-plays, simulations, drama, and various other tasks. It may be useful to consider for a moment why such activities are, in fact, necessary, especially (but not only) in foreign language teaching.

124

CHAPTER 6
The Role of
Pragmatics in
Language Teacher
Education

It is well-documented that in teacher-fronted instruction—the classic mode of teaching language or any other subject—the person doing most of the talking is the teacher (cf. Chaudron 1988). Although this is to the detriment of students' speaking opportunities, it could be argued that through the sheer quantity of teacher talk, students are provided with the input they need for language development. Apart from other problems with such a position, however, studies show that compared to conversation outside instructional settings, teacher-fronted classroom discourse displays the following:

- A narrow range of speech acts (Long, Adams, McLean & Castanos 1976);
- Lack of politeness markings (Lörscher & Schulze 1988);
- Shorter and less complex openings and closings (Kasper 1989; Lörscher 1986); and,
- A limited range of gambits used for turn-taking and politeness marking (DuFon 1991; Kasper 1989).

The reason for such differences is not that classroom discourse is "artificial." Classroom discourse is just as authentic as any other kind of discourse. Rather, classroom interaction is an institutional activity in which participants' roles are asymmetrically distributed. The activities associated with the teacher's and students' roles are epitomized in the basic interactional pattern of classical teacher-fronted instruction: the (in)famous pedagogical exchange of elicitation (by the teacher)–response (by a student)–feedback (by the teacher) (cf. Chaudron 1988, p. 37). In the classic scenario, the teacher is solely responsible for the main functions of teaching: imparting new information to students, helping them process such information, and controlling whether the new information has become part of students' knowledge. The goals of teaching are thus mainly referential and transactional and can be achieved through a quite limited range of linguistic acts. Furthermore, even within this restricted range of speech activities, teachers have dominance, both in quantitative and qualitative terms, because they are the ones who initiate most (if not all) exchanges and take care of complex instructional and classroom management tasks.

When we map the linguistic actions in classic language classroom discourse against the pragmatic competence that non-native speakers need to communicate in the world outside, it becomes immediately obvious that the language classroom in its classic format does not offer the students what they need, neither in terms of teacher's input, nor in terms of students' productive language use. As comparisons of teacher-fronted instruction and small group work show, the range of linguistic acts performed by the students increases dramatically in student-centered activities (Long et al. 1976). Student-centered activities do more than just increase students' speaking time: They also give them opportunities to practice conversational management, perform a larger range of speech acts, and interact with other participants in completing a task. It is precisely its interactional property that makes conversation so complex and demanding for the less proficient non-native speaker. Conversationalists have to listen to and understand their partner's contributions while also planning and carrying out their own. They have to attend not just to their own and the other person's utterances, but also to the relationship of these utterances to the preceding talk and the situational context. In order to interpret their partner's contributions and make appropriate choices for their own, they constantly have to assess and reassess assumptions, knowledge and beliefs, goals, attitudes, and affective states. When the topic is cognitively demanding and the whole encounter stressful, as in gatekeeping encounters or interpersonal conflicts, even native speakers' communicative competence can be stretched to its maximum capacity. Therefore, it stands to reason that non-native speakers need plenty of occasions to exercise their conversational ability in the L2, especially when the sociopragmatic norms for different types of conversation contrast between the L1 and L2.

---

*P*ause to consider . . .

the characteristics of teacher-fronted instruction in terms of input for L2 pragmatic development. What characteristics of student-centered activities are beneficial in terms of input to the learner and in terms of communicative demand on the learner?

   What types of activities do you usually associate with student-centered activities? Do these also run the risk of embodying a limited range of speech acts? If so, how can the range be broadened?

Although student-centered interaction requires shared turn-taking and, thus, alternating discourse roles as speaker and hearer, conversation alone does not ensure that students practice a larger variety of speech acts. Structuring a language course around different topics is good for vocabulary learning, but when the associated activities are invariably of the discourse type "discussion," little is done for the development of students' illocutionary and sociolinguistic competence. This is so because the typical type of speech act performed in discussions are representatives (e.g., claiming, arguing, clarifying, describing, objecting) the functions of which are mainly referential and to some extent directive—because the speaker may want to persuade the other discussants of his/her point of view—and expressive—because the speaker may express his/her attitude about some aspect of the topic. Other speech acts, which regularly occur in everyday interaction and which emphasize the relational function (opening and closing conversations, thanking, complimenting, apologizing, requesting, inviting, offering, refusing), do not regularly occur in discussions. It is, therefore, essential to include activities, such as drama, simulations and role-play, where a wide range of roles, speech acts, and language functions can be practiced.

Such student-centered activities should be based on authentic native speaker input, brought into the classroom through audiovisual media (including students' recorded observations of native speaker interaction as much as possible). Authentic discourse is crucial not because students should imitate native speakers' action patterns, but rather in order to build their own pragmatic knowledge of the L2 on the right kind of input. Comparisons of textbook

126

CHAPTER 6
The Role of
Pragmatics in
Language Teacher
Education

dialogues and authentic discourse show that a mismatch often occurs between the two. For instance, Bardovi-Harlig et al. (1991) examined conversational closings in twenty textbooks for American English and found that few of them represented closing phases accurately. Similar discrepancies were discovered between the representation of many other conversational features in authentic discourse and textbook dialogues (Berendt 1991; Myers-Scotton & Bernstein 1988). The reason for such inaccurate representations is that native speakers are only partially aware of their pragmatic competence (the same is true of their language competence generally). Most of native speakers' pragmatic knowledge is tacit, or implicit knowledge: It underlies their linguistic action, but they cannot describe it (cf. Wolfson [1989] and Schmidt [1993]). Even the most proficient conversationalist has little conscious awareness about turn-taking rules, for example. Miscommunication or pragmatic failure is often vaguely diagnosed as "impolite" behavior on the part of the other person, whereas the specific source of the irritation remains unclear (e.g., Gumperz 1992; Tyler & Davies 1990). Because the intuitions of native speakers are a notoriously unreliable source of information about the pragmatic norms of their own community, it is vital that pragmatic input to students be research-based (Bardovi-Harlig et al. 1991; Myers-Scotton & Bernstein 1988; Wolfson 1989; Olshtain & Cohen 1992).

Pragmatics theory and research, thus, help teachers to evaluate and choose materials and learning activities inside and outside the classroom. Yet, another important way in which especially cross-cultural pragmatics is helpful for language teachers exists. As any kind of teaching, language teaching has an official and a hidden agenda to it. The official agenda of a communicative curriculum is to enable students to know and to use relevant parts of the target language in order to accomplish their communicative goals. The hidden agenda, unknown not only to students but also to teachers, aims at more than that. Through the classroom interaction itself, the way the teacher's and students' roles are orchestrated by the teacher, the teacher's own actions, and his/her response to students' behaviors, students are informed about the cultural practices of the target community. Interaction in the second language classroom, thus, functions as language socialization, or perhaps more precisely, resocialization. In a recent study, Poole (1992) identifies a number of discourse features in ESL classrooms that encode cultural messages to students. In order to help students supply responses that exceed their L2 competence, teachers simplify their utterances, guess what students may want to say, and jointly construct responses with the students. The message is thus that experts accommodate novice incompetence. Such downward convergence from expert to novices is also characteristic of child socialization by white, middle-class American caregivers (Snow 1988) and contrasts strongly with the socialization practices of working-class African Americans (Heath 1983) or Samoans (Ochs 1988) where such expert-to-novice convergence is uncommon. A second message includes task accomplishment, in which experts provide help for novices; however, successful task completion is attributed to the novice. Thus, while setting and carrying out a task, the teacher encodes joint agency in plural markers *(let's, we, our)* and carries out most of the tasks—him/herself; however, in evaluation, the teacher praises the students for their accomplishments. A third cultural message includes the avoidance of overt displays of status differentials. Teachers downplay status asymmetry by soliciting students' suggestions on how to proceed with an activity and to implement their own agendas covertly. The unequal power balance between teacher and students is further deemphasized by the informal style of classroom interaction evident in Poole's (1992) transcripts.

Pause to consider . . .

an ordinary foreign or second language lesson. If you can, record such a lesson on audio- or videotape. What kinds of speech acts occur? Who performs them? How (i.e. by what strategies and linguistic means) are the speech acts realized? How are turns at talk distributed among students and teacher? Is the pattern of speech acts and turn distribution appropriate for the development of students' pragmatic competence? If not, how would you change it?

Ironically, the cultural messages encoded in second language classroom discourse may be more salient for the foreign students than for teachers who are members of the L2 community. Students bring their own culturally informed expectations to second language classrooms and are often bewildered to find that these expectations are not fulfilled. For many foreign students, observing quite a different style of classroom interaction is a consciousness-raising experience of major proportions and can be a serious element of culture-shock. Because modifying well-rehearsed role behaviors takes time and is sometimes never accomplished, culturally varying norms and beliefs about who does what, and when, in classrooms are visible in different patterns of student participation. Four studies examined three types of turn-taking in second language classrooms: response to general (whole class) solicits, response to personal (specific student) solicits, and self-selection. In all three categories, Asian students were outperformed by non-Asians (Sato 1982), Japanese by non-Japanese (McLean 1983), Japanese-Americans by Caucasians (in a JFL classroom; Doi 1988), and Japanese by Chinese (Shimura 1988); however, the last study did not find different participation patterns in response to personal solicits.

The example of the Japanese students may serve to illustrate that the resocialization that foreign students are tacitly expected to undergo can be quite a formidable task for all participants, but mostly perhaps for the students themselves. The unisonal complaint of "Western" teachers about Japanese students is the lack of classroom participation found in the cited studies. Especially when grades are partly based on participation, students' passivity is clearly to their own detriment. From the teachers' point of view, students' nonparticipatory behavior is an instance of sociopragmatic failure: The expected linguistic actions (e.g., responses to teacher's elicitations, requests for information or

128

*CHAPTER 6
The Role of
Pragmatics in
Language Teacher
Education*

clarification in self-selected turns, or comments challenging the teacher's or another student's contribution) are not forthcoming. Pragmatic failure can have many causes; however, in the case of the reticent Japanese students, sociopragmatic transfer from their experience in Japanese classrooms is a very likely source.

Based on studies of classroom behavior in Japanese elementary schools, high schools, and colleges, Anderson (1993) notes that appropriate student behavior is characterized by four features: group-mindedness, consensual decision-making, formalized speech-making, and listener responsibility. Group-mindedness is evident in the emphasis, beginning in preschool, on team-work and group study, and collective rather than individual responsibility. Consensual decision-making is reflected in students' reluctance to offer their own responses to a teacher elicit. In a typical response pattern, the nominated student confers with his/her classmates sitting next to him/her before responding. The basic pattern of the pedagogical exchange is still intact, but the second step, namely the student's response, is expanded to "consensus check–response." The nominated student's response, thus, reflects the opinion or knowledge display of the consulted group rather than his/her own.

Just as expressing personal views is deemphasized in Japanese classrooms, original impromptu contributions in informal style—typical of American classroom discourse—are not encouraged. Japanese students are trained at a young age in formal presentations, characterized by ritual language use and an elevated style that sets such classroom contributions apart from the casual language of everyday spoken interaction. Students not yet acculturated to American[3] classroom style may feel they have to use an equivalent formality level in English, and realizing that this overtaxes their L2 competence, they may prefer not to respond. Finally, listener responsibility refers to the well-documented feature of Japanese communicative style to place the burden of making sense of a conversation on the listener, one outcome of the "empathy training" in the socialization of Japanese children (Clancy 1986). Again, this is in marked contrast to American norms of communication, where it is the speaker's job to give the necessary information in a form that is optimally comprehensible to the listener. The different responsibility assigned to the roles of listener and speaker in Japanese and American communication raises questions about whether a universal consensus exists as to how people communicate.

Pause to consider . . .

the relationship of cultural background and classroom interaction. This chapter provides examples from one culture. Can you provide other examples from your experience where cultural backgrounds influence interactional styles in the classroom? What can happen in multicultural classes where interactional styles among the students are diverse?

A particularly clear example is the "cooperative principle" proposed by Grice (1975) with its four maxims:

1. Give the right amount of information;
2. Tell the truth;
3. Say what is relevant; and
4. Be brief and clear.

As can be seen, the cooperative principle articulates how speakers ensure successful communication. The listener's job is to assume that the speaker is cooperative, even if an utterance on the surface were to violate one or more of the four maxims. However, comprehending what a speaker means by what he/she says can be taxing for the listener in conversations between Americans and is not always achieved successfully. Moreover, the cooperative principle is a cultural construct itself, revealing the American view of speaker's responsibility in communication.

As a cultural belief, listener responsibility explains why Japanese students are reluctant to ask questions in class. They assume that an assigned text or the teacher's lecture is a non-negotiable piece of discourse. When they do not understand something, it must be because of their lack of knowledge or attention. Such comprehension problems are solved by asking classmates or, occasionally, the teacher after class. The student thereby avoids presenting himself/herself as a "poor listener" (or reader) in public. Public requests for clarification are also avoided because they could be seen as a challenge to the teacher's authority. Unlike in the American ESL classrooms examined by Poole (1992), where the de facto inequality between teacher and students was minimized in classroom interaction, Japanese classroom discourse accentuates the status differential. Consequently, status-incongruent acts are not desired by Japanese teachers and duly avoided by the students.

The formal, lecture-style arrangement of Japanese instructional settings with the teacher as authority figure and students as interactionally passive recipients, thus, contrasts sharply with American ideas of good teaching and productive learning, especially when language learning is on the agenda. "Meaning negotiation" between teacher and students, a favorite strategy in American classroom discourse (Poole 1992), is "not on" in a Japanese classroom setting because it presupposes the "polite fiction" that "you and I are equal" (Sakamoto & Naotsuka 1982). From an American (and this writer's) cultural perspective, meaning negotiation is desirable because of its multifunctional potential as a learning and teaching strategy: Clarification requests and comprehension and confirmation checks function as a diagnostic for the teacher about students' current state of knowledge and for the students as a means to test hypotheses and solicit from the teacher the input they currently need. However, as the preceding discussion suggests, theories of teaching and learning, both implicit teacher theories (Poole 1992) and explicit scientific theories, are of necessity culturally informed and hence unlikely to be shared when teacher and students have different cultural backgrounds.

The discussion of differential participation structures in language teaching has several implications—and throwing up one's hands in despair in the face of what looks like firm cultural barriers need not and should not be one of

130

CHAPTER 6
The Role of
Pragmatics in
Language Teacher
Education

them. Awareness is the first step towards change, and understanding that Japanese students' reticence is a perfectly functional classroom behavior in their own cultural context is such a first step. Miller (1993, p. 3) notes critically about foreign English teachers in Japan that "the very teachers who mercifully overlook linguistic errors in order to bolster a learner's self-confidence may take that learner to task for failing to adhere to their own ethnocentric standards concerning student participation." Awareness of the cross-culturally varying sociopragmatics of classroom interaction is a potent antidote to ethnocentric bias.

Awareness alone makes a bad conscience but does not change anything. What are the pedagogic options for the cross-culturally-conscious language teacher? The first option is to insist on the participation patterns characteristic of target culture classrooms. Imposing such one-sided convergence on the students amounts to a form of cultural imperialism and power display which cross-culturally-sensitive teachers would hopefully shy away from. It is not likely to be successful either, and is of doubtful usefulness in a foreign language context where only few students may have the possibility or desire to live in the L2 community. A second possibility is the reverse scenario, namely, the teacher converging to the students' cultural expectations. In a content classroom where the foreign instructor only teaches for a short time, this may be the most effective option. The same is true when the goal of language instruction is explicit knowledge of grammar and ability to translate. However, when communicative competence is on the agenda, it is difficult to justify a lecture-style classroom. The third alternative is a compromise solution of sorts, which has been recommended by experienced foreign teachers in Japan (cf., Anderson 1993). Rather than imposing completely new participatory demands on the students, this option takes advantage of activities that are both familiar to the students and consistent with the teacher's desire to increase student activity. Although it appears to be used less commonly in high schools and in colleges, students are used to group work from as early as preschool. It seems that adult students can reactivate this experience, because they usually perform group tasks competently and with all group members participating to the best of their abilities. Eventually, many students discover that they actually enjoy a style of classroom interaction that allows for more personal expression and responsibility, and welcome the informal style of their foreign teacher (Yamashita & Miller 1994). However, students' convergence to American ways of classroom participation should not be taken as indication of an ultimately superior teaching style. It should be seen as students grasping the opportunity of building on skills which they first developed in their own cultural context and expanding those skills into new territories of interaction and self-expression.

---

*P*ause to consider . . .

the factors that may affect the structure of classroom interaction. Cultural beliefs and students' purpose for learning the language have been mentioned as two such factors. What are some of the other factors that you can think of?

CONCLUSION

In this chapter, I argue that knowing pragmatic theory and research is helpful to language teachers in two important ways. First, pragmatic theory provides the basis for deciding what to teach. It is useful to distinguish between students' receptive and productive pragmatic ability because students' learning tasks are different in the two modalities. Several problems exist with adopting a native speaker standard for productive pragmatic ability, suggesting that communicative success is a matter of optimal rather than total convergence to native speaker action patterns.

The second reason for a pragmatic perspective on language teaching is that it affords teachers a framework to assess and improve alternative learning activities and classroom interaction. Because traditional teacher-fronted instruction imposes severe limits on the pragmatic information and skills that students need outside the classroom, different discourse types and activities must be introduced into the classroom. Although such activities aim at providing useful communicative practice to students and raise their pragmatic awareness, the need for pragmatic consciousness-raising extends to the teacher as well. It is vital for teachers to understand the pragmatics of classroom instruction. Such understanding implies, first and foremost, teachers' self-reflexive awareness of their own assumptions about language instruction and willingness to explore how their implicit theories match or don't match with students' ideas about "good language teaching."

This conclusion implies a strong plea for classroom research from a pragmatic perspective, in the various senses proposed in this chapter. Teachers' and students' actions and interactions in language classrooms need to be examined with a view to assessing their contribution to the development of students' pragmatic competence. One important goal of such research is to identify "optimal levels of convergence" (Giles, Coupland & Coupland 1991) between students and teacher in second and foreign language classrooms.

Pause to consider . . .

how, after reading this chapter, you see pragmatics influencing your decisions as a teacher.

NOTES

[1] See also discussions of the role of L1 in Bardovi-Harlig (Ch. 2) and Pennington (Ch. 4).
[2] See references at the end of this chapter on institutional discourse.
[3] Here and elsewhere in this chapter, the generalizing descriptor "American" is not intended to suggest that all American classrooms or classes taught by American teachers are the same; obviously they are not. In a language teaching context, "American" refers to a teaching approach adopted by many North-American and

132

CHAPTER 6
*The Role of
Pragmatics in
Language Teacher
Education*

Anglo-European teachers, namely an approach informed by the current educational ideal of a student-oriented, participatory style that fosters autonomy, expressivity, critical thinking, and creativity. Sociocultural and individual variation in teaching and communication practices throughout North America, while herewith acknowledged, is not the point of this chapter.

KEY TERMS, CONCEPTS, AND ISSUES

competence
  communicative competence
  grammatical competence
  linguistic competence
  illocutionary competence
  pragmatic competence
  sociolinguistic competence
discourse
language function
language socialization
illocutionary act

illocutionary force
interlanguage pragmatics
metalinguistic/metacommunicative
pragmalinguistic/sociopragmatic
pragmatic awareness/practice
pragmatic development
pragmatic transfer
pragmatics
sociolinguistic variation
speech act

EXPLORING THE TOPICS FURTHER

1. *Classroom issues.* A recent review of approaches to communicative competence in second language teaching is provided in Savignon (1991). A view of second language classrooms as cultural spaces is discussed in Breen (1985). For the difference between studies of language acquisition and language socialization, see Schieffelin & Ochs (1986).
2. *Establishing the target norm.* The problem of a native speaker norm in second language theory and research is discussed by Kachru (1994) and Sridhar (1994). A bilingual perspective on the issue is proposed by Grosjean (1985).
3. *The development of pragmatic competence.* For studies examining the development of pragmatic competence, see Bouton (1992) for the comprehension of implicature, Schmidt (1983) and Ellis (1992) for directives, and Bardovi-Harlig & Hartford (1993) for suggestions and rejections. *Studies in Second Language Acquisition 16,* no. 2 (1996) is a special issue on this topic.
4. *Journals of interest.* For serial publications with a focus on pragmatics, consult *Journal of Pragmatics, Pragmatics,* and the monograph series *Pragmatics and Language Learning* (published by The University of Illinois, Division of English as an International Language).

REFERENCES

Anderson, F. E. (1993). The enigma of the college classroom: Nails that don't stick up. In P. Wadden (Ed.), *A handbook for teaching English at Japanese colleges and universities* (pp. 101–110). Oxford: Oxford University Press.

Aston, G. (1993). Notes on the interlanguage of comity. In G. Kasper & S. Blum-Kulka (Eds.), *Interlanguage pragmatics* (pp. 224–250). New York: Oxford University Press.

Bachman, L. (1990). *Fundamental considerations in language testing.* Oxford: Oxford University Press.

Bardovi-Harlig, K. & Hartford, B. (1990). Congruence in native and nonnative conversations: Status balance in the academic advising session. *Language Learning, 40,* 467–501.

Bardovi-Harlig, K. & Hartford, B. (1993). Learning the rules of academic talk: A longitudinal study of pragmatic development. *Studies in Second Language Acquisition, 15,* 279–304.

Bardovi-Harlig, K., Hartford, B .A. S., Mahan-Taylor, R., Morgan, M. J. & Reynolds, D. W. (1991). Developing pragmatic awareness: Closing the conversation. *ELT Journal, 45,* 4–15.

Berendt, E. (1991). Conversation from a cross-cultural perspective, and implications for language teaching. *Studies in Language, 14,* 161–170. Center for Foreign Language Studies, Kanagawa University, Yokohama.

Billmyer, K. (1990). "I really like your lifestyle": ESL learners learning how to compliment. *Penn Working Papers in Educational Linguistics, 6*(2), 31–48.

Blum-Kulka, S., (1982). Learning how to say what you mean in a second language: A study of speech act performance of learners of Hebrew as a second language. *Applied Linguistics, 3,* 29–59.

Blum-Kulka, S. (1991). Interlanguage pragmatics: The case of requests. In R. Phillipson, E. Kellerman, L. Selinker, M. Sharwood Smith & M. Swain (Eds.), *Foreign/second language pedagogy research* (pp. 255–272). Clevedon: Multilingual Matters.

Blum-Kulka, S. & Sheffer, H. (1993). The metapragmatic discourse of American-Israeli families at dinner. In G. Kasper & S. Blum-Kulka (Eds.), *Interlanguage pragmatics* (pp. 196–223). New York: Oxford University Press.

Bouton, L. F. (1988). A cross-cultural study of ability to interpret implicatures in English. *World Englishes, 17,* 183–196.

Bouton, L. F. (1990). The effective use of implicature in English: Why and how it should be taught in the ESL classroom. In L. F. Bouton & Y. Kachru (Eds.), *Pragmatics and language learning,* Vol. 1 (pp. 43–51). Urbana, IL: University of Illinois at Urbana-Champaign, Division of English as an International Language.

Bouton, L. (1994). Can NNS skill in interpreting implicature in American English be improved through explicit instruction? – A pilot study. In L. F. Bouton & Y. Kachru (Eds.), *Pragmatics and language learning,* Vol. 4 (pp. 88–109). Urbana, IL: University of Illinois at Urbana-Champaign, Division of English as an International Language.

Breen, M. (1985). The social context for language learning – A neglected situation? *Studies in Second Language Acquisition, 7,* 135–158.

Canale, M., & Swain, M. (1980). Theoretical bases of communicative approaches to second language teaching and testing. *Applied Linguistics, 1,* 1–47.

Chaudron, C. (1988). *Second language classrooms. Research on teaching and learning.* Cambridge: Cambridge University Press.

Clancy, P. M. (1986). The acquisition of communicative style in Japanese. In B. B. Schieffelin & E. Ochs (Eds.), *Language socialization across cultures* (pp. 213–249). New York: Cambridge University Press.

Clyne, M. (1979). Communicative competence in contact. *ITL Bulletin, 43,* 17–37.

Coulmas, F. (Ed.) (1981). *Conversational routine.* The Hague: Mouton.

Doi, T. (1988). An ethnographic study of a Japanese as a foreign language class in Hawai'i. Analyses and retrospective notes. Paper presented at Second Language Research Forum, Honolulu.

134

CHAPTER 6
The Role of
Pragmatics in
Language Teacher
Education

DuFon, M. A. (1991). The acquisition of gambits by beginning learners of Indonesian in a foreign language classroom. Unpublished manuscript, University of Hawai'i.

Eisenstein, M. & Bodman, J. (1993). Expressing gratitude in American English. In G. Kasper & S. Blum-Kulka (Eds.), *Interlanguage pragmatics* (pp. 64–81). New York: Oxford University Press.

Ellis, R. (1992). Learning to communicate in the classroom. *Studies in Second Language Acquisition,* 14, 1–23.

Ellis, R. (1994). *The study of second language acquisition.* Oxford: Oxford University Press.

Erickson, F., & Shultz, J. (1982). *The counselor as gatekeeper: Social interaction in interviews.* New York: Academic Press.

Færch, C. & Kasper, G. (1989). Internal and external modification in interlanguage request realization. In S. Blum-Kulka, J. House, & G. Kasper (Eds.), *Cross-cultural pragmatics* (pp. 221–247). Norwood, N. J.: Ablex.

Fiksdal, S. (1990). *The right time and pace: A microanalysis of cross-cultural gatekeeping interviews.* Norwood, NJ: Ablex.

Giles, H., Coupland, J. & Coupland, N. (Eds.) (1991). *Contexts of accommodation.* Cambridge: Cambridge University Press.

Grandcolas, B., & Soulé-Susbielles, N. (1986). The analysis of foreign language classrooms. *Studies in Second Language Acquisition,* 8, 293–308.

Grice, H. P. (1975). Logic and conversation. In P. Cole & J. L. Morgan (Eds.), *Syntax and semantics,* Vol. 3: Speech acts (pp. 41–58). New York: Academic Press.

Grosjean, François. (1985). The bilingual as a competent but specific speaker-hearer. *Journal of Multilingual and Multicultural Development,* 6, 467–477.

Gumperz, J. (1982) *Discourse strategies.* Cambridge: Cambridge University Press.

Gumperz, J. (1992). Contextualization and understanding. In A. Duranti & C. Goodwin (Eds.), *Rethinking context.* Cambridge: Cambridge University Press.

Habermas, J. (1971). Vorbereitende Bemerkungen zu einer Theorie der kommunikativen Kompetenz. In J. Habermas & N. Luhmann, *Theorie der Gesellschaft oder Sozialtechnologie?* (pp. 101–141). Frankfurt: Suhrkamp.

Heath, S. B. (1983). *Ways with words: Language, life, work in communities and classrooms.* Cambridge: Cambridge University Press.

House, J. & Kasper, G. (1987). Interlanguage pragmatics: Requesting in a foreign language. In W. Lörscher & R. Schulze (Eds.), *Perspectives on language in performance* (pp. 1250–1288). Tübingen: Narr.

Hymes, D. (1964). Introduction: Towards ethnographies of communication. *American Anthropologist,* 66, 12–25.

Hymes, D. (1971). *On communicative competence.* Philadelphia: University of Pennsylvania Press.

Kachru, Y. (1994). Monolingual bias in SLA research. *TESOL Quarterly,* 28, 795–800.

Kasper, G. (1989). Interactive procedures in interlanguage discourse. In W. Olesky (Ed.), *Contrastive pragmatics* (pp. 189–229). Amsterdam: Benjamins.

Kasper, G. (1992). Pragmatic transfer. *Second Language Research,* 8, 203–231.

Kasper, G. & Blum-Kulka, S. (Eds.) (1993a). *Interlanguage pragmatics.* New York: Oxford University Press.

Kasper, G. & Blum-Kulka, S. (Eds.) (1993b). Interlanguage pragmatics: An introduction. In G. Kasper & S. Blum-Kulka (Eds.), *Interlanguage pragmatics* (pp. 3–17). New York: Oxford University Press.

Kasper, G. & Kellerman, E. (Eds.) (1997). *Communication strategies: Psycholinguistic and sociolinguistic perspectives.* London: Longman.

Kasper, G. & Schmidt, R. (1996). Developmental issues in interlanguage pragmatics. *Studies in Second Language Acquisition,* 18, 149–169.

Kasper, G. & Zhang, Y. (1995). 'It's good to be a bit Chinese': Foreign students' experience of Chinese pragmatics. In G. Kasper (Ed.), *Pragmatics of Chinese as native and target language*. Technical Report #5 (pp. 1–22). Honolulu: University of Hawai'i, Second Language Teaching & Curriculum Center.

Larsen-Freeman, D. & Long, M. H. (1991). *An introduction to second language acquisition research*. London: Longman.

Lörscher, W. (1986). Conversational structures in the foreign language classroom. In G. Kasper (Ed.), *Learning, teaching and communication in the foreign language classroom* (pp. 11–22). Århus: Aarhus University Press.

Lörscher, W. & Schulze, R. (1988). On polite speaking and foreign language classroom discourse. *International Review of Applied Linguistics in Language Teaching*, 26, 183–199.

Long, M. H. (1992). Maturational constraints on language development. *Studies in Second Language Acquisition*, 12, 251–286.

Long, M. H., Adams, L., McLean, M. & Castaños, F. (1976). Doing things with words: verbal interaction in lockstep and small group classroom situations. In J. F. Fanselow & R. Crymes (Eds.), *On TESOL '76* (pp. 137–153). Washington, D.C.: TESOL.

Michaelis, K. (1992). Regional variation in request realization. Unpublished Scholarly Paper, University of Hawai'i at Manoa.

McLean, K. P. (1983). Japanese/non-Japanese differences in classroom discourse turn-taking. In C. Ward & D. Wren (Eds.), *Selected papers in TESOL 59–67*. Monterey, CA: Monterey Institute for International Studies.

Miller, T. (1993). Cross-cultural classroom interactional styles in Japan and North America. Unpublished term paper, Temple University Japan, Tokyo.

Myers-Scotton, C. & Bernstein, J. (1988). Natural conversation as a model for textbook dialogue. *Applied Linguistics*, 9, 372–384.

Nattinger, J. R. & DeCarrico, J. S. (1992). *Lexical phrases and language teaching*. Oxford: Oxford University Press.

Ochs, E. (1988). *Culture and language development: Language acquisition and language socialization in a Samoan village*. Cambridge: Cambridge University Press.

Olshtain, E. & Cohen, A. (1991). Teaching speech act behavior to nonnative speakers. In M. Celce-Murcia (Ed.), *Teaching English as a second or foreign language* (2nd edition, pp. 154–190). New York: Newbury House.

Poole, D. (1992). Language socialization in the second language classroom. *Language Learning*, 42, 593–616.

Rehbein, J. (1986). Institutioneller Ablauf und interkulturelle Missverständnisse in der Allgemeinpraxis. *Curare*, 9, 297–328.

Robinson, M. A. (1992). Introspective methodology in interlanguage pragmatics research. In G. Kasper (Ed.), *Pragmatics of Japanese as a native and foreign language*. Technical Report #3 (pp. 27–82). Honolulu: University of Hawai'i, Second Language Teaching & Curriculum Center.

Rose, K. R. 1994. Pragmatic consciousness-raising in an EFL context. In L. F . Bouton & Y. Kachru (Eds.), *Pragmatics and language learning* monograph series, Vol. 5 (pp. 52–63). Urbana, IL: University of Illinois at Urbana-Champaign, Division of English as an International Language.

Ross, S. (1995). *The discourse of accommodation in oral proficiency interviews*. Unpublished Ph.D. dissertation, University of Hawai'i at Manoa.

Sakamoto, N. & Naotsuka, R. (1982). *Polite fictions: Why Japanese and Americans seem rude to each other*. Tokyo: Kinseido.

Sato, C. (1982). Ethnic styles in classroom discourse. In M. Hines & W. Rutherford (Eds.), *On TESOL '80* (pp. 11–24). Washington D.C.: TESOL.

136

CHAPTER 6
*The Role of
Pragmatics in
Language Teacher
Education*

Savignon, S. (1991). Communicative language teaching: State of the art. *TESOL Quarterly, 25,* 261–277.

Sawyer, M. (1992). The development of pragmatics in Japanese as a second language: The sentence-final particle *ne*. In G. Kasper (Eds.), *Pragmatics of Japanese as a native and foreign language*. Technical Report #3 (pp. 83–125). Honolulu: University of Hawai'i, Second Language Teaching & Curriculum Center.

Scarcella, R. (1979). On speaking politely in a second language. In C. A. Yorio, K. Peters, & J. Schachter (Eds.), *ON TESOL '79—The learner in focus* (pp. 275–287). Washington, DC: TESOL.

Schieffelin, B. B. & Ochs, E. (1986). Language socialization. *Annual Review of Anthropology, 15,* 163–191.

Schmidt, R. (1983). Interaction, acculturation and the acquisition of communicative competence. In N. Wolfson & E. Judd (Eds.), *Sociolinguistics and second language acquisition* (pp. 137–174). Rowley, MA: Newbury House.

Schmidt, R. (1993). Consciousness, learning and interlanguage pragmatics. In G. Kasper & S. Blum-Kulka (Eds.), *Interlanguage pragmatics* (pp. 21–42). New York: Oxford University Press.

Scollon, R. & Scollon, S. B. K. (1983). Face in interethnic communication. In J. C. Richards & R. W. Schmidt (Eds.), *Language and communication* (pp. 156–188). London: Longman.

Searle, J. (1976). A classification of illocutionary acts. *Language in Society, 5,* 1–23.

Shimura, A. (1988). The effect of Chinese-Japanese differences on turn-taking in an ESL classroom. *University of Hawai'i Working Papers in ESL, 7*(2), 99–115.

Snow, C. E. (1988). Conversations with children. In P. Fletcher & M. Garman (Eds.), *Language acquisition* (pp. 69–89). Cambridge: Cambridge University Press.

Sridhar, S. N. (1994). A reality check for SLA theories. *TESOL Quarterly, 28,* 800–805.

Takahashi, S. & Roitblat, H. (1994). Comprehension of nonliteral utterances by nonnative speakers. *Applied Psycholinguistics, 15,* 475–506.

Takahashi, T. & Beebe, L. M. (1993). Cross-linguistic influence in the speech act of correction. In G. Kasper & S. Blum-Kulka (Eds.), *Interlanguage pragmatics* (pp. 138–157). New York: Oxford University Press.

Tannen, D. (1981). The machine-gun question: An example of conversational style. *Journal of Pragmatics, 5,* 383–397.

Thomas, J. (1983). Cross-cultural pragmatic failure. *Applied Linguistics, 4,* 91–112.

Tyler, A. & Davies, C. (1990). Cross-linguistic communication missteps. *Text, 10,* 385–411.

Wetzel, P. (1994). Contemporary Japanese attitudes towards honorifics (*keigo*). *Language Variation and Change, 6,* 113–147.

Wildner-Bassett, M. (1984). *Improving pragmatic aspects of learners' interlanguage*. Tübingen: Narr.

Wolfson, N. (1989). *Perspectives: Sociolinguistics and TESOL*. Cambridge, MA: Newbury House.

Yamashita, S. & Miller, T. (1994). Japanese and American students' attitudes toward classroom interaction. *ICU Language Research Bulletin, 9,* 51–73.

A World Language Perspective: English, French, and Spanish

Kimberley Brown

INTRODUCTION

Recent research in the domain of World Englishes provides support for the argument that it is time to move beyond what B. Kachru (1983) terms a "monomodel" of ideal speaker-hearers. It is time to acknowledge that in addition to speaking with native speakers, language learners may be speaking with each other: that is, with non-native speakers from the same or different countries. Thus, the pivotal question is not whether non-native speakers should attempt to approximate native speaker norms but rather what non-native speakers need to do in order to be intelligible to their interlocutors. Answering these questions entails the adoption of a world languages perspective on the part of language teachers.

A world languages perspective is a framework of knowledge that accords as much importance to the socio-political context and the human needs of its users as to the attributes of the language itself. It neither assumes that one variety of the language is "better" than another variety, nor that by studying for a longer period that learners will move through fluency stages finally to become skilled users of a native variety of the language. Rather, it establishes intelligibility, that is, the ability to be understood by an educated speaker of the language, whatever the variety, as a higher order goal than proximity to native norms. A world languages perspective looks at the local cultural context as a creative source of innovation in language use. Finally, a world languages perspective looks at what Kramsch (1995) terms the "privilege of the non-native speaker[s]" to own the languages they are studying, which acknowledges that part of their identity is as a speaker/user of a language other than their mother tongue.

This perspective allows greater flexibility in the classroom in terms of materials and curriculum. It realistically connects students with the world around them. Within many social sciences and humanities fields, discussion now occurs about how to improve the internationalization of the discipline (cf. Hamnett, Porter, Singh & Kumar 1984). Within the fields of second and foreign language education, such a commitment entails embracing a world languages

138

CHAPTER 7
A World Language
Perspective:
English, French, and
Spanish

perspective that, in turn, calls for movement beyond North Americentric and Eurocentric models and theories of language learning and teaching, a redefinition of appropriate norms for classroom instruction (Andreasson 1994; Valdman 1982), and an avoidance of linguicism (de facto and de jure language planning which promotes one language at the expense of another) (Skutnabb-Kangas & Phillipson 1992, p. 47).

WHAT IS A WORLD LANGUAGES PERSPECTIVE?

Three of the major world languages (English, French, and Spanish) share the following characteristics: Each is located in extensive and diverse areas around the world, and each has large numbers of both native and non-native speakers. Historically these were colonial languages, established during the eras of western European expansionism. In the present day they tend to be the preeminent languages in the areas of technology and development in their respective regions. Among the three, the most extensively researched is English, because of its wide geographical distribution and rapid expansion throughout the globe. One group of scholars extensively investigating the socio-political context of English refer to their framework as a "World Englishes" framework. The discussion of world languages in this chapter is based on this framework.

Kachru (1988) introduces three terms in his framework: "Inner Circle," "Outer Circle," and "Expanding Circle." What Kachru terms Inner Circle English is English spoken in Britain, the United States, Canada, Australia, and New Zealand. Similarly, French as is it spoken in France and Spanish as it is spoken in Spain are Inner Circle varieties. Canadian French and Latin American Spanish are also Inner Circle varieties by most definitions even though the languages were introduced to these countries as exogenous administrative languages of power (cf. Milan, 1983). They are now the primary languages of the majority of citizens of these countries.

Pause to consider . . .

the prestige variety of the language you teach. Who owns this language? What does it mean to own a language?

The Outer Circle comprises those countries where English, French, or Spanish have become official or national languages but where they were first introduced as colonial languages for administrative purposes. West African Frenches, such as Cameroonian and Senegalese, fit in the Outer Circle as do Haitian and Martinique French. The Spanishes spoken by indigenous populations, such as in Peru, Guatemala, and Mexico, may be regarded as Outer Circle Spanishes. Terms used synonymously with Outer Circle are "nativized" and "institutionalized" varieties, the former referring to the process of language contact with the endogenous languages of the country and the latter referring to the setting in which such varieties have developed: that is, within school and civic infrastructures. These varieties are characterized by extensive borrowing from other indigenous languages, distinctive lexical and phonological markings, and gradations or what B. Kachru (1983, p. 154) terms "clines of participants, roles and intelligibility." "Clines of participants" refers to the level of bilingualism of particular individuals, some users of world languages being more bilingual than others. "Clines of roles" refers to greater or lesser mastery of various functions and registers of a language. "Clines of intelligibility" refers to a scale of greater or lesser intelligibility. For example, a speaker of bazaari Pakistani English is less intelligible to a variety of listeners than is a political speaker giving a speech at an urban rally in a major city, such as Lahore.

The Expanding Circle is comprised of countries where English as a foreign language is widespread and its use is growing. Such countries include Japan, Korea, and Saudi Arabia. Spanish as a foreign language in the United States and Japan—the second most studied foreign language in Japan—would also be Expanding Circle varieties.

B. Kachru (1988, p. 1) suggests that three elements characterize a World Englishes perspective. First is the notion that no single model of English meets local, regional, and international needs simultaneously. Like an orchestra with many pieces in its repertoire, an individual or a nation-state may have many Englishes in its repertoire. Second, Kachru suggests that various innovations in nativized varieties of English have developed for practical, pragmatic reasons as English comes in contact with and is affected by the local languages of a particular country. Finally, Kachru adds a sociolinguistic dimension, indicating that English belongs not only to Inner Circle speakers but to all individuals who use it.

Pennycook discusses what he calls the "worldliness" of English (1994, p. 34). He suggests that:

> the issue, then is not so much how "using English as an international language" involves the users in various syntactic or phonological, or lexical diversity from central English norms, but rather how those acts of language use always imply a position within a social order, a cultural politics, a struggle over different representations of the self and other.

The dimensions outlined by Kachru and those discussed by Pennycook apply not only to English, but to French and Spanish as well.

PEDAGOGIC NORMS IN THE LANGUAGE CLASSROOM

Whether one is teaching teachers or teaching language students of English, French, or Spanish, it becomes important to articulate one's beliefs about the role of these languages in world communication. In many language class-

CHAPTER 7
*A World Language
Perspective:
English, French, and
Spanish*

rooms, teachers see their primary responsibility as one of helping to create a vanguard of loyal "languagephiles" whose ideal speaker-hearers are native speakers of those languages. In English, this means that the target model is a speaker of Inner Circle English. In French, the target model is a speaker of standard Parisian French; in Spanish, the target speaker model is frequently from Spain, and not Mexico, or any of the other Latin American Spanish-dominant countries.

The Inner Circle variety is the standard and the acrolectal or highest level of language used by educated native speakers as idealized by Chomsky (1965). Rather than automatically adopting the Inner Circle variety of a language as a target, what may be more appropriate is for teachers throughout the world to look at the reasons why students are studying a particular language and to define more specifically the purposes for which the language is used. Gill (1993, p. 230) suggests the endorsement of varieties which are "acceptable to [a country's population] and which [are] intelligible for international communication." Thus, one reason for teacher educators to develop pedagogic norms that embrace a world languages perspective is that their learners will have a better understanding of who all the speaker-hearers of their language may be. Teacher educators will be better able to help their pre-service and in-service teachers understand the contexts in which their languages are used. Another reason is to improve the support of international students in their programs who intend to return to their home countries to teach. In other words, education in Inner Circle countries can better meet needs of students from Outer and Expanding Circle countries when a world languages perspective is adopted.

For example, many students studying French in North American universities are just as likely to travel to Montreal, Quebec, or parts of the French-speaking Caribbean such as Martinique as to France. It becomes important for their teachers to help them to recognize phonological features of these Frenches and to understand the sociolinguistic consequences of their choosing a Parisian French model when traveling in these areas. A student in rural Malaysia may not be interacting with any speakers of Inner Circle varieties of English but may need to use English frequently for intra-country use with fellow Malaysians whose first language is Chinese or Tamil. Taking these different targets into account would lead teachers to develop different types of course materials and activities.

Valdman (1988) suggests that typical participants in foreign language classrooms do not succeed in attaining functional proficiency when "educated native speaker planned discourse remains the target." (1988, p. 235). He argues instead for adopting a "pedagogical norm . . . that involve[s] the simplest syntactic machinery and that form[s] the most regular pattern" (p. 235).

In the second/foreign language classroom, a focus on Valdman's proposed pedagogical norm would mean noticeable changes in syllabus and textbook design throughout the world. In the French or Spanish class, it would be necessary for teachers to identify whether Parisian French or Madrid Spanish was indeed the target desired by the students. In like manner, in the ESL/EFL classroom, American, Australian, British, Canadian, or New Zealand models may be augmented or substituted by Outer Circle models, such as Malaysian, Nigerian, or Indian English.

Andreasson (1994, p. 402f) suggests that three elements must be considered when developing a pedagogical paradigm: the functions of language (that is, the purposes for which it will be used and the context or language events involved); intelligibility, which involves word or utterance recognition, meaning and speaker intent (Smith & Nelson 1983, p. 334); and student expectations. Language teachers and learners in the Inner Circle may have different needs from those in Outer and Expanding Circle countries. Teachers who are familiar with these three circles can create more appropriate curricula which are truly tied to learner needs. Identification of the three elements proposed by Andreasson is important to avoid dosing "linguistic medicine for one geographic area [that] may prove linguistic poison for another area" (B. Kachru 1983, p. 154).

A student hoping to live and work in West Africa or in Latin America has different needs than a student expecting to travel to Paris or Madrid. A Nigerian student who expects to study engineering in the United States has different communicative needs than a Nigerian student who will use English for intra-country purposes in Lagos in the market or court system. It is critically important for teachers to identify what the context of situation will be for their learners, who their learners need to sound like, and the reasons why students are studying a particular language. The language acquisition goals of the students cited above all differ from each other. An understanding of this will allow language teachers to provide this information to their teachers-in-training so that they, in turn, can provide necessary resources to their learners.

For example, we may ask what variety of English should be taught in Puerto Rico. There, argue Blau and Dayton (1992), English is neither a foreign language nor a second language; rather, its functions vary between these two poles. An examination of who uses English for what purposes there reveals a difference across ages, with older speakers using English in a broader range of settings than do younger learners. English is used by many in grocery stores because of the number of products whose labels are only in English. Many television shows also broadcast only in English. Blau and Dayton suggest that some day an Outer Circle variety of Puerto Rican English may evolve.

In like manner, we may ask what variety of Spanish is the target in Puerto Rico. Although a Puerto Rican standard is appropriate for residents of the island, some researchers have found this variety to be devalued when compared with a Madridian standard (Fayer & Krasinski 1987). Betancourt (1985) found a significant level of what he termed "linguistic insecurity" in speakers of the Spanish vernacular of Puerto Rico. The high school teacher of Spanish in New York City may be hard pressed to ignore key elements of a Puerto Rican model of Spanish because many of his/her students are more likely to interact with such users than to travel to Spain. However, the textbook models and standardized tests that his/her students take probably do not use the acrolectal or most educated variety of Puerto Rican Spanish; rather, the Spanish of Spain or Mexico is the model.

142

CHAPTER 7
*A World Language
Perspective:
English, French, and
Spanish*

> *Pause to consider . . .*
>
> how the Puerto Rican situation discussed in this chapter relates to the
> French-Canadian situation discussed by Hartford in Chapter 5.

Whatever model is chosen, students need to become more familiar with
what Valdman (1988) terms "unplanned discourse" in the desired variety.
Valdman suggests that unplanned discourse has three primary features: It is
"highly context-embedded [and] features syntactic reduction and semantic
simplification" (p. 235). In other words, unplanned discourse is usually spoken, not written. It is not formal or planned ahead of time. Examples of
unplanned discourse can be found on television or radio talk shows, and
examples of planned discourse can be found in situations such as public lead-
ers delivering radio addresses or press releases.

Kramsch (1995) suggests that students acquire the kinds of rights that
native speakers possess through the competency that they develop in a school
setting where competence of use is more important than, for example, a particular accent. Thus, it is perhaps inappropriate to push learners of English,
French, or Spanish to sound like speakers from Inner Circle countries. A more
appropriate target to aim for is intelligibility among an educated circle of users
of the language who may hold any variety of passports and citizenship (Smith
& Nelson 1983).

INTERNATIONALIZATION OF FOREIGN LANGUAGE
EDUCATION

Three key movements characterize second/foreign language research in the
past decade: the proficiency movement (Omaggio 1986); design of tasks and
activities that promote authentic communication (Johnson 1982; Scarcella,
Anderson & Krashen 1990); and, most recently, a focus on the learner-centered
classroom and attendant research in language learning styles and strategy
preferences (Nunan 1986; Oxford 1990). All of these movements originated in
what are sometimes termed the "North" or "developed" countries of Europe,
North America, New Zealand, and Australia. Yet the consumers of language
education—be they English, Spanish, French, or others—live throughout the
world, and teachers from all nations are involved in language education.
Many countries have used what may seem to be unpopular or outdated methods to teach language with outstanding results. Yet language teaching experts
who are sent out from Inner Circle countries often seem bent on molding
teachers after themselves. Pennycook (1995) and Phillipson (1992) suggest that
a type of dependency mentality is fostered when educators perpetually turn
towards the Inner Circle nations for texts and theories.

A commitment to an internationalization of second/foreign language education includes an investigation of conceptual frameworks and theories that originate in other countries as well and that draw upon the local context. Hamnett, Porter, Singh, and Kumar (1984) call this "theoretic indigenization." We need to ask where pre-service language teachers can gain access to such information. One answer is to look towards professional language education journals written in Outer Circle countries. This means that it is just as important for pre-service teachers to become familiar with what language educators from Nigeria, India, Singapore, and Malaysia have to say about the teaching of English as it is to know what Inner Circle scholars have said. It is just as important for recently certified French and Spanish teachers to know what West African, Caribbean, Central, and South American scholars say about the teaching of these languages as it is to know what North American and European scholars have said.

In addition to exploring theories which originate in a variety of places, Hamnett, Porter, Kumar, & Singh (1984) indicate that it is also important for pre-service teachers to look at the structure of language education throughout the world: that is, who the researchers are and what they are writing about. Teachers also need to be aware of the content of language lessons around the world and to question whether the needs of language students within those countries are actually being met.

Pause to consider . . .

the internationalization of the discipline of language teaching. Where does much of the theory traditionally provided in language methodology courses come from? What do teachers need to know about the sociolinguistic aspects of the languages they teach? Where could one go to gather more information about varieties of English, French, and Spanish?

"Linguicism" in Foreign and Second Language Education

Related to the issue of identifying a target variety is the issue of "linguicism." As previously stated, linguicism is any type of language planning that promotes one language at the expense of another. Skutnabb-Kangas and Phillipson (1992) introduce the term and define it as:

> ideologies, structures, and practices which are used to legitimate, effectuate, and reproduce an unequal division of power and resources (both material and immaterial) between groups which are defined on the basis of language (p. 47).

144

CHAPTER 7
A World Language
Perspective:
English, French, and
Spanish

In likening linguicism to racism, one could look at whether particular structures promote such inequality. Thus, an individual may not purposefully engage in an activity that devalued one language, but that same individual may promote the continuation of structures which esteem one language at the expense of another.[1] In like manner, an individual may firmly believe that he/she does not devalue other varieties of a language but, in fact, by promoting only an Inner Circle variety of a language, that individual may be sending a message to his/her learners that other varieties are incorrect or deviant rather than simply different (Vavrus 1991).

Pennycook (1995) sees a positive role for non-Inner Circle users of English and other world language speakers in their creation of what he terms "counter-discourses" and "the articulation of insurgent knowledge and cultural practices in English" (p. 326). He suggests that if such users were to permit themselves to own the new language and were to find their own voices in it, they would be combating linguicism and moving far beyond it.

Teachers of English, French, and Spanish must not only become aware of their roles in the international arena of language education but need to make active choices in their classrooms to avoid promoting linguicism. They need to develop pedagogical norms within an ethical framework which takes into account all the speakers and users of the target language.

In their classrooms, learners of French, English, and Spanish need to learn about all the global users of their languages. They need to become familiar with what B. Kachru (1992) calls the "cline" of users, and they must come to see themselves as legitimate users of the language. In a thought-provoking volume, Paikeday (1985) suggests that English belongs to all those who use it; he even suggests that there is something mythological about the concept "native speaker," likening it to the abominable snowman.

What does this mean for the language classroom? Pedagogic norms, which do not take into account the sociocultural realities of context of use, promote inequality. It is important for pre-service teachers and ultimately professional language educators to become familiar with what linguicism is and to avoid promoting one variety of a language over another or one language over another.

In the French classroom, if learners never hear French Canadians or West Africans, they may assume that the ideal speaker-hearer uses Parisian French. In a business English class, if learners only hear Australians negotiating with British or American colleagues, they will be unaware of the power of English as it is used by Saudi, German, and Japanese business people. In the Spanish classroom, if learners never hear various users of Spanish from Central and South America as well as the Caribbean speaking with each other, they may perpetuate the notion of unequal status among speakers of Castillian Spanish and speakers of all other varieties.

Thus, instructors should familiarize their learners with the full range of users of the language they teach. Tapes of Inner Circle, Outer Circle, and Expanding Circle users, as well as examples of writers from these various places writing in English, French, and Spanish, should be part of classroom materials students use.[2]

*P*ause to consider . . .

whether the language you teach is being promoted at the expense of another language or to the exclusion of other established varieties of the same language.

Contributions of the World Englishes Framework to Foreign and Second Language Education

Over the past quarter century, research in the field of World Englishes has been growing. A rich tradition of empirical research and descriptive data is now available for English as it is spoken in Inner, Outer, and Expanding Circle countries. World Englishes scholars have challenged current assumptions in second language acquisition, in particular conceptualizations of interlanguage and fossilization. Y. Kachru (1994, p. 796) states:

> The evidence available on the acquisition and use of a second or additional language from research on world varieties of English . . . has been either ignored in SLA-related literature, normalized as supporting the IL interlanguage] hypothesis . . . or mentioned only very briefly (in Preston, 1993); (cf. Y. Kachru 1994; S.N. Sridhar 1994; Sridhar & Sridhar 1992).

It is now appropriate to ask how this framework can contribute to second/foreign language education. In the first part of this chapter the three elements of a world Englishes perspective were identified: a repertoire of models for English; pragmatic bases for the localized innovations that characterize world varieties of English; and inclusive group membership for more than Inner Circle speakers. If we adopt these notions as we design and teach in the second/foreign language classroom, our own repertoire of material from which to teach will increase.

*P*ause to consider . . .

how the recognition of a concept such as "World Language" variety affects the concept of "interlanguage." What sort of ramifications does this have for the classroom?

First, whether we teach English, French, or Spanish, it is important to introduce learners to sociolinguistic variation depending on topic, setting, and interlocutor. Learners need to read, hear, and appreciate the voices of Inner, Outer, and Expanding Circle speakers of these languages. They need to understand that a lectal range exists which moves from how those with little formal education speak to how those who are highly educated speak in

146

CHAPTER 7
A World Language
Perspective:
English, French, and
Spanish

formal settings (cf. Platt & Weber 1980, p. 271). With the help and encourage-ment of their teachers, these learners can decide who their ideal speaker-hearer will be.

In addition to the notion of a lectal range, Kachru (1990) also discusses what he terms the "cline of bilingualism," that is, variation on the part of indi-vidual speakers depending on their interlocutors and what indicators they wish to provide of socioeconomic status, as well as their membership in a par-ticular group. This dimension is part of the sociocultural aspect of commu-nicative competence (Bachman 1990). Although some language textbooks are formally including identification of such ranges (cf. the *Tapestry* ESL series from Heinle & Heinle Publishers) and actively promoting the development of such a cline of bilingualism, others lag far behind. Pre-service language teach-ers need to feel comfortable examining potential textbooks for presentation of such a range of language choices. In like manner, pre-service language teach-ers need to feel comfortable demonstrating to their learners how local envi-ronment and cultural contact have changed English, French, and Spanish. These changes need to be explored as creative responses to practical needs and not as mistakes or fossilizations (Sridhar & Sridhar 1986).

Language learners frequently do not see themselves as owners of the lan-guage they are studying, that is, they do not feel they have the same language rights as do Inner Circle speakers. This is a psychological or language attitude issue. Adoption of a World Englishes perspective in the classroom means that learners of English, French, or Spanish would come to believe that these lan-guages belong to all of those who use them. In a practical sense, this may call for learners in the language classroom to actually practice saying to them-selves "I am a speaker of English (French, or Spanish)."

IMPLEMENTING A WORLD
LANGUAGES PERSPECTIVE

Once teachers decide to internationalize their classrooms, the next step is imple-mentation. Kachru (1992, p. 10) lists eight elements of a World Englishes course that can serve as a basis for any language course that takes a World Languages perspective. These can easily be adapted to French and Spanish as well:

1. An overview of World Englishes from a sociolinguistic perspective;
2. An introduction to particular varieties;
3. The validity of such varieties on their own terms;
4. The functional and pragmatic range of particular varieties;
5. The contrasting pragmatic functions and realities of particular varieties;
6. The multidimensionality of functions: That is, the "implications of the functional ranges of English" in various settings;
7. An expanded understanding of various canons of English; and,
8. The importance of cross-cultural intelligibility of particular varieties of English.

Language teachers can draw upon these elements to create a type of checklist to use in designing their curricula.

On a practical level, the following questions may aid in such planning:

1. Have I provided a sociolinguistic overview of how this language is used throughout the world?
2. Have I actually introduced my students to a number of varieties of the language?
3. Have I demonstrated that one variety is not necessarily superior to another, but rather that each possesses validity on its own terms?
4. Have I introduced the concept of "lectal range" by looking at particular functions of a variety of the language as determined by practical needs in a particular country?
5. How may the pragmatic functions of one variety of my language contrast with the pragmatic functions of another variety of my language? For example, are there different rules for apologizing in Canadian, Caribbean, and Parisian French?
6. How does setting affect the functional range of the language I am teaching? For example, in a business language course versus a language-for-academic purposes course, what functions would need to be taught?
7. What is the global literary tradition of writing in the language I will teach?
8. What aspects of these varieties may make them unintelligible to speakers of other varieties of these languages? What does it mean for a particular variety to possess cross-cultural intelligibility?

CONCLUSION

The discussion in earlier sections focused on two primary issues: (1) whether an Inner Circle standard is always the most appropriate pedagogical norm and, if so, which Inner Circle variety it should be; and (2) whether the acrolect or variety spoken by the most educated members of a society should always be the most appropriate pedagogical norm. I suggest that the definition of Inner and Outer Circle is complicated, and question whether Inner Circle varieties should be the only target norm. With respect to the sociolectal cline, I suggest, following B. Kachru (1983) and Andreasson (1994), that the context of situation should determine which lect is used as the pedagogical norm. Further, I indicate that historical vestiges of dependency sometimes govern textbook and testing decisions and that these decisions are not always in the best interest or expectations of the learners.

It has been the intent of this chapter to demonstrate the need to internationalize our teaching of foreign languages by drawing upon lessons from World Englishes to aid in the determination of pedagogical norms and to avoid the practice of linguistic colonialism. This chapter looked at three elements that are needed in the field of second/foreign language education to improve the internationalization of its perspective: an identification of and acceptance of model and theory building in language education from around the world; a redefinition of pedagogical norms; and a movement away from "linguicist" practices that promote inequality. These elements are all part of what is termed the "World Englishes Paradigm."

148

CHAPTER 7
*A World Language
Perspective
English, French, and
Spanish*

It is fitting perhaps to close with a piece of graffiti found on the walls of an English medium college in Tehran where I taught during the Islamic Revolution:

Teacher, you must teach me what I need, not what you want.

---

*P*ause to consider . . .
_____

what the world languages perspective has to offer you as a language teacher. How will you implement this perspective into your own teaching?

NOTES

[1]For example, early pre-school language immersion programs for non-English-speaking children are designed to promote English language mastery to enable children to succeed in school. Yet frequently this promotion of English ultimately contributes to the loss of fluency in the home language and, in some cases, to the complete suppression of L1 use in the home setting.

[2]In fact, an acquisitional benefit from this practice may also occur. Speech communication research has demonstrated that when individuals are in more frequent contact with individuals with accents different from their own, they become better able to understand those accents (Gass & Varonis 1984).

KEY TERMS, CONCEPTS, AND ISSUES

Inner Circle
Outer Circle
Expanding Circle
lect
   acrolect
   mesolect
   basilect
   lectal range

sociolectal cline
North Americentric/Eurocentric
linguicism
interlocutor
unplanned discourse
indigenization
cline of bilingualism

EXPLORING THE TOPICS FURTHER

1. *Overview of world languages perspective.* Kachru's (1992) seminal article provides a complete overview of research and practice in World Englishes. Because of its scope, a great deal of information is introduced quickly and with a minimum of detail. Smith (1981) provides an expanded explanation of many of the issues raised in the Kachru paper.

2. *World Languages and language teaching.* Berns (1990) provides a solid integration of general work in communicative language teaching with an extensive section dealing with English in West Germany, Japan, and India.

For teacher educators hoping for a way to integrate country-specific examples from both Outer and Expanding Circles, Berns's volume is quite accessible. For a discussion of World Englishes in TESOL programs, see Brown (1993, 1995). Baxter (1980) presents an interesting discussion of target and ownership.

3. *SLA and the world languages perspective.* Sridhar & Sridhar (1986) focuses on differences between traditional perspectives on interlanguage and fossilization and a World Englishes perspective. Along with Williams (1989) and Berns (1990), this paper provides solid complementary information to that traditionally presented in second language acquisition texts.

4. *Assessment.* For teacher educators interested in the issue of world standards in testing, Davidson (1993) provides a set of five papers that summarize a testing symposium from the 1992 World Englishes meeting. These papers provide a solid historical context as well as up-to-date information on how to become part of LTEST-L, an international electronic mail discussion group on language testing.

5. *Politics.* Pennycook (1994) explores broader contextual variables associated with the role of English in the world. It is an excellent complement to much of Kachru's work and moves past much early work in World Englishes to explore what Pennycook terms "a critical pedagogy for teaching English as a worldly language" (p. vi).

6. *Journals of interest.* Two main journals focus on World Englishes: *English Worldwide* and *World Englishes.*

REFERENCES

Andreasson, A.-M. (1994). Norm as a pedagogical paradigm. *World Englishes, 13,* 395–410.

Bachman, L. (1990). *Fundamental considerations in language testing.* New York: Oxford University Press.

Baxter, J. (1980). How should I speak English? American-ly, Japanese-ly, or international-ly? *JALT Journal, 2,* 31–61.

Berns, M. (1990). *Contexts of competence: Social and cultural considerations in communicative language teaching.* New York: Plenum.

Betancourt, F. (1985). Puerto Rican Spanish: Linguistic insecurity. ERIC Document ED265738.

Blau, D. & Dayton D. (1992). Puerto Rico as an English-using society. Paper presented at World Englishes Conference. Urbana, IL.

Brown, K. (1993). World Englishes in TESOL programs: An infusion model of curricular innovation. *World Englishes, 12,* 59–73.

Brown, K. (1995). World Englishes: To teach or not to teach? *World Englishes, 14,* 281–293.

Chomsky, N.A. (1965). *Aspects of a theory of syntax.* Cambridge, MA: MIT Press.

Davidson, F. (Ed.) (1993). *World Englishes, 12 (1),* (Thematic issue: Symposium on Testing English Across Cultures.)

Fayer, J. & Krasinski, E. (1987). Native and non-native judgments of intelligibility and irritation. *Language Learning, 37,* 313–326.

Gass, S. & Varonis, E. (1984). The effect of familiarity on the comprehensibility of non-native speech. *Language Learning, 34,* 65–87.

150

CHAPTER 7
A World Language
Perspective
English, French, and
Spanish

Gill, S.K. (1993). Standards and pedagogical norms for teaching English in Malaysia. *World Englishes, 12,* 223–238.

Hamnett, M., Porter, D., Singh, A., & Kumar, K. (1984). *Ethics, politics, and international social science research: From critique to praxis.* Honolulu, Hawaii: University of Hawaii Press.

Johnson, K. (1982). *Communicative syllabus design and methodology.* Oxford: Pergamon Press.

Kachru, B. (1983). Models of new Englishes. In J. Cobarrubias & J. Fishman, (Eds.) *Progress in language planning* (pp. 145–170). Berlin: de Gruyter.

Kachru, B. (1988). *Teaching World Englishes. ERIC/CLL News Bulletin, 12 (1),* 1,3,4,8.

Kachru, B. (1990). World Englishes and applied linguistics. *World Englishes, 9,* 3–20.

Kachru, B. (1992). World Englishes: Approaches, issues and resources. *Language teaching: The international abstracting journal for language teachers and applied linguistics.* Cambridge: Cambridge University Press, pp. 1–14.

Kachru, Y. (1994). Sources of bias in SLA research: Monolingual bias in SLA research. *TESOL Quarterly, 28,* 795–799.

Kramsch, C. (1995). The privilege of the non-native speaker. Plenary Address. International TESOL Convention. Long Beach, CA.

Milan, W.G. (1983). Contemporary models of standardized New World Spanish: Origin, development, and use. In J. Cobarrubias & J. Fishman, (Eds.) *Progress in language planning* (pp. 121–144). Berlin: de Gruyter.

Nunan, D. (1986). *The learner-centred curriculum.* London: Cambridge University Press.

Omaggio, A. (1986). *Teaching language in context: Proficiency-oriented instruction.* Boston: Heinle and Heinle.

Oxford, R.L. (1990). *Language learning strategies: What every teacher should know.* New York: Harper and Row.

Paikeday, T. (1985). *The native speaker is dead!* Toronto: Paikeday Publishers.

Pennycook, A. (1994). *The cultural politics of English as an international language.* London: Longman.

Pennycook, A. (1995). English in the world/The world in English. In J. B. Tollefson (Ed.), *Power and inequality in language education* (pp. 34–59). Cambridge: Cambridge University Press.

Phillipson, R. (1992). *Linguistic imperialism.* London: Oxford University Press.

Platt, J. & Weber, H. (1980). *English in Singapore and Malaysia: Status; Features; Functions* (pp. 167–182). Kuala Lumpur: Oxford University Press.

Preston, D. 1993. *Sociolinguistics and second language acquisition.* Oxford: Blackwell.

Scarcella, R., Anderson, E. & Krashen, S. (Eds.) (1990). *Developing communicative competence in a second language.* New York: Newbury House.

Skutnabb-Kangas, T. & Phillipson, R. (1992). Wanted: Linguistic human rights! Roskilde Papir. Roskilde University.

Smith, L.E. & Nelson, C. (1983). International intelligibility of English: Directions and resources. *World Englishes, 4,* 333–342.

Smith, L.E. (Ed.). (1981). *English for cross-cultural communication.* London: Macmillan.

Sridhar, K.K. & Sridhar, S.N. (1986). *Bridging the paradigm gap: Second-language acquisition theory and indigenized varieties of English in World Englishes, 5,* 3–14.

Sridhar, S.N. (1994). A reality check for SLA theories. *TESOL Quarterly, 28,* 800–805.

Sridhar, S.N. & Sridhar, K.K. (1992). The empire speaks back: English as a non-native language. In P. Nelde (Ed.) *Plurilingua XIII: It's easy to mingle when you are bilingual* (pp. 187–198). Bonn: Dummler.

Tapestry series. (1993). Boston, MA: Heinle & Heinle.

Valdman, A. (1982). Francais standard et francais populaire: Sociolectes ou fictions? *The French Review, LVI,* 218–227.

Valdman, A. (1988). Classroom foreign language learning and language variation: The notion of pedagogical norms. *World Englishes, 7,* 221–236.

Vavrus, F. (1991). When paradigms clash: The role of institutionalized varieties in language teacher education. *World Englishes, 10,* 181–196.

Williams, J. (1989). Language acquisition, language contact, and nativized varieties of English. *RELC Journal, 20,* 39–67.

CHAPTER 8

Non-native Reading Research and Theory

James F. Lee
University of Illinois at Urbana-Champaign

INTRODUCTION

What is Reading? The American Heritage Dictionary (1973, p. 1085) provides twelve meanings for the word *read*. Among them are:

1. "to perceive, receive, or comprehend a signal, message or the like"; and,
2. "to learn or get knowledge from something written or printed"

The first of these two definitions acknowledges three sets of processes involved in reading: perceiving or decoding; receiving or encoding; and comprehending. The second underscores what I consider the goal of reading instruction: to learn information. Yet these definitions are popular conceptualizations of reading, but are not scientific. The problem with the first definition is that the "or" separates reading into three equal parts. In other words, reading is perceiving; or reading is receiving; or reading is comprehending. Certainly, reading research has investigated all three sets of processes, but for the purposes of this chapter, I define reading as follows:

> the activation, application and interaction of decoding, encoding, and comprehension processes that result in knowledge gain from something written or printed.

WHY LANGUAGE TEACHERS SHOULD UNDERSTAND READING PROCESSES

The mistaken, yet popular, belief that all you need to know to teach the language is the language itself can find a parallel in reading. In other words, it is widely believed that if you know the language, you can teach it. Can people believe that they can teach others to read based solely on the fact that they know how to read? Many language teachers believe that if their students knew the grammar and the vocabulary, then they should also know how to read. This belief, too, is mistaken. If it were true, then no adult illiteracy would exist. Adult illiterates know the grammar and they have the vocabulary, still they cannot read.

Acquisition order research established a clear difference between instructional orders and acquisition orders that points out that instructional materials are not the sole driving force in language development. What is, then? The learners, or to be more explicit, the learners' cognitive and psycholinguistic processes constitute the driving force of acquisition. Let's draw a reading parallel: Reading research has shown that differences exist between textual content and what a reader extracts from a text. Clearly then, the text alone is not the driving force of comprehension; the reader plays a significant role in the comprehension process, as is demonstrated in the next section.

Language teachers should understand reading processes because it is a means to several ends:

1. To gain an appreciation for the workings of the reader's mind;
2. To develop a set of expectations for reader performance; and,
3. To have a knowledge base around which to evaluate and develop reading materials.

*P*ause to consider . . .

what learners bring to the reading process. What types of knowledge are accessed in the learner's understanding of a text?

FROM MISCOMPREHENSION TO MODELS OF READING PROCESSES

Corder's landmark 1967 essay (reprinted in 1981) on the significance of learners' errors demonstrates that errors are not merely examples of random mistaken learning but rather reflections of underlying processes purposefully and systematically applied to language production. The whole theory of error analysis is based on the concept that errors are systematic and reveal underlying processes. The same concept extends to non-native reading. In the following three examples, the non-native readers miscomprehended the passages they read. As you read these passages, try to identify the elements of the passages that were miscomprehended in order to begin to understand the underlying processes involved in comprehension.

The first example comes from the research of Steffensen, Joag-Dev & Anderson (1979, pp. 20–21). The passage fragment is part of a letter describing an American wedding and is followed by the recall of the same information by an Indian and American subject:

Passage fragment:

Did you know that Pam was going to wear her grandmother's wedding dress? That gave her something that was old, and borrowed, too. It was made of lace over satin, with very large puff sleeves and looked absolutely charming on her. The front was decorated with seed pearls.

Indian reader's recall:

She was looking alright except that the dress was too old and out of fashion.

American reader's recall:

Pam's mother wants Pam to carry on the tradition of wearing the family wedding gown.

The second example is taken from Bernhardt's research (1986, pp. 100–101):

Passage fragment:

The hollow window in the lonely wall yawned bluish-red full of the early evening sun. Clouds of dust flickered between the crooked remains of the chimneys. The wasteland of rubble was dozing.

Non-native reader's recall:

The evening sun shone through the window. There were clouds in the sky. The boy was in the desert sleeping.

Perhaps you did not completely comprehend the passage fragment, a translation of Wolfgang Borchert's *Nachts schlafen die Ratten doch*, a frequently anthologized German short story. You may want to reread it now with the knowledge that the author describes the bombed remains of World War II Berlin. Does this information help you to comprehend better?

The final example passage is used in Lee's (1990) research. The passage fragment is the beginning of the second paragraph in a three-paragraph expository essay on feudalism. The original text was in Spanish (translated from *El feudalismo*):

Passage fragment:

Feudalism was based on an agreement of honor between two men. One, called a lord or don, controlled a lot of land. The other, called a vassal, promised to serve and protect the lord so that the latter would permit him to use part of his land. While the agreement was in place, the vassal could use the land, including the buildings and peons, to make himself richer. In exchange for these rights, he gave part of his earnings to the lord and served him faithfully in time of war.

Non-native reader's recall:

. . . there were two people who feuded over land. One was rich and already had a lot of land, his name was Mr. Don. The other was a simple farmer who owned just a little land. Mr. Don wanted this other man's land because it would make him more rich. . . .

As you tried to identify the elements of the original texts that were miscomprehended you probably were able to match words in the original passages to words in the recall, words whose meanings had been reconstructed by the non-native readers. This is not to imply that vocabulary knowledge is at the root of these readers' miscomprehensions. The processes involved are much more complex because words appear in clauses that form sentences of varying structures and these sentences combine to create discourse. Moreover, the readers themselves contribute to the process. The Indian reader does not understand the sentiment of wearing what he calls an old dress. The student of German can't take in the imagery expressed, perhaps because he has no personal experience of war-torn Berlin. The student of Spanish interpreted the passage in terms of two people feuding rather than in terms of a sociopolitical structure.

These examples serve to establish that reading, be it in a first, second, or third language, is a dynamic interplay between a reader and a text, with each making contributions to the processes by which the reader creates for himself/herself, a model of the text's meaning. In the remainder of this chapter, I explore these contributions as a means to understanding the underlying processes involved in comprehension.

Non-native Readers' Contributions to Comprehension

Beginning in the late sixties and early seventies, research emerged that demonstrated the roles that individual readers play in the comprehension process. Such research was conducted under the rubric of schema theory:

> According to schema theories, all knowledge is packaged into units. These units are the schemata [schema in the singular]. Embedded in these packages of knowledge is, in addition to the knowledge itself, information about how this knowledge is to be used. A schema, then, is a data structure for representing the generic concepts stored in memory (Rumelhart 1980, p. 34).

Therefore, the readers' contributions to comprehension are their schemata, their personal data structures for representing concepts. For example, two learners of Italian with the same language proficiency may both read an article on Italian politics but with different results. The reader who has a political science background will most likely comprehend more of the article than will the reader who has a music background, because they possess different schemata.

For comprehension to take place, a reader's schema must be activated: That is, conditions must be favorable for readers to bring their knowledge and experiences to the task of reading. Otherwise, the eyes may move horizontally and vertically across the page without the mind being engaged. How do schemata function? What do they do? They function to constrain the interpretation of incoming information ("constrain" is used here in a positive sense) in several ways: Schemata are used to disambiguate, elaborate, filter, and compensate. Finally, readers possess formal schemata: That is, they have data structures for representing exposition, narration, fables, and fairy tales. These schemata function to organize textual information. Examples of each function follow.

To Disambiguate

One way in which schemata constrain our interpretations is to disambiguate passage information. That is, readers tend to interpret passage information consistent with their background knowledge. To demonstrate, Anderson et al. (1976) gave two ambiguous passages to two groups of readers, physical education majors and musicians. The first passage could have been interpreted either as a prison break or a wrestling match, the second passage either as a card playing session or a musical practice session. Segments of each passage are given below to show their ambiguous qualities:

Prison/Wrestling:

Rocky slowly got up from the mat, planning his escape . . . What bothered him most was being held, especially since the charge against him had been weak. He considered his present situation. The lock that held him was strong but he thought he could break it.

Card/Music:

When Jerry, Mike, and Pat arrived, Karen was sitting in her living room writing some notes. She quickly gathered the cards and stood up to greet her friends at the door. They followed her into the living room, but as usual they couldn't agree on exactly what to play.

Anderson et al. shows that physical education majors consistently interpreted the Prison/Wrestling passage as a wrestling match, whereas the music majors interpreted it as a prison break. Conversely, the music majors consistently interpreted the Card/Music passage as being about playing music, whereas the physical education majors interpreted it as playing cards.

To Elaborate

Schemata also play an elaborative function in comprehension in that readers can use their knowledge to fill in gaps either in what they did not comprehend or in what was missing from the passage, that is, readers make inferences. The elaborative function of schemata, for example, leads readers to indicate that information was present in a text when it was not, as long as that information could be logically inferred from the content of the text (Perkins 1983).

Research on narrative texts shows a definite structural pattern to elaborations. Fairy tales, for example, are organized around a highly predictable structure, a structure readily used by readers to organize and recall information. Riley (1990) finds that her L2 readers are sensitive to the kinds of information present in fairy tales. In her study, subjects tend to provide endings to the episodes that comprise the story whether such endings appear in the original. "For example, many subjects stated that the wife divorced her husband, the werewolf, in order to end the episode before recounting the [next] episode that contained the wife's marriage to the second knight" (p. 130). In the minds of the readers, a divorce from one husband logically precedes a marriage to another, even though no such divorce takes place in this story.

To Filter

Schemata also have a filtering function. That is, once a schema is activated, all incoming information is filtered through it. This function is not exactly the same as that of disambiguating a text, rather, a schematic filter provides an evaluative perspective on unambiguous incoming information. This function of schemata is demonstrated in first language reading by Pichert & Anderson (1977) (cited by Bransford, 1979). Two groups of readers are given the same passage about two boys and a house in which they are playing. One group of readers is told that they are potential house buyers, the other group that they are thieves. The information recalled by the two groups is different, reflecting their different perspectives on the information presented in the text. For example, the "house buyers" recall that the house has a leaky roof, while the "thieves" recall that there is a color television set. The "house buyers" recall the spaciousness of the dining room, while the "thieves" recall the open drawer of sterling silver. In a certain sense, what readers get out of a passage depends on what perspective they bring to it.

Readers need not be provided an external perspective in order to filter information. Steffensen et al. (1979), cited above, demonstrate how Indians and Americans who read letters describing marriage ceremonies in the two cultures, interpret information about the two ceremonies through a culturally-generated schematic filter. As Steffensen et al. point out:

> Wearing an heirloom wedding dress is a completely acceptable aspect of the pageantry of the American marriage ceremony and reflects interest in tradition that surfaces on this occasion. [An Indian subject] appears to have completely missed this and, on the basis of the Indian emphasis on the relative financial power of the two families (which can be shown by even such a small detail as wearing an up-to-date, fashionable sari), has inferred that the dress was out of fashion (p. 21).

What was an unambiguous sentence to Americans about wearing grandmother's wedding dress was filtered through the reader's cultural perspective on weddings.

To Compensate

Another function that schemata can play in comprehension is to compensate for other knowledge sources (e.g., underdeveloped orthographic knowledge, lexical knowledge, syntactic knowledge). Just as the word "constrain" was not used with negative connotations earlier, "compensate" is not used here with any negative connotations. For example, a non-native speaker of English would not have to know anything about the morphology of the past tense to interpret correctly that each of the following sentences refers to a past event. These sentences demonstrate that certain knowledge sources can compensate for underdeveloped linguistic knowledge. What contextual cues are available in the following three sentences that indicate a past time?

1. The Louisiana Purchase in 1804 dramatically increased the size of the United States;
2. The last time I saw him, he was getting better; and,
3. Armstrong and Aldrich walked on the moon before anyone else.

By utilizing such contextual cues as dates, adverbials, and historical knowledge, readers could construct meaning from these sentences. The intent of the example is not, however, to discount the role of linguistic knowledge in comprehension. To rely on a small set of knowledge sources without complete recourse to linguistic knowledge may lead a reader to construct inaccurate meanings, which happened in the Bernhardt and Lee examples presented above.

In the Lee example, the subject's knowledge of the target language is not sufficient to correct his (mis)interpretation of the passage. Rather, he feeds the incoming information through his knowledge of (or schema for) feuds in order to construct meaning. Clearly, his background knowledge compensates for his other knowledge sources. Yet, if not for his background knowledge, the reader would not be able to interpret any information from the text. This reader's reconstruction demonstrates that not only must a schema be activated for comprehension to take place, but the *appropriate* schema must be activated for accurate comprehension to result.

To Organize Incoming Information

Carrell (1984a) refers to our knowledge of the overall organization of a text and its conventional structures as formal schemata. Such conventional orders include chronological order in narratives and cause-effect relationships and problem-solution discourse in expository texts. Following work on first language reading, she found that second language readers are better able to comprehend stories that follow a conventional organization. Importantly, she found that even when readers do not read a text that is organized conventionally, they tend to recall it in a conventional order. In other words, formal schemata operate both to encode information as well as to retrieve it. Riley (1990) reviewed the research on formal schema for stories and found that the research base was composed entirely of studies on invented stories that have few episodes. She addressed this shortcoming in previous research by using an authentic story comprised of twelve episodes. Her findings parallel those of Carrell and the L1 research. Readers comprehend best a story presented in conventional order and use the conventional structure to recall the content of what they read.

Carrell (1984b) and Lee & Riley (1990) investigate non-native readers' formal schemata for expository texts. In both studies, the non-native readers, who recognized and then utilized the organization of the text to organize their recall, were able to recall more than those who did not. Additionally, Lee & Riley provided a group of non-native readers information about the organization of the text as a prereading, advance organizer. Those who received the advance organizer recalled more than those who were not provided it.

Pause to consider . . .

the functions of schemata in interpreting incoming information. Give examples of some of the functions of schemata from your own experience as a reader.

The research on schema theory clearly establishes that readers contribute various knowledge sources in a variety of ways to the reading process. Schema theory tends to emphasize content as is evidenced by the somewhat simplistic equation of schemata with background knowledge. As schema-theoretic research developed, researchers began to examine readers' interactions with texts in order to document the strategies they used to comprehend them. Barnett (1989, pp. 66–70) provides a historical context for various developments in strategy research.

Hosenfeld was an early pioneer of strategy research (1977, 1984). She attempted to create inventories of good versus poor reading strategies based on case studies of what good and poor readers did when reading in the second language. Block (1986) proposes two categories of strategies: "general" versus "local". General strategies are comprehension-gathering and comprehension-monitoring strategies, whereas local strategies are attempts to understand specific linguistic data. These categories parallel other research that examines global versus local context. Sarig (1987) proposes that strategies can be organized around two global categories related to outcome: "comprehension promoting strategies" versus "comprehension deterring strategies". Within these two categories, Sarig classifies strategies into four types: technical aid; clarification and simplification; coherence-detecting; and monitoring. Sarig found that each strategy type both promotes and deters comprehension in almost equal proportions! She also found that a reader's strategy usage, as she categorizes and classifies strategies, is stable in both native and non-native reading.

Not only has non-native strategy research attempted to categorize and classify strategies, it has also investigated the teachability of strategies. The results of this line of research is not very consistent and it is difficult to determine a way to account for these differences. Hamp-Lyons (1985) reports that comprehension is better for the group who receives a semester's worth of reading strategy training than for the group who receives traditional reading instruction. Carrell (1985) demonstrates that non-native reader's comprehension improves after receiving one week of training in identifying a text's rhetorical organization. Kern (1989) integrates strategy training into a semester-long intermediate French course. He focuses training on word analysis, sentence analysis, discourse analysis, and reading for specific purposes. The strategy group's gains in comprehension are significantly higher than are the control group's. He also groups subjects as "low", "middle", and "high" ability according to their general language and reading abilities. When he analyzes the gains according to ability level, he reports that only the low-ability subjects show significant gains in comprehension. The gains of the middle and high ability groups are not significant. Barnett (1988) conducted strategy training for fourth semester learners of French. She found no effect for direct training in strategy use, the strategies being to predict, self analyze one's reading style, skim, scan, and infer word meanings from context. Laufer & Sim (1985) tried to teach word inferencing skills and found no effects for instruction among lower proficiency readers because these readers could not determine when they had sufficient context to make a correct inference. Yet it was Kern's low ability group that benefited most from strategy training.

> ## *Pause to consider . . .*
>
> the case of a learner with high grammatical and lexical proficiency who has low reading comprehension. What factors could contribute to the learner's profile? What type of classroom activities might help such a learner?

The Effects of Language on Reading Comprehension

Instructional materials for reading in a second language were once tied to the grammatical structures and vocabulary that learners were being taught. It was assumed, incorrectly, that learners could not understand language they had not been taught. Research has challenged these assumptions. For example, Lee (1987) showed that learners who had never been taught the Spanish subjunctive (either forms or functions) could understand the information being conveyed by the subjunctive forms just as well as learners who had been taught the subjunctive. Johnson (1981) gave original and simplified versions of a passage to ESL learners. The passages had been simplified by reducing the number of relative clauses and the figurative language, using higher frequency vocabulary and simplifying the sentence structure. She showed that the learners' comprehension was simply not affected one way or another by these simplifications. Strother & Ulijn (1987) presented ESL learners with an original and simplified version of a passage. They simplified passive structures, nominalizations, and particles. They found no difference in comprehension across the simplified and unsimplified versions of the passage.

Even though the results of the three studies converge, one should not conclude that language plays no role in second language reading comprehension. Language does have a role in reading comprehension, but instructors should not view the language of the text as the only criterion for judging a text's appropriateness. Text characteristics need to be judged and evaluated in light of the readers' characteristics. Whereas many researchers have found that simplification does not affect comprehension, others have found evidence that it does; we know that the language of the text can make a difference. Let's look at some examples where differences in comprehension have resulted from differences in the language learners read.

Word specificity in a text can make a difference. First and second language readers comprehend the passage better when the lexical items are transparent and specific rather than opaque and general (Bransford & Johnson 1972; Carrell 1983; Lee 1986). Transparent words explicitly refer to the topic, while opaque words do so only indirectly. For example, *things* for *clothes* and *facilities* for *washing machines* as seen in the following sets of sentences:

Transparent version:

The procedure is actually quite simple. First you arrange the clothes into different groups. Of course, one pile may be enough depending on how much wash there is to do. If you have to do it somewhere else due to lack of washing machines that is the next step, otherwise you are ready to begin.

Opaque version:

The procedure is actually quite simple. First you arrange things into different groups. Of course, one pile may be enough depending on how much there is to do. If you have to do it somewhere else due to lack of facilities that is the next step, otherwise you are ready to begin.

Not only does choice of lexical item affect comprehension, the way information is organized does, too. Carrell (1984b) presented the same information to ESL learners but organized it in four ways:

1. As a comparison/contrast;
2. As a problem with a solution;
3. As a collection or series of descriptions; and,
4. As a cause and effect relationship.

Both comprehension and retention of information were best for more highly organized information (i.e., comparison/contrast, problem/solution, and cause/effect) than for more loosely organized information (i.e., collection of descriptions). Lee & Riley (1990) found similar results on text organization with learners of French. They also found that providing learners with information about text organization prior to reading improved their comprehension. As discussed in the section on readers' contributions to comprehension, activating readers' formal schema for a text improves comprehension.

Discourse can be organized differently not just at the text level but also at more local levels within the text. Flick & Anderson (1980) presented first and second language readers short passages that contained explicit and implicit definitions. Examples of each type of definition follow (pp. 345–346):

Explicit:

Negative pressure is that type of pressure whose value is below atmospheric.

Implicit:

From fluid mechanics it can be shown that as a fluid or gas passes through a venturi, its velocity increases; but its pressure decreases to some value below atmospheric. This negative pressure is greatest at the point in the throat where the fuel pick-up is located.

They found that both first and second language readers comprehended explicit definitions better than they did implicit ones.

The research results presented above are only examples of the many investigations into the effects of text characteristics on comprehension. Even from this small sample of research, one can see that no facile conclusion can be reached. The language of the text both does and does not affect comprehension. No established rules account for when text characteristics prevent readers from making contributions to the construction of meaning.

> ## *Pause to consider . . .*
>
> that texts are often modified for second/foreign language learners by simplifying grammar and vocabulary. What alternative classroom practices would facilitate the comprehension of authentic texts by learners?

Interactive Models of Reading

The research on reader contributions and language demonstrate that comprehension involves both reader-based and text-based factors. The two sets of factors are not easily isolated because they tend to interact. Perhaps the clearest demonstration of how the two interact can be found in an experiment conducted by Mohammed & Swales (1984). They asked four groups of subjects to read an instruction booklet for an alarm clock and then use the instructions to set the alarm on the clock. Their subjects were native and non-native readers of English who had either a science or humanities background. They found that those with a science background, whether they were native or non-native readers, completed the two tasks more quickly than the others. Among the slowest to finish were two native readers with humanities backgrounds. Two subjects were unable to complete the tasks; both were non-native readers, one with a science background, the other with a humanities background who had low-level second language proficiency. Mohammed & Swales concluded that a particular level of language proficiency was required to comprehend the technical instructions; yet once that level was attained, background knowledge was a better predictor of success than was language proficiency. One cannot read in a second language without some knowledge of that language. By the same token, one cannot comprehend much, in either a first or second language, unless one can bring more to the task of reading than just linguistic knowledge.

One still hears "that passage was really hard" or "the passage was too difficult." We know now that not just characteristics of the passage, but those of the readers, combine to make a particular reading difficult or easy. Schema-theoretic research demonstrated the roles that individual readers play in the comprehension process:

> According to schema theories, all knowledge is packaged into units. These units are the schemata [schema in the singular]. Embedded in these packages of knowledge is, in addition to the knowledge itself, information about how this knowledge is to be used. A schema, then, is a data structure for representing the generic concepts stored in memory (Rumelhart 1980, p. 34).

The readers' contributions to comprehension are their schemata, their personal data structures for representing concepts. That they are personal reflects individual experience as well as group characteristics (cf. Steffensen et al., cited above).

Schema-theoretic research led to new types of interactive models for the reading process. Rumelhart (1977) proposed an interactive model of processing consisting of several knowledge sources representing different levels of linguistic representation, that is, feature, letter, letter-cluster, lexical, syntactic, and semantic knowledges. Interactive models of reading posit that the components of the model, that is, the knowledge sources, all act simultaneously and in parallel ways on the incoming written input. For example, semantic knowledge can be used to decide which letters comprise a word at the same time that letters in words may trigger the semantic knowledge to be used. In a passage on medical care the reader would expect certain words to appear such as *doctor* and *nurse*. When the reader arrives at these words in the passage, his/her brain does not need to analyze each letter and letter cluster to arrive at their meanings. In a certain sense the brain is "ready" for these words and may only need the *d-o* of *doctor* or the *n-u-r* of *nurse* to access their meanings.

Interactive models fundamentally redefined the relationship among knowledge sources. Figure 8.1 contains a graphic representation of a prototypical interactive model. Note that in the interactive model, each knowledge source is connected to each of the others. Each can influence the others, singly or in combination, so that semantic knowledge can aid feature analysis or the syntactic knowledge can aid letter analysis. What follows is a brief description of the elements of the model. Feature analysis entails recognizing that a letter has a loop and the direction of the loop, (e.g., *p*), whereas letter analysis involves recognizing that the loops make a specific letter (e.g., *p* vs. *d* vs. *b*). Certain letters may cluster in particular languages and the clusters syllabify in particular ways. The letters *th* cluster in English as in *the* and *ar-thri-tis*. Syntactic knowledge concerns knowledge of the order of words in a language, for example, knowing that subjects often precede verbs so that the agent of an

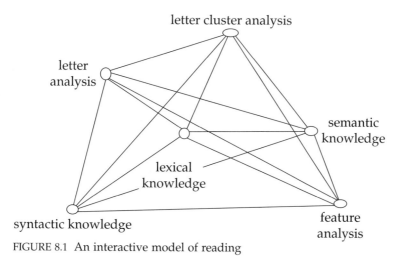

FIGURE 8.1 An interactive model of reading

action is correctly identified. For example, *John hit Charlie* is not the same as *Charlie hit John*. The same words ordered in different ways can produce different meanings as in *plan to fail* versus *fail to plan*. Our syntactic knowledge identifies the order of the words. Lexical knowledge concerns word properties and meanings such that the word *work* is identified rather than similar words such as *word* or *fork*. Semantic knowledge concerns meaning at all levels: words, phrases, clauses, sentences, paragraphs. For example, semantic knowledge tells us that the differences between the following two sentences are minimal: *Terry met Chris* versus *Chris met Terry*.

According to interactive models, comprehension is constructed from these knowledge sources interacting with each other on the input from the written page. Comprehension, by definition, is the process of relating new or incoming information to information already stored in memory. Readers make connections between the new information on the printed page and their existing knowledge. They must allow the new information to enter and become a part of their knowledge store. Anderson & Pearson state "To say that one has comprehended a text is to say that she has found a mental 'home' for the information in the text, or else that she has modified an existing mental home in order to accommodate that new information" (1984, p. 255).

Once interactive models of mental processes began to guide research and the interpretation of experimental results, reading was referred to as an interactive process. Educators quickly adopted the terminology to refer to readers and texts, that is, the people and objects of reading. Educators began to refer to reading as the "interaction" between a reader and a text so that we now talk about "interactive" approaches to teaching reading. McNeil provides a useful example; the process of reading involves "actively constructing meaning among the parts of the text and between the text and personal experience. The text itself is [but] a blueprint for meaning" (1984, p. 5). The blueprint metaphor is appropriate because it originated in the construction field; someone must take the blueprint and make it a building. The blueprint guides the construction of the building, but it is not the building itself. Similarly, the text guides comprehension, but it is not comprehension itself. The reader takes the text and gives it meaning.

> ## *P*ause to consider . . .
>
> the similarities and differences between text-based and reader-based factors. How can they be distinguished? How do they interact?

WHAT IF THE L1 ORTHOGRAPHY WERE DIFFERENT FROM THE L2 ORTHOGRAPHY?

As a fluent, adult reader of your native language, feature and letter cluster analyses are automatic processes for you; you exert no mental effort in distinguishing a *p* from a *b*. These processes may be quite effortful, however, for some second language readers particularly when the second language uses a different alphabetic, logographic, or syllabic writing system than their native language. What differences can you detect between the following pairs of symbols?

$$\begin{array}{cc} \Theta & \theta \\ \Phi & \phi \\ \sigma & \varpi \\ \varphi & \Psi \end{array}$$

FIGURE 8.2. Differences between symbols

How do you know which differences are significant? For example, is it the roundness of the first pair of symbols that changes their meaning or the thickness of the center bar? Are the last pair of symbols really different from each other or is one symbol used at the beginning of words and the other inside words? If these symbols were part of our native language writing system, we would already know the answers to these questions and use the information automatically when reading. Imagine the task of the second language reader who encounters these symbols in words along with other symbols whose features must be detected and deciphered. How much effort does that reader expend on feature recognition? How much mental energy does he/she have left to uncover the meaning of the sentence or paragraph in which he/she encounters the word?

At least two consequences arise from shifting writing systems when learning to read another language. First, the initial stages of learning must include learning the writing system. The second consequence stems from humans being limited capacity processors. In other words, we have finite processing capacity. If any one of the six components of the interactive model described above becomes effortful, it takes up processing capacity, which means less capacity is available to the other processes. Comprehension under these circumstances suffers.

---

*P*ause to consider . . .

cases in which first and second language orthographies differ. How may a learner's reading process be enhanced by integrating writing practice and reading instruction?

THE ROLE OF READING IN LANGUAGE ACQUISITION

In a previous section we examined the effects of textual characteristics on comprehension. In general, the way information is expressed seems to have a greater impact on comprehension than on the linguistic elements (words and phrases) themselves. Given this situation between language and comprehension, what is the relationship between comprehension and language acquisition?

VanPatten's extensive research on input processing establishes that language learners process meaning before they process form (cf. Lee & VanPatten [1995] and VanPatten [1996] for reviews). In their attempts to comprehend, learners pay attention to lexical items before they pay attention to grammatical features. In some cases, when the language learner can arrive at a satisfactory interpretation, then he/she may not even process the grammatical features in the input. Some may misinterpret these findings and conclude that language learners are not learning the grammar from the input. On the contrary, VanPatten demonstrates how learners acquire the grammar from the input and documents stages of development.

Let's approach written language as input for language acquisition. Previous reading research demonstrated that non-native readers can construct accurate meaning without knowing the forms that encode that meaning (Lee 1987). New research sheds more light on some of the intricacies of this phenomenon. Lee (in progress) gave the same passages to four different groups of non-native readers of Spanish. They were instructed to read the passage and then recall as much as they could in English (the native language of the readers). The passages contained a set of targeted verb forms. In the correct versions of the passage, the target verbs were in the third person singular preterite tense, which is encoded in regular verbs with an *ó*, for example, *habló*. These preterite tense verbs were substituted in the other versions of the passage with an infinitive (e.g., *hablar*), an invented form (e.g., *hablu*), and a periphrastic future (e.g., *va a hablar*). As expected, comprehension was not affected by the form of the verb. Each group comprehended the passages just as well as the others no matter the forms. After measuring comprehension, readers were presented word and sentence recognition tasks for which they were to indicate whether a word or sentence appeared in the passage they had read. For these tasks, form was a significant factor. Readers who read the correct version with preterite tense verbs recognized the forms more accurately than did the other groups, but the other groups indicated that they had seen words, such as *hablu*. Importantly, in determining the patterns that emerged from the recognition task, Lee found that when the readers did not indicate that they had seen an infinitive, an invented form, or the periphrastic future, then they overwhelmingly indicated that they had seen the preterite. Whereas subjects in the preterite group only identified preterite forms, the subjects in the other three groups identified a mixture of forms. These results provide some evidence that forms in the input are decoded; non-native readers comprehend form as well as meaning. The results strongly indicate that knowledge sources, other than those for linguistic form, are at work during encoding, ensuring that the correct meaning is generated (as any interactive model of reading would predict). Finally, the results indicate that during retrieval, forms get "reassigned" correctly, which is beneficial for language acquisition.

*P*ause to consider . . .

how reading contributes to language acquisition in general. What role does reading play in the acquisition of second/foreign language writing in particular? Can writing contribute to the development of reading in any way?

Krashen (1993) explores the research on the power of reading, particularly free, voluntary reading, to increase literacy (which contrasts with overt reading strategy instruction). Throughout his examination of the research, he draws many parallels between the results of first and second language research. He writes:

> My conclusions are simple. When children read for pleasure, when they get "hooked on books," they acquire, involuntarily and without conscious effort, nearly all of the so-called "language skills" many people are so concerned about: They will become adequate readers, acquire a large vocabulary, develop the ability to understand and use complex grammatical constructions, develop a good writing style, and become good (but not necessarily perfect) spellers . . . When second language acquirers read for pleasure, they develop the competence they need to move from the beginning "ordinary conversational" level to a level where they can use the second language for more demanding purposes, such as the serious study of literature, business, and so on. When they read for pleasure, they can continue to improve in their second language without classes, without teachers, without study, and even without people to converse with (p. 84).

*P*ause to consider . . .

what characteristics you would look for when selecting second/foreign language reading texts or textbooks, or when developing your own materials.

CONCLUSION

This chapter on non-native reading research and theory began with a definition of reading as the activation, application, and interaction of decoding, encoding, and comprehension processes that result in knowledge gained from something written or printed. This chapter presented a broad overview of the research, the understanding of which should lead language teachers toward an appreciation for the workings of the reader's mind. Even though they utilize an incomplete linguistic system while comprehending, language learners do not randomly or haphazardly apply processes. Understanding this research should also lead to a coherent set of expectations for reader performance and a basis for evaluating and developing classroom materials. What is a difficult text? How can it be made more comprehensible?

Also discussed in this chapter were the reader's own contributions to comprehension, that is, the schemata and how they operate with relation to the type of text being read. In addition to the schemata, a reader also brings to the task of reading his/her strategic competence. Although the research is somewhat ambiguous on the effects of teaching strategies to non-native readers, it does seem to indicate that strategies are probably helpful, particularly for less proficient readers. Whereas some teachers believe that successful reading results from teaching vocabulary and grammar, many others do not. Clearly, some linguistic base is needed, if only to recognize words. For example, having to read a logographic language when your native language is alphabetic presents a challenge! Although the effects of specific linguistic structures on comprehension do not seem to be significant, the effects of how information is organized in a text do. The final point explored in this chapter was how reading may play a role in language acquisition, an area of investigation open to considerable empirical examination.

P*ause to consider . . .*

what you consider to be the most important ways in which knowing more about reading research and theory will help you as a language teacher.

KEY TERMS, CONCEPTS, AND ISSUES

reading
comprehension
significance of learners' errors
significance of miscomprehensions
reader's contributions to
   comprehension
schemata
inference
functions of schemata
   to disambiguate
   to elaborate
   to filter

to compensate
to organize incoming information
strategic competence
effects of language on comprehension
   particular linguistic structures
   simplified texts
   lexical choice
   organization of information
interactive models of reading
shifting writing systems from L1 to L2
input
reading and language acquisition

EXPLORING THE TOPICS FURTHER

1. *Descriptions of what learners do with texts.* An early pioneer of describing what language learners were actually doing with texts was Carol Hosen-

feld. She published several readable works on the topic (e.g. 1977, 1984). For analyses of what readers do with texts within an interactive framework, see Lee (1990) and Bernhardt (1991, especially Chapter 5).

2. *Readers' contributions to comprehension.* One of the best works on this subject is Bransford's book, *Human Cognition.* Although the entire work is recommended, the chapters specifically treating schema theory are particulary pertinent.

3. *Reading strategies and skills.* Barnett (1989), Swaffar, Arens & Byrnes (1991), and several chapters of Dubin, Eskey & Grabe (1986) address reading skills in instructional settings.

4. *Journals of interest. Reading in a Foreign Language,* is the only international journal dedicated to second language studies. *Reading Research Quarterly* is the premier journal of first language research.

REFERENCES

Anderson, R.C., Pichert, J., Goetz, E., Schallert, D.L., Stevens, K. & Trollip, S. (1976). Instantiation of general terms. *Journal of Verbal Learning and Verbal Behavior, 15,* 667–679.

Anderson, R.C. & Pearson, P.D. (1984). A schema-theoretic view of basic processes in reading comprehension. In P.D. Pearson (Ed.), *Handbook of reading research* (pp. 255–292). New York: Longman.

Barnett, M. (1989). Teaching reading strategies: How methodology affects course articulation. *Foreign Language Annals, 21,* 109–21.

Barnett, M. (1990). *More than meets the eye: Foreign language reading theory and practice.* Englewood Cliffs, NJ: Prentice Hall.

Bernhardt, E.B. (1986). Reading in the foreign language. In B.H. Wing (Ed.), *Listening, reading and writing: Analysis and application* (pp. 93–115). Middlebury, VT: The Northeast Conference on the Teaching of Languages.

Bernhardt, E.B. (1991). *Reading development in a second language: Theoretical, empirical and classroom perspectives.* Norwood, NJ: Ablex.

Block, E. (1986). The comprehension strategies of second language readers. *TESOL Quarterly, 20,* 436 494.

Bransford, J.D. (1979). *Human cognition: Learning, remembering, understanding.* Belmont, CA: Wadsworth.

Bransford, J.D. & Johnson, M.K. (1972). Contextual prerequisites for understanding: Some investigations of comprehension and recall. *Journal of Verbal Learning and Verbal Behavior, 11,* 717–726.

Carrell, P.L. (1983). Three components of background knowledge in reading comprehension. *Language Learning, 33,* 183–207.

Carrell, P.L. (1984a). Evidence of a formal schema in second language comprehension. *Language Learning, 34,* 87–112.

Carrell, P.L. (1984b). The effects of rhetorical organization on ESL readers. *TESOL Quarterly, 18,* 441–469.

Carrell, P.L. (1985). Facilitating ESL reading by teaching text structure. *TESOL Quarterly, 19,* 727–52.

Corder, S.P. (1991). *Error analysis and interlanguage.* Oxford: Oxford University Press.

Dubin, F., Eskey, D. & Grabe, W. (1986). *Teaching second language reading for academic purposes.* Reading, MA: Addison-Wesley.

Flick, W.C. & Anderson, J.I. (1980). Rhetorical difficulty in scientific English: A study in reading comprehension. *TESOL Quarterly, 14,* 345–351.

Hamp-Lyons, L. (1985). Two approaches to teaching reading: A classroom based study. *Reading in a Foreign Language, 3,* 363–73.

Hosenfeld, C. (1977). A preliminary investigation of the reading strategies of successful and nonsuccessful second language learners. *System, 5,* 110–23.

Hosenfeld, C. (1984). Case studies of ninth grade readers. In J.C. Alderson & A.H. Urquhart (Eds.), *Reading in a Foreign Language.* New York: Longman.

Johnson, P. (1981). Effects on reading comprehension of language complexity and cultural background. *TESOL Quarterly, 15,* 169–181.

Kern, R. (1989). Second language reading strategy instruction: Its effects on comprehension and word inferencing ability. *Modern Language Journal, 73,* 135–49.

Krashen, S. (1993). *The power of reading: Insights from the research.* Englewood, CA: Libraries Unlimited.

Laufer, B. & Sim, D. (1989). Measuring and explaining the reading threshold needed for English for academic purposes texts. *Foreign Language Annals, 18,* 405–11.

Lee, J.F. (1986). Background knowledge and L2 reading. *Modern Language Journal, 70,* 350–354.

Lee, J.F. (1987). Comprehending the Spanish subjunctive: An information processing perspective. *Modern Language Journal, 71,* 50–57.

Lee, J.F. (1990). Constructive processes evidenced by early stage non-native readers of Spanish in comprehending an expository text. *Hispanic Linguistics, 4* (1), 129–148.

Lee, J.F. (in progress). Do forms have meaning or does meaning have form?

Lee, J.F. & Riley, G.L. (1990). The effects of prereading, rhetorically-oriented frameworks on the recall of two structurally different expository texts. *Studies in Second Language Acquisition, 12,* 25–41.

Lee, J.F. & VanPatten, B. (1995). *Making communicative language teaching happen.* New York: McGraw-Hill.

McNeil, J.D. (1984). *Reading comprehension: New directions for classroom practice.* Glenview, IL: Scott Foresman.

Mohammed, M.A.H. & Swales, J.M. (1984). Factors affecting the successful reading of technical instructions. *Reading in a Foreign Language, 2,* 206–217.

Perkins, K.L. (1983). Semantic constructivity in ESL reading comprehension. *TESOL Quarterly, 17,* 19–27.

Pichert, J.W. & Anderson, R.C. (1977). Taking different perspectives on a story. *Journal of Education Psychology, 69,* 309–15.

Riley, G.L. (1990). *Effects of story grammar on reading comprehension of L2 readers of French.* Unpublished doctoral dissertation, University of Illinois, Urbana-Champaign.

Rumelhart, D. (1977). Toward an interactive model of reading. In S. Dornic (Ed.), *Attention and performance,* (pp. 573–603). New York: Academic Press.

Rumelhart, D. (1980). Schemata: The building blocks of cognition. In R. Spiro, B. Bruce, & W. Brewer (Eds.), *Theoretical issues in reading comprehension* (pp. 33–35). Hillsdale, NJ: Lawrence Erlbaum.

Sarig, G. (1987). High level reading in the first and in the foreign languages: Some comparative process data. In J. Devine, P.L. Carrell & D. Eskey (Eds.), *Research in reading in English as a second language* (pp. 105–20), Washington, DC: TESOL.

Steffensen, M., Joag-Dev, C. & Anderson, R.C. (1979). A cross-cultural perspective on reading comprehension. *Reading Research Quarterly, 15,* 10–29.

Strother, J.B. & Ulijn, J.M. (1987). Does syntactic rewriting affect English for science and technology text comprehension? In J. Devine, P.L. Carrell & D.E. Eskey (Eds.), *Research in reading in English as a second language* (pp. 89–100). Washington, DC: TESOL.

Swaffar, J.K., Arens, K., & Byrnes, H. (1991). *Reading for meaning: An integrated approach to language learning.* Englewood Cliffs, NJ: Prentice Hall.

VanPatten, B. (1996). *Input processing and grammar instruction.* Norwood, NJ: Ablex.

CHAPTER 9

The Writing Course

William Grabe
Northern Arizona University
Robert B. Kaplan
University of Southern California

INTRODUCTION

Why, given the variety of areas in which teachers-in-training should be versed, is a course in the teaching of writing a necessary part of their training? In fact, several reasons exist for taking such a course: Aside from improving their instructional techniques and expanding their curricular knowledge, teachers-in-training also derive self-development benefits from such a course. As course participants, they must be engaged intensively with their own writing, and in doing so will improve their own writing skills. A course in the teaching of writing will also raise their awareness of the demands of writing tasks and motivational issues that represent such an important dimension of the teaching of writing. The points below summarize the benefits of a course in the teaching of writing. These same points can also be used to justify specific courses in each of the four language skills as well as courses in integrated skills and content-based instruction. Nonetheless, the relatively advanced demands and complexity of writing typically expected in academic settings make the following reasons particularly appropriate:

1. Knowing how to write is among the most important advanced abilities that L2 learners need to develop;
2. Being able to teach writing is an important skill expected of any well-trained teacher;
3. Taking a course in writing instruction will lead teachers-in-training to explore theories of writing;
4. Apart from theories of cognitive processing, language structure and text construction, and social contexts of writing, course participants also explore theories of writing and literacy development; and,
5. For participants, a course in the teaching of writing will:
   A. Explore the relationship between writing theories and other foundational courses, such as teaching methods, introduction to linguistics, syntax, sociolinguistics, psycholinguistics, applied linguistics, and literacy;

B. Explore a wide range of issues associated with curriculum design and especially address the move from theoretical insights to practical applications;

C. Offer them many practical activities and techniques for conducting a well-designed curriculum and for building L2 learners' writing skills;

D. Lead them to appreciate what is involved in writing in different languages;

E. Lead them to consider fair and appropriate feedback and assessment procedures;

F. Encourage them to explore consciously why writing should be part of L2 learner preparation, including what sorts of writing abilities complement the learner or institutional goals, raising awareness of the place that writing has in the integrated curriculum; and,

G. Give them practice and experience in writing, and help them build their teaching skills, and confidence as they engage in writing.

---

*P*ause to consider . . .

which of the above reasons for taking a course in the teaching of writing seem most persuasive to you. The points above are intentionally not in rank order. Rank them in order of priority and justify your ranking.

THE IMPORTANCE OF WRITING

Knowing how to write is among the most important abilities that academically oriented L2 learners need to develop. Skill in writing represents the difference between beginning and advanced learners as well as the difference between those who are only fulfilling a basic second language requirement and those who are studying a second language further. Although one may argue that not every L2 learner needs to become a good L2 writer, many L2 learners need to develop strong skills in writing. We argue in this chapter that all L2 learners need to attain some proficiency in writing and that all second language teachers need to know how to teach a writing class in the L2. At advanced levels of writing in college, some L2 learners may even need to write research papers, reports, abstracts, and proposals in the L2. The need to teach these skills in the college setting involves specialized skills in specific content areas. In contexts outside of college, writing needs may involve collaborative writing and require skills with specific occupational genres as well as careful attention to features of form and usage. Many L2 learners may need to write memos, professional letters, and project analyses in the L2. Writing is also typically taught in foreign language courses; thus, being able to teach writing skills is valuable (Kaplan 1995). Although the demands of writing may require specialized courses and training for language learners, a teacher well-grounded in more general writing theory and practice is able, with some additional preparation, to teach specific genres of writing to language learners when specialized teachers are not available.

Although it is not controversial that many L2 learners need to develop writing skills, it is important to recognize that writing is a unique language skill. Writing places more complex demands on both teachers and learners, and it requires greater metacognitive awareness, typically fostered through the act of writing itself (e.g., awareness of audience, of specific goals, of problem-solving demands, of genre constraints) (Bereiter & Scardamalia 1987; Gordon & Braun 1985; Kellogg 1994; Perfetti & McCutchen 1987). These complexities make writing instruction a more specialized extension of the general L2 curriculum. For these reasons, second/foreign teachers who are well trained in writing instruction have an advantage when applying for a teaching position.

THEORIES OF WRITING

Taking a course in the teaching of writing requires teachers-in-training to explore theories of writing. In a few cases, such a writing course may do little more than introduce participants to writing-process notions and provide relatively simplistic formulas for writing instruction. More sophisticated courses in writing, however, emphasize the popular writing-process orientation (e.g., Graves 1983) within a much broader and more complex set of writing theories. This better-developed orientation to writing exposes teachers-in-training to a wide range of concepts, issues, dilemmas, and responses, all within a complex interpretation of:

- How language is used for different purposes in different contexts;
- How the individual writer performs writing tasks; and,
- What writing resources are available to the writer.

This orientation to writing must be developed on at least two levels. First, a theory of writing must integrate:

- A theory of language;
- A theory of written language processing;
- A theory of social context influences; and,
- A theory of affective influences.

Second, a theory of writing must evaluate the relative strengths and weaknesses of the various explanations of how writing is done. We sketch briefly how these two levels may be developed, leaving details to be pursued in the sources cited.

---

*P*ause to consider . . .

what learners bring to the writing process. What types of knowledge and resources may be used in writing in academic contexts?

Any theory of language appropriate for and relevant to writing, whether for language instruction more generally or for applied linguistic concerns dealing with language use in real-world contexts, must account for at least the following four dimensions:

1. Epistemological beliefs and supporting evidence (Chomsky 1986; Halliday 1995; Hymes 1974);
2. Analytic explanations for structure and lexicon (Haegeman 1991; Givón 1995; Grabe 1992; Halliday 1995);
3. Textual organization and coherence (Beck et al. 1991; Britton and Gulgoz 1991; Gernsbacher 1990; Singer 1990); and,
4. Genre and register variation (Berkenkotter & Huckin 1995; Kellogg 1994; Martin 1992; Swales 1990).

Epistemological belief and supporting evidence refer to first premises of a given theory of language. For example, a Chomskyan theory of language assumes that many of the important issues of language development center around a universal biological predisposition (e.g. Chomsky 1986). Chomsky's view also holds that a theory should:

- Have generative capacity (describing all and only the possible sentences of a language);
- Assume an ideal speaker-listener as the model for language use;
- Allow for intuitive data as evidence; and,
- Represent a psychological theory of mind.

Chomsky's theory does not address language use (performance): It ignores the social contexts of language use; it disregards patterned variability in language; it ignores the pattern and organization of discourse above the level of the sentence; and it disregards the influence of affective factors. Such a theory of language is essentially irrelevant to research and practice in writing instruction.

In contrast, the Hallidayan theory of language is based on the premise that language use is the only reliable observational evidence that should be analyzed and explained. His systemic functional theory is based on the assumptions that:

- Language use occurs only in social contexts;
- An interpersonal metafunction is an essential component for understanding language use and language structuring; and,
- All language use is textual and, thus, the only verifiable level of language use in real-world contexts (Halliday 1995).

Although limitations and drawbacks to systemic functional theory exist, its first premises make this approach a far more compatible foundation for understanding how language represents the material resources through which meaningful interaction occurs; that is, meaning is instantiated through language use.

A third orientation to language is that of a descriptive, functional approach to language (Givón 1984/1990, 1995). Such an approach accepts the idea that some aspects of language development may be biologically predisposed in humans, but that a much larger proportion of language form and use is likely to be shaped by socialization practices and by language in use. Such a view is compatible with much work in sociolinguistics, applied linguistics, and discourse analysis (including text linguistics and cognitive psychological research on comprehension, inferencing, and learning) (cf. Hartford, Ch. 5.) It is also compatible with sociocultural interpretations of literacy development and with Vygotskean theories of cognitive development (see "Vygotskean Approaches" below).

Perhaps one of the most serious drawbacks to current composition and rhetoric research and practice in the United States is the willingness to accept a Chomskyan orientation to language as correct and therefore to see language as irrelevant to concerns of composition and writing studies. It is true that a Chomskyan orientation may be irrelevant, but it is not correct to assume that a theory of writing can be fully developed without accounting for the ways that words, sentences, and larger discourse structuring all shape and instantiate the meanings intended by the writer (Gernsbacher 1990). In some respects, the work being done in applied linguistics, and to some extent in second language acquisition, is filling in part of the gap, at least for L2 theory, by including issues of language form and discourse structure in an integrated orientation to writing theory and instruction (Connor 1995; Leki 1992; Raimes 1991, 1992; Reid 1993).

---

*P*ause to consider . . .

that different theories of language (also called *grammars*) may have different purposes and account for different characteristics of language. According to Grabe & Kaplan, what type(s) of theories of language are most compatibly integrated into a theory of writing? Why?

In Chapter 4, Beck presents a generative theory of language. What are the strengths of this type of grammar? What type of linguistic knowledge is best accounted for by generative grammar? According to Grabe & Kaplan, why is generative grammar less likely to be integrated into a theory of writing than other grammars?

A Theory of Written Language Processing

Any effort to make sense of what L2 learners need to learn and what teachers have to provide must address what happens when individuals perform a writing task. Current theories are fairly consistent in recognizing basic cognitive processes that appear to be central to the writing activity. These processes include planning, on-line processing, and evaluation of processing output to see how well it fits with planning goals.[1]

The earliest, and still the most popular, of these theories of writing processes is that of Flower & Hayes (1977, 1980, 1981). They established the planning-writing-reviewing framework based on extensive protocol analyses of writers who thought aloud while writing. Still important in the 1990s, Flower & Hayes, together and separately, have extended their basic model to explore and describe problem-solving processes, revision processes, the integration of writing with content resources, and planning procedures (cf. Grabe & Kaplan 1996). Flower (1994) also elaborated the model to integrate cognitive and social factors in the writing process.

Bereiter & Scardamalia (1987) also developed a model of writing processes that builds upon the Flower & Hayes approach but that extends concepts of problem-solving in writing and emphasizes a much greater role for the interplay of social/rhetorical factors with content resources. As a result, their model makes somewhat different predictions about the development of writing ability. Bereiter & Scardamalia (1993; Scardamalia & Bereiter 1991) also explore writing in terms of the growth of expertise. This perspective argues that consistently good writers have developed expertise in writing, and teaching writing should be examined in line with current research on the development of expertise.

Two additional models of writing processes seek to combine the above two perspectives. Kellogg (1994) extends the basic processes involved to include the "collection of resources" for writing in addition to planning, writing, and reviewing. He also incorporates the Bereiter & Scardamalia concepts of "knowledge telling" and "knowledge transforming" as two distinct ways of writing. The latter concept is related to the cognitive psychology notion of knowledge restructuring, though at a conscious and deliberate level (cf. McLaughlin 1990). Kellogg also begins to integrate social context issues and affective issues as background concerns for cognitive processing theory to a greater extent than do either of the above two models. Finally, he explores issues related to expertise and to the role of knowledge in writing, two factors that have also been developed recently by Bereiter & Scardamalia (1993).

Grabe & Kaplan (1996) similarly integrate recent research and model building from earlier work. They integrate the processing mechanisms involved, the importance of developing expertise, the complexities of problem-solving routines in ill-defined tasks, and the importance of linguistic and discourse knowledge in writing. Their model also stresses the many and varied social-context influences on writing and the development of writing abilities. In addition, they present an effort to model a communicative competence orientation to writing from an applied linguistics perspective. As such, the model is intended to be adaptable for the exploration of other language skills (cf. Celce-Murcia, Dörnyei & Thurell 1995; Chapelle, Grabe & Berns 1993; Grabe & Kaplan 1996).

---

*P*ause to consider . . .

to what extent reading constitutes a "resource" for writing (to use Kellogg's term). How does reading contribute to the underlying linguistic competence used in writing, to rhetorical or discourse knowledge, to content resources, or to simply providing a model for L2 writing?

A Theory of Social Context Influences

All language is produced in contexts of use. Writing does not escape this constraint, though there are popular notions of the solitary writer toiling away by himself/herself. A critical foundation for a theory of writing capable of informing both L1 and L2 contexts is one that takes seriously the full range of social-context factors that may influence the student. Such a theory would provide a framework that at least accounts for the range of factors involved, even when it does not interpret their interactions while students engage in writing (a much harder task). Both Flower (1994) and Kellogg (1994) consider these issues but do not provide a full framework. A more intense effort to do so is found in Grabe & Kaplan's (1996) exploration of an ethnography of writing (primarily for the student context). They argue that a theory of social factors needs to include at least the following:

Situation
    Settings
    Texts
    Participants and interaction patterns
        Audience
        Gricean maxims
        Politeness, power, and face
        Functional purposes
        Parameters of register variation
    Tasks (Activities)
    Topics

Performance outcomes

The cultural/social variation between L1 and L2

The "situation" is comprised of settings, texts, participants and interaction patterns, tasks, and topics. Each of these components deserves extended discussion, as any good sociolinguistics course would reveal.[2] The situation in which writing is done is likely to influence both the writing and the writer. "Setting" refers to the physical location of the act of writing and the physical conditions under which the act of writing is done. It also refers to the larger cultural expectations and constraints that may be associated with given environments for writing. "Text" (as a singular cover concept) refers to all the informational resources—including computer resources, visual resources, text resources, and media resources—available to support the writing activity. "Participants and interaction patterns" cover audience issues, possible constraints on interaction routines, genre constraints, functional purposes for writing, the degrees of formality and status recognition required, and the levels of knowledge complexity required.[3] "Tasks" and "topics" run the gamut of writing activities and concepts that L2 learners may encounter. A fairly extensive taxonomy of these factors is developed in Grabe & Kaplan (1996).

"Performance outcomes" represent an emergent feature of the social contexts that invariably influence the on-going writing process. In a sense, the emerging written text represents a secondary situation for the writer, one that is shaped not only by the initial context, but also by the cognitive processing, affective factors, and production constraints of the writing act. Kellogg (1994) discusses these issues under the heading of "situated cognition" which, in the writing context, argues that the text produced becomes an important resource for the writer. As Kellogg notes:

> The text produced at any point actively reshapes the task initially perceived by the author, and the nature of the writing problem shifts as the text develops. Thus, the writer's thinking and behavior change the physical and task environments (1994, p. 37).

Finally, the role of L1/L2 cultural and social variation is a factor that, in theory, may be explained by the other social factors noted above. However, it is important to emphasize the many aspects of L1/L2 writing differences. L2 learners typically have quite different orientations to linguistic dimensions of writing, including metalinguistic knowledge of learning the language and using it for various purposes (Connor 1995; Kaplan 1995). Moreover, L2 learners bring a different set of linguistic resources to the writing task (Berman & Slobin 1994). In addition, L2 learners typically are less averse to specific feedback on linguistic aspects of their writing, because corrections in their second language represent no evaluation of their writing abilities in their L1. L2 learners also often bring with them distinct notions of appropriate teacher behavior and instructional practices. These and other factors become part of the mix of social and contextual factors influencing writing development (Grabe & Kaplan 1996; Leki 1992).

A Theory of Affective Influences

If a relatively neglected area of theory in writing research were to exist, it would the area of affective and motivational factors that influence writing and writing development. Although many interesting studies of affective factors in writing have been published, no consistent effort has arisen to integrate these factors into a model alongside linguistic, cognitive, and social factors. As a prominent neurologist Damascio (1994) argues, the separation of the cognitive from the emotional and affective states of thinking is a serious limitation on how we understand cognition. Similarly, from a second language acquisition perspective, Schumann (1994; Pulvermuller & Schumann 1994) has argued that language learning research has been mistaken in ignoring the affective and attitudinal factors in learning.

Kellogg (1994) provides a good current overview of affective factors that may influence writing abilities and writing development. He reviews motivation for writing, addressing achievement motivation, intrinsic motivation, and extrinsic motivation. He also considers cognitive styles of individual writers and the impact of styles on a writer's disposition to engage in various writing activities. On topics more commonly noted for writing, he discusses the research on anxiety, on writing apprehension, and on writer's block. He argues that all three phenomena are real and important issues for writing and writing instruction. He also covers in some detail theories of creative flow and the resulting positive affect that arises from flow experiences (cf. Csikszentmihalyi 1990, 1991). His perspective offers an interesting explanation for a skilled writer's engagement with ever more complex writing tasks.

Aside from Kellogg's integration of affective factors within a cognitive model of writing, relatively little effort has been generated to synthesize affective factors in general theories of writing. Increasingly, however, such an integration is required. In the related area of reading comprehension, a number of serious efforts has occurred to link reading achievement and learning to read to affective theories (Mathewson 1994; McCombs 1988; McKenna 1995). Researchers consider the impact of major affective systems on learner performance and, in some cases, outline the causal-path contributions of various components of affect on learner achievement. Aside from motivation and creativity, research in this area explores such factors as emotional attitudes, self image, self regulation, learner autonomy, performance attributions, and interest (cf. Andersson & Maehr 1994; Chapman & Tunmer 1995; Reed & Schallert 1993; Shraw, Bruning & Svoboda 1995; Tobias 1994).

Interest in affective factors in second language acquisition has grown more generally (Crookes & Schmidt 1991; Dörnyei 1994; Gardner & Tremblay 1994a, 1994b; Tremblay & Gardner 1995; Hartford, Ch. 5). Research in affective factors can provide further perspectives for the L2 writer (as well as in all language learning settings). It is important to recognize that a large research field in cognitive psychology and educational psychology examines affective theories, such as motivation, interest, self-regulation, performance attributions, and self-esteem. This research has already included extensive work in the area of reading comprehension development; this work would also provide an important foundation for extending research on affective factors more systematically into writing development.

P*ause to consider* . . .

the importance of affective factors in writing development or in L2 development more generally. Can you suggest how affective factors might influence writing?

The Complexity of Theories of Writing

What future language teachers need to realize is that the combination of linguistic, cognitive, social, and affective factors is an appropriate theoretical grounding for a theory of any language skill and may represent an appropriately complex grounding for any theory of learning. The fact that this view generates a fairly complex interplay of factors is not a reason to disregard it. In fact, if teachers were to be able to make well-reasoned decisions for curriculum and instruction, they would need to know not only how to move from theory to practice, but also need to be familiar with sufficiently complex and appropriate theories so that they could move from such theories to the implementation of sound practical decisions. Current theories of writing need to represent:

- Some combination of the psycholinguistic processing in which writers engage;
- A theory of social contexts that influence writing at any point; and,
- A theory of motivation/attitude.

Such theories require both an exploration of cognitive differences in individual L2 learners as well as a theory of language that subsumes a reasonable theory of text construction (discourse analysis). Disregarding these issues in a teacher preparation course may lead to an unproductive situation in which the ignorant lead the blind (to mix a metaphor). Although a competent and aware teacher with advanced training should know many techniques and activities for engaging students on any given day, he/she must also know quite a bit more. Teachers need to know which activities and techniques within a coherent curriculum lead most efficiently to L2 learner development. Only a teacher who understands theories and who is able to make the transition from theory to practice can make the most appropriate decisions for a successful and meaningful writing course.

THEORIES OF WRITING DEVELOPMENT

Apart from theories of cognitive processing, language structure and text construction, and social contexts of writing, participants in a course in the teaching of writing also need to explore theories of writing (and literacy) development. Future teachers could be given a list of activities or a textbook and told to follow them, but such a scenario does not promote the development of an informed L2 teacher who can take responsibility for his/her students' learning or make the necessary adjustments to the curriculum so that his/her students receive the most effective instruction. Issues of concern for theories of writing development include both the general stages of writing development and the various paths that such development can take. This latter notion of variable paths of development depends on:

- Student and institution goals and histories;
- General theories of learning that may inform teachers of alternative choices; and,
- Alternative readings of the ways that students are developing (or not developing).

Freirean orientations, Vygotskean theories, and general instructional approaches that assume a developmental theory (e.g., whole language approaches), among others, would all be included under the designation of theories of learning (see below).

General stages of writing development are typically discussed in terms of early literacy development among L1 writers. Children learning to write are typically seen as moving from an egocentric stage to a stage in which audience considerations and reader needs are incorporated (Bereiter & Scardamalia 1987; Hillocks 1986). Moreover, longitudinal studies of L1 student writing as well as extended cross-sectional studies of student writing across grades has demonstrated rather straightforward development of more complex uses of language structure and more complex writing organization (Hillocks 1986; Hunt 1965; Loban 1976; Perera 1984). In second language settings, no general language development research is devoted specifically to writing. General second language acquisition theories of language development are not likely to be of much use because they abstract away from the complexities of writing and are typically decontextualized theories (cf. Ellis 1994; Larsen-Freeman & Long 1991). It remains to be seen whether a viable theory of writing development will emerge for L2 contexts, or even if one is possible, given the extraordinarily broad range of variation among learner backgrounds and goals, instructional contexts, and institutional demands (cf. Silva 1990, 1993).

---

*P*ause to consider . . .

the skills and abilities that may make someone a good writer. Can these abilities be taught, encouraged, supported?

In contrast to the limited work on stages of writing development and patterns of context variation in writing, an extensive and growing set of theoretical arguments and research studies supports various general learning approaches for writing instruction. A thorough review of these approaches would require its own chapter (and would make excellent research papers for teachers-in-training). In the following sections, we note seven approaches and comment on them briefly:

1. Writing process instruction and natural literacy development;
2. Directed writing instruction;
3. Strategy instruction;
4. Freirien approaches;
5. Vygotskean approaches;
6. Cooperative learning; and,
7. Expertise and second-order communities.

Writing Process Instruction and Natural Literacy Development

One of the most popular orientations to writing development is to introduce L2 learners to "the writing process approach" and let them develop their writing abilities naturally in a non-threatening environment. The teacher is seen as a facilitator and guide rather than as an instructor, and learners will grow when given the appropriate conditions in which to write (Freeman & Freeman 1992; Graves 1983; Harste, Woodward & Burke 1984; Rigg 1991). These ideas actually represent one extension of a Chomskean view of language development, namely, the assumption that literacy development occurs as naturally as spoken language development when learners are placed in the correct environment.

Of course, sufficient evidence supports the belief that L1 literacy abilities do not develop in the same natural ways that L1 spoken language skills do. The most obvious evidence is the fact that one quarter of the world's population is illiterate. It is also unlikely that assumptions for the natural development of writing abilities is relevant to L2 instructional contexts. Furthermore, no persuasive evidence exists that natural language development theories are applicable to writing. The point of this critique is not to belittle the process approach as instructional practice, but rather to point out that instructional practices alone do not meet the requirements for a theory of learning—a good lesson for any teacher-in-training to recognize.

---

*P*ause to consider . . .

the contrast between Grabe & Kaplan's position on natural development in the preceding section and Krashen's (1993) stance on the power of reading in acquisition, including the development of good writing (cf. Lee, Ch. 8). What type of empirical studies could you suggest that would contribute to the debate on "natural development" in writing?

Directed Writing Instruction

In second language contexts, many traditional orientations to the development of writing exist. These traditions include direct instruction in grammar and usage, practice with paragraph writing and short essays, writing with models, moving from controlled to free writing, and so forth. Many of these general techniques represent instructional practices that have been elevated to the status of learning theories. In a sense, they represent what teachers and textbooks have claimed work for writing instruction. These practices do not represent general theories of learning as much as techniques that may be useful in various instructional contexts.

A number of directed instruction frameworks genuinely appear to reflect principles of learning theories. Many directed instruction frameworks are also supported by converging research evidence. For example, the appropriate use of writing models to assist students in learning how to write is often viewed disparagingly as "current traditional" practice; however, a growing set of research studies argue strongly in favor of the appropriate use of writing models to support writing development (Charney & Carlson 1995; Hillocks 1986;

Smagorinsky 1992; Stolarek 1994). The reason that models should be useful follows from learning theory in cognitive psychology: This view argues that learning is effective when instruction is scaffolded, when reasonable genre and discourse frames are provided, when the functional purposes for the model are understood, and when instruction limits the complexity of the task to manageable levels.

Similarly, another disparaged "current traditional" practice in writing instruction, the use of outlining, appears to be an effective means for writing development when used appropriately with writers (Kellogg 1994). Supporting research arguments for this approach include the benefits derived from the specification of hierarchy in organizing ideas, the planning of content, and the restructuring of content to fit writing goals. Similar arguments can be forwarded for strategy instruction (i.e., metacognitive and metalinguistic awareness and monitoring, goal planning and development, strategic flexibility), reciprocal teaching (i.e., a Vygotskean orientation to learning, combined with effective strategy instruction), and cooperative learning (i.e., a Vygotskean orientation, strategy instruction, individual responsibility, and group support).

One general lesson from direct instruction approaches that should not be lost on teachers-in-training is that extensive evidence points to the effectiveness of direct instruction when one looks beyond second language acquisition research. The demonstrated effectiveness of general instructional programs in real classroom environments, like Reading Recovery (DeFord et al. 1991), cooperative learning (Slavin 1995), transactional strategy instruction (Brown et al. 1996; Pressley & Woloshyn 1995), and reciprocal teaching (Brown & Campione 1994; Brown & Palincsar 1989), all in the area of L1 literacy, leave little room for notions such as the idea that direct instruction does not assist literacy development or the idea that acquisition and learning are unrelated.

Strategy Instruction

An increasingly important orientation to literacy learning has been the emphasis given to strategy development which would include the use of specific strategies that have proved to be successful in instructional contexts, strategies that develop metacognitive awareness, and strategy instruction that leads to the flexible applications of combinations of strategies. The goal is not the development of specific strategies, but rather the development of the strategic writer (Harris & Graham 1995; Pressley & Woloshyn 1995).

Current views on strategy instruction in L1 literacy contexts stress the integrated teaching of strategies embedded within general content and language learning lessons rather than as a separate component (Brown et al. 1996; Gaskins 1994; Pressley et al. 1995a, 1995b). Whether one examines the roles of outlining, text structure awareness, main idea summarizing, or planning and goal setting in writing classes, or examines the effectiveness of general literacy training programs, such as reciprocal teaching (Brown & Palincsar 1989), guided inquiry (Brown & Campione 1994), Project READ (Calfee & Patrick 1995), or cooperative learning (Slavin 1995), one finds clear evidence that a strategy orientation to writing development is an important aspect of any learning theory (cf. Pressley et al. 1995b).

Freirean Approaches

Another view of writing development, which has taken on the status of a learning approach, is a Freirean orientation to writing. Based on a social theory of personal human development and social liberation, the Freirean approach centers on student autonomy and self-actualization through literacy skills development. Generative words and ideas that provoke reflection on the part of learners lead them to explore their relationships to the world and to other words that are potentially generative. The heightened awareness of language use for empowerment, along with practical direct instruction of language form and a supporting collaborative environment, lead the learners to better literacy skills (Bartholomae & Petrosky 1986; Freire 1985; Freire & Macedo 1987; Shor 1987).

***P**ause to consider . . .*

the role of reading in the acquisition of second/foreign language writing in light of the approaches to writing that emphasize literacy. How can reading contribute to the development of L2 writing in the instructional setting (short of the "natural development" position discussed earlier)?

Vygotskean Approaches

Vygotskean approaches to writing development (and to learning more generally) emphasize a number of features of an effective learning environment. Learning best occurs when learners are asked to engage in tasks and activities that are manageable within their "Zone of Proximal Development" (ZPD), the space that exists between what learners can do independently and what they can do when assisted by a more knowledgeable person (i.e., "scaffolded instruction"). Learning evolves out of verbal interaction and task negotiation with a more knowledgeable person, leading to an emphasis on teacher modeling, facilitation, and then participation; direct instruction by the teacher is a necessary beginning component to the learning cycle. Gradually, the learner assimilates the task demands and appropriate procedures for performing the task successfully: that is, the learner internalizes the skills needed for these purposes. In addition, a Vygotskean approach requires a degree of learner autonomy and self regulation; thus, an emphasis is given to meaningful learning to match students' learning purposes (Moll 1990; Newman et al. 1989; Rogoff 1990).

Recently, Vygotskean orientations have been emerging in second language acquisition research as well (Lantolf 1994; Lantolf & Appel 1994; Lantolf & Pavlenko 1995; Schinke-Llano 1993; Swain 1995). To what extent these orientations can be extended directly into a wide range of L2 writing contexts is an open question, one that deserves exploration by teachers-in-training as they engage in action research.

Cooperative Learning

Cooperative learning approaches have also become popular in L1 literacy contexts over the past 15 years. These approaches stress the benefits of groups working together cooperatively, of the importance of direct instruction, of the benefits of strategy instruction, and of group goals and individual responsibility for learning. Many variations in cooperative learning exist, with the strongest research support for the various approaches advocated by Slavin (1995) and by Johnson & Johnson (1994; Qin et al. 1995; cf. also Kagan 1992; Stahl 1994). These approaches should not be confused with discussions in composition research on the uses of collaborative learning, approaches that, despite their popularity, have yet to demonstrate significant improvements in learners' writing abilities. In cooperative learning, much less work has been conducted in L2 contexts. Fathman & Kessler (1993) review general principles for using cooperative learning in L2 contexts and suggest specific instructional practices relevant for writing instruction. Again, the potential applicability of cooperative learning principles for many L2 writing instruction contexts would be an ideal action research topic.

Expertise and Second-Order Communities

A final learning orientation, which has emerged in the past ten years, consists of a range of approaches centered on issues of expertise, expertise acquisition, and cooperative integrated skills approaches, with a strong emphasis on strategy instruction. Typically, a primary goal is the establishment of learning communities that undertake extended inquiry into interesting themes and projects. In the process, students develop abilities to work with supporting groups, improve skills for strategic inquiry, receive direct instruction and guidance as needed, learn appropriate language skills, and build more complex knowledge bases and problem-solving skills for future projects. All of these skills and supports are essential for the development of advanced writing abilities. These approaches are discussed under such names as "second-order communities" (Bereiter & Scardamalia 1993), "inquiry communities" or "community of learners" (Brown & Campione 1994), "learning communities" (Calfee & Patrick 1995), "transactional instruction" (Pressley et al. 1995a, 1996), and certain cooperative learning designations (Slavin 1995).

The development of expertise requires the development of various types of knowledge and metacognitive skills. Carter (1990) discusses the need for a balance between general strategic knowledge and a strong grounding in local domain-specific knowledge in advanced writing contexts (cf. also Scardamalia & Bereiter 1991). Moreover, Ericsson et al. (1993) discuss the development of expertise as requiring extended periods of deliberate practice (cf. also Ericsson 1996; Kellogg 1994). Finally, research on problem-solving in ill-defined learning contexts (such as writing) has indicated the need to gain extensive practice with related sets of problems to be solved (McGinley & Tierney 1989; Spiro et al. 1994). All of these notions are likely to be central concepts for a modern theory of writing development, particularly for advanced writing abilities.

Applying Learning Approaches, and L1 vs. L2
Influences on Learning

187

Writing and
Disciplinary
Knowledge

As is evident from the discussion of learning approaches to literacy and writing noted above, many competing ideas are currently vying for the teacher's attention. Several of these learning approaches are yet to be adapted to L2 writing contexts and need to be subjected to more intensive research. Many of the newer approaches hold real promise for L2 writing instruction and curriculum development (e.g., strategy orientations, cooperative learning environments, support through appropriate direct instruction, and the creation of an effective and structured support community for inquiry). Teachers-in-training have many opportunities to gain specialized knowledge of these approaches, to explore their applicability in L2 teaching contexts and, in the process, to gain insights into other orientations to writing instruction.

It is also likely that exploration of these ideas by teachers-in-training will lead them to greater skill in adapting ideas, less dogmatism with respect to a "right" approach, and increased flexibility in planning curricula. These ideas also reveal central notions for learning beyond the teaching of writing, extending to the teaching of other language skills, to integrated-skills instruction, and to content-based language instruction.

---

*P**ause to consider . . .*

what approaches to writing best fit the components of writing theory outlined in the previous section ("Theories of Writing Development"). Which approaches are most adaptable to L2 teaching contexts? Which approaches fit best with your own orientation to teaching and learning?

WRITING AND DISCIPLINARY KNOWLEDGE

Theories of writing and theories of writing development not only represent information and resources that permit one to be a better writing teacher, but they also inform the teacher as a language specialist in his/her own right: A training course in writing leads participants to consider the very foundations of language structure and use. Beyond writing instruction, participants need to consider, or reconsider, the earlier training they may have received in psycholinguistics, sociolinguistics, learning theories, literacy, formal linguistics, and applied linguistics—all through the filter of writing and writing instruction.

In this way, a writing course may lead teachers-in-training to consider the connections between writing and literacy, more generally, and may also lead them to explore connections with psycholinguistics, sociolinguistics, second language acquisition, linguistic theories, anthropology, sociology, psychology, education, and applied linguistics, more specifically. All of these potential connections can be important sources of exploration, discussion, and awareness raising.

ISSUES OF CURRICULUM DEVELOPMENT

A writing course also explores a wide range of pedagogical issues, including ways to draw on theory to inform instruction, to design curricula, to develop syllabi, to generate activities that match instructional goals and motivate students, and to prepare effective materials as support. Perhaps the most complex of these issues lies in the procedures for moving from theory to practice; this latter issue may also constitute a major rationale for a good writing course in a teacher-preparation program.

A standard approach for making the transition from theory to practice follows generally from the "approach-design-procedure" framework developed by Richards & Rodgers (1986), though also adding an initial increment of theory development. Richards & Rodgers suggest that an approach to instruction should include consideration of philosophies of teaching, language learning assumptions, and relevant research findings. We argue that the theoretical foundation, which informs these three issues, should be addressed as well.

The "design" component incorporates a number of major factors in the preparation of a curriculum plan. A well-designed and appropriate "needs analysis instrument" needs to be used with learners and instructors to ensure a reasonable match between learner and institutional goals. A reasonably comprehensive taxonomy of research and learning assumptions that can inform instruction needs to be developed as well, to ensure that important concerns and features of a curriculum are not overlooked; however, the taxonomy itself is not intended to be a blueprint for instruction. Other factors for the design component include specification of the role of the teacher (and the level of teacher abilities), the role of the learner, the resources available for instruction, and those instructional approaches known to be effective in the given setting. From these factors, a multidimensional set of guidelines may be developed to account for the major variables influencing a curriculum. The resulting guidelines should establish instructional procedures and activities that lead to learner (and institutional) goals. Such procedures for curriculum design in writing contexts can also be generalized to curriculum development for any language learning program.

Recognizing that any instructional situation calls for specific solutions for specific contexts, it is nevertheless possible to draw on a wide range of converging evidence from research and instructional practices to develop a generalized set of principles for effective writing instruction. A beginning framework of this type allows planners to assess the relevance of each principle to a given curriculum setting. In this way, a general set of principles for writing instruction provides a useful entry point for initial development of a writing curriculum. Below, we list ten general principles for a writing curriculum, recognizing that any of these principles may or may not be incorporated into a final specific curriculum for a variety of possible reasons. Generally, the writing course should:

1. Develop a curriculum around a coherent set of content-themes and relevant topics for learners;
2. See writing as apprenticeship training, including extensive practice in defined genres, teacher modeling and support, and instruction in strate-

gies for writing, as well as activities that engage learners in problem solving and in the gradual transfer of skills to related tasks;
3. Engage learners in the writing process;
4. Incorporate cooperative learning activities;
5. Require the integration of language skills: That is, writing should evolve in conjunction with extensive reading and supportive discussions;
6. Attend to the formal constraints of the language which serve to signal writing purposes, the role of genre in reader expectations, the coherence of text organization, and the flow of discourse information;
7. Provide careful consideration of audience constraints, as well as the influence of many social and contextual variables, on the writing task;
8. Introduce writing activities that encourage experimentation without harsh penalties and promote a sense of language play;
9. Offer a variety of options for feedback; and,
10. Practice a range of writing tasks that cover a number of important genres for learners' needs: That is, learners should write extensively.

Many of these principles follow from theories of writing and writing development; others reflect effective learning practices that are applicable to writing; still others follow from innovative approaches to learning that have been demonstrated effective in research studies.

We would like to offer a final comment concerning the applicability of these principles for specific L2 writing instruction: Many concepts and practices developed in L1 contexts may not transfer well into L2 teaching situations or may require specific adaptations. The design procedures described here provide one way to assist in decision making in specific L2 contexts. These issues are also discussed by Leki (1992) and Reid (1993).

---

*P*ause to consider . . .

how specific L2 teaching contexts require adaptation in approaches to writing instruction. What curriculum design issues would be critical in adaptation efforts? Describe a specific L2 context and discuss the adaptations needed. For the specific context created, prioritize the usefulness of the ten general principles for curriculum development noted above. Finally, which approaches to writing instruction, if any, may not be adaptable to certain L2 contexts?

ISSUES OF INSTRUCTION—ACTIVITIES AND TECHNIQUES

Instruction in writing ultimately rests with the set of tasks and activities that are created. We believe that many writing activities and tasks follow naturally from the implementation of the principles discussed above. In fact, hundreds of techniques and teaching ideas can be listed; the teacher, as a well-trained professional, must inform himself/herself about which tasks and activities are the most appropriate for the evolution of learning and the goals of the curriculum. Rather than cataloguing an array of specific techniques for instruction, we simply note that instructional practices, as they are implemented from day to day, need to conform to the established curriculum design and the goals for instruction.[4]

---

*P*ause to consider . . .

what suggestion for techniques are given in a well-known "techniques" book on L2 writing. Decide which techniques may be most useful within a coherent theory of writing and a well-planned writing curriculum.

WRITING AND ISSUES OF CROSS CULTURAL DEVELOPMENT

A good teacher preparation course leads participants to consider what it means to write in different languages: What differences may occur across languages in the discourse structuring of writing, and how can teachers address these issues (cf., Connor 1995; Grabe & Kaplan 1996; Kaplan 1995)? This is not an issue that is likely to lead to many specific instructional techniques, but it indicates types of difficulties that learners from different L1s may encounter when they write in a given L2. The difficulties that L2 learners are likely to encounter include a limited vocabulary for expressing complex ideas and concepts, limited experiences with organizing more complex genres in academic contexts (developing coherence), difficulties in recognizing the appropriate linguistic mechanisms for persuasion and argumentation (e.g., what is evidence), and the limitations on acceptable uses of maxims, proverbs, and literary quotations in technical writing.

Many cultural aspects of the L2 writing setting can also create difficulties for the learner coming from a different academic culture. For example, many Asian students may find the transition to a writing process approach difficult, particularly when the task involves personal expression and divulging private thoughts. Similarly, a learner who has done little writing may be overwhelmed in a writing course that emphasizes extensive writing, particularly given the limited fluency and vocabulary resources in the L2. Learners may not be comfortable with the more relaxed instructional styles of teachers in the United States; they may find the lack of a strong structural framework for instruction to be ambiguous and thus may not respond positively. Further, learners may not understand the Western concept of plagiarism; they may need to be trained in the notion of ownership of ideas. Finally, many may expect specific linguistic corrections with teacher feedback on their writing; they may be perplexed by the use of peer-correction.

A writing course also leads participants to consider fair and appropriate feedback and assessment procedures. Not only are matters of feedback and assessment crucial for writing, they are also important for all areas of language teaching (cf. Gradman & Reed, Ch. 10). These matters, considered from the perspective of writing, provide additional insights for teachers that may otherwise be overlooked in a teaching methodology survey course or in a course on language learning theories. Specific issues for assessment and feedback in L2 contexts include the choice of approaches for providing feedback on student writing (e.g., whole class, peer group, teacher guided, written comments on papers). The more formal aspects of assessment require teachers to consider whether writing abilities can best be assessed through indirect measures of writing, direct essay prompt writing, or writing portfolios. Teachers need to be aware of these as well as other options, and the difficulties that each choice entails (Grabe & Kaplan 1996; Hamp-Lyons 1991; Purves et al. 1995; Tierney et al. 1991; White 1994; Williamson & Huot 1993).

CONCLUSION

Much as a teacher-preparation program must consider how the writing course can be integrated as part of the teacher training curriculum, teachers must also consider how writing may be integrated into general language learner preparation. As new teachers teach writing, they must consider the connection between a writing course and other courses in their student's total curriculum, and they must base their own expectations for writing on an understanding of the writing expectations and needs of other courses in the curriculum.

A writing course for future teachers should also teach them how to be better writers. The teacher who lacks reasonably powerful writing skills is in the position of a tennis coach who does not actually play tennis. A writing teacher is expected to model successful writing for his/her students. A writing course should not only make a teacher-in-training more aware of what is actually involved in the teaching of writing, but it should also make him/her more aware of his/her own writing skills, and it should provide opportunities for the teacher to practice and improve his/her own writing. This final benefit should not be underestimated.

*P*ause to consider . . .

the ways in which knowing more about writing will help you as a teacher.

NOTES

[1]For a discussion of processing in language learning in general, see VanPatten, Chapter 1.
[2]Thus the importance of sociolinguistics for prospective language teachers. See also Hartford, Chapter 5.
[3]"Situations," "settings," and "participants and interaction patterns" are also the concern of pragmatics (cf. Vasper, Ch. 6), and sociolinguistics more broadly (cf. Hartford, Ch. 5).
[4]For listings of specific instructional techniques, see Frank 1979; Grabe & Kaplan 1996; Hedge 1988; Leki 1992; Newkirk 1993; Raimes 1983, 1992; Reid 1993; Tompkins 1990; White & Arndt 1991.

KEY TERMS, CONCEPTS, AND ISSUES

theory of writing
theory of language
   the uses and limitations of explicit teaching of *grammar* (and if so, what grammar), *vocabulary* (and if so, what vocabulary), spelling, and various *writing conventions* (and if so, what conventions), and whether these are prerequisite or co-requisite to writing instruction
theories of language processing
models of writing processes
theory of social-context effects
theory of affective influences

theories of writing development
   writing process instruction and natural learning
   directed instruction
   strategy instruction
   Freirean approaches
   Vygotskean approaches
   cooperative learning
   expertise and second-order communities
curriculum development
instructional activities and techniques
writing assessment
student feedback

EXPLORING THE TOPICS FURTHER

1. *Essential texts on theories of writing.* Texts that are important resources for writing theory include Bereiter & Scardamalia (1987), Flower (1994), Grabe & Kaplan (1996), Hillocks (1986), Kellogg (1994), Kroll (1990).

2. *Important resources from learning theory and strategy instruction.* Resources that provide overviews of cognitive approaches to learning include Bereiter & Scardamalia (1993), Harris & Graham (1995), McGilly (1994), Pressley & Woloshyn (1995), Slavin (1995).

3. *Insights into writing development and writing instruction.* Resources that provide important insights into writing curriculum and writing instruction include Bartholomae & Petrosky (1986), Hedge (1988), Leki (1992), Reid (1993), White & Arndt (1991).

4. *Journals of interest.* Important journals for writing research include *College Composition and Communication, Journal of Second Language Writing, Research in the Teaching of English, Text,* and *Written Communication.* Other journals with regularly appearing articles on writing include: *Discourse Processes, English for Special Purposes, Linguistics and Education, Language Learning, Studies in Second Language Acquisition,* and *TESOL Quarterly.*

REFERENCES

Andersson, E. & Maehr, M. (1994). Motivation and schooling in the middle grades. *Review of Educational Research, 64,* 287–309.

Bartholomae, D. & Petrosky, A. (1986). *Facts, artifacts and counterfacts: Theory and method for a reading and writing course.* Upper Montclair, NJ: Boynton/Cook.

Beck, I., McKeown, M., Sinatra, G. & Loxterman, J. (1991). Revising social studies texts from a text-processing perspective: Evidence of improved comprehensibility. *Reading Research Quarterly, 26,* 251–276.

Bereiter, C. & Scardamalia, M. (1987). *The psychology of written composition.* Hillsdale, NJ: L. Erlbaum.

Bereiter, C. & Scardamalia, M. (1993). *Surpassing ourselves: An inquiry into the nature and implications of expertise.* Chicago: Open Court Press.

Berkenkotter, C. & Huckin, T. (Eds.). (1995). *Genre knowledge in disciplinary communication.* Hillsdale, NJ: L. Erlbaum.

Berman, R. & Slobin, D. (1994). *Relating events in narrative: A crosslinguistic developmental study.* Hillsdale: NJ, Lawrence Erlbaum.

Britton, B. & Gulgoz, S. (1991). Using Kintsch's computational model to improve instructional text: Effects of repairing inference calls on recall and cognitive structures. *Journal of Educational Psychology, 83,* 329–345.

Brown, A., & Campione, J. (1994). Guided discovery in a community of learners. In K. McGilly (Ed.), *Classroom lessons: Integrating cognitive science* (pp. 229–270). Cambridge, MA: MIT Press.

Brown, A. & Palincsar, A. (1989). Guided, cooperative learning and individual knowledge acquisition. In L. Resnick (Ed.), *Knowing, learning, and instruction: Essays in honor of Robert Glaser* (pp. 393–451). Hillsdale, NJ: L. Erlbaum.

Brown, R., Pressley, M., Van Meter, P. & Schuder, T. (1996). A quasi-experimental validation of transactional strategy instruction with low-achieving second-grade readers. *Journal of Educational Psychology, 88,* 18–37.

Calfee, R. & Patrick, C. (1995). *Teach our children well.* Stanford, CA: Stanford Alumni Association.

Carter, M. (1990). The idea of expertise: An exploration of cognitive and social dimensions of writing. *College Composition and Communication, 41,* 265–286.

Celce-Murcia, M., Dörnyei, Z. & Thurell, S. (1995). Communicative competence: A pedagogically motivated model with content specifications. *Issues in Applied Linguistics, 6,* 5–35.

Chapelle, C., Grabe, W. & Berns, M. (1993). *Communicative language proficiency: Definitions and implications for TOEFL 2000.* Princeton, NJ: ETS Report.

Chapman, J. & Tunmer, W. (1995). Development of young children's reading self-concepts: An examination of emerging subcomponents and their relationship with reading achievement. *Journal of Educational Psychology, 87,* 154–167.

Charney, D. & Carlson, R. (1995). Learning to write in a genre: What student writers take from model texts. *Research in the Teaching of English, 29,* 88–125.

Chomsky, N. (1986). *Knowledge of language.* New York: Praeger.

Connor, U. (1995). *Contrastive rhetoric: Cross-cultural aspects of second language writing.* New York: Cambridge University Press.

Crookes, G. & Schmidt, R. (1991). Motivation: Reopening the research agenda. *Language Learning, 41,* 469–512.

Csikszentmihalyi, M. (1990). *Flow: The psychology of optimal experience.* New York: Harper Collins.

Csikszentmihalyi, M. (1991). Literacy and intrinsic motivation. In S. Graubard (Ed.), *Literacy: An overview by 14 experts* (pp. 115–140). New York: Noonday Press.

Damascio, A. (1994). *Descartes' error: Emotion, reason, and the human brain.* New York: Grosset/Putnam.

DeFord, D., Lyon, C. & Pinnell, G. (Eds.). (1991). *Bridge to literacy: Learning from reading recovery.* Portsmouth, NH: Heinemann.

Dörnyei, Z. (1994). Motivation and motivating in the foreign language classroom. *Modern Language Journal, 78,* 273–284.

Ellis, R. (1994). *The study of second language acquisition.* Oxford: Oxford University Press.

Ericsson, K. A. (Ed.). (1996). *The road to excellence.* Mahwah, NJ: L. Erlbaum.

Ericsson, K., Krampe, R. & Tesch-Romer, C. (1993). The role of deliberate practice in the acquisition of expert performance. *Psychological Review, 100,* 363–406.

Fathman, A. & Kessler, C. (1993). Cooperative language learning in school contexts. In W. Grabe, et al, (Eds.), *Annual review of applied linguistics, 13. Issues in second language teaching and learning* (pp. 127–140). New York: Cambridge University Press.

Flower, L. (1994). *The construction of negotiated meaning: A social cognitive theory of writing.* Carbondale, IL: Southern Illinois University Press.

Flower, L. & Hayes, J. (1977). Problem-solving strategies and the writing process. *College English, 39,* 449–461.

Flower, L. & Hayes, J. (1980). The dynamics of composing: Making plans and juggling constraints. In L. Gregg & E. Steinberg (Eds.), *Cognitive processes in writing* (pp. 31–50). Hillsdale, NJ: L. Erlbaum.

Flower, L. & Hayes, J. (1981). A cognitive process theory of writing. *College Composition and Communication, 32,* 365–387.

Frank, M. (1979). *If you're trying to teach kids how to write, you've gotta have this book.* Nashville, TN: Incentive Publications.

Freeman, D. & Freeman, Y. (1992). *Whole language for second language learners.* Portsmouth, NH: Heinemann.

Freire, P. (1985). *The politics of education.* South Hadley, MA: Bergin & Garvey.

Freire, P. & Macedo, D. (1987). *Literacy: Reading the word and the world.* South Hadley, MA: Bergin & Garvey.

Gardner, R. & Tremblay, P. (1994a). On motivation, research agendas, and theoretical frameworks. *Modern Language Journal, 78,* 359–368.

Gardner, R. & Tremblay, P. (1994b). On motivation: Measurement and conceptual considerations. *Modern Language Journal, 78,* 524–527.

Gaskins, I. (1994). Classroom applications of cognitive science: *Teaching poor readers how to learn, think, and problem solve.* In K. McGilly (Ed.). Classroom lessons: Integrating cognitive theory (pp. 129–154). Cambridge, MA: MIT Press.

Gernsbacher, M. A. (1990). *Language comprehension as structure building.* Hillsdale, NJ: Lawrence Erlbaum.

Givón, T. (1984/1990). *Syntax: A functional/typological introduction.* 2 Volumes. Philadelphia, PA: J. Benjamins.

Givón, T. (1995). *Functionalism and grammar.* Philadelphia, PA: John Benjamins.

Gordon, C. & Braun, C. (1985). Metacognitive processes: Reading and writing narrative discussion. In D. L. Forrest-Pressley, G. E. Mackinnon, & T. G. Waller (Eds.). *Metacognition, cognition and human performance* (Vol. 2), (pp. 1–75). New York, NY: Academic Press.

Grabe, W. (1992). Applied linguistics and linguistics. In W. Grabe & R.B. Kaplan (Eds.), *Introduction to applied linguistics* (pp. 35–58). Reading, MA: Addison-Wesley.

Grabe, W. & Kaplan, R.B. (1996). *Theory and practice of writing: An applied linguistics perspective.* New York, NY: Longman.

Graves, D. (1983). *Writing: Teachers and children at work.* Portsmouth, NH: Heinemann.

Haegeman, L. (1991). *Introduction to Government and Binding theory.* New York, NY: Blackwell.

Halliday, M.A.K. (1995). *An introduction to functional grammar,* 2nd ed. London: Edward Arnold.

Hamp-Lyons, L. (Ed.), (1991). *Assessing second language writing in academic contexts.* Norwood, NJ: Ablex.

Harris, K. & Graham, S. (Eds.). (1995). *Making the writing process work: Strategies for composition and self-regulation.* Cambridge, MA: Brookline Books.

Harste, J., Woodward, V. & Burke, C. (1984). *Language stories and literacy lessons.* Portsmouth, NH: Heinemann.

Hedge, T. (1988). *Writing.* New York, NY: Oxford University Press.

Hillocks, G. (1986). *Research on written composition.* Urbana, IL: National Council of Research on English.

Hymes, D. (1974). *Foundations of sociolinguistics.* Philadelphia, PA: University of Pennsylvania Press.

Hunt, K. (1965). *Grammatical structures written at three grade levels.* Urbana, IL: National Council of Teachers of English.

Johnson, D. & Johnson, R. (1994). *Learning together and alone: Cooperative, competitive, and individualistic learning* (4th ed.). Boston, MA: Allyn and Bacon.

Kagan, S. (1992). *Cooperative learning.* San Juan Capistrano, CA: Kagan Cooperative Learning.

Kaplan, R.B. (1995). Contrastive rhetoric. In T. Miller (Ed.), *Functional approaches to written texts: Classroom applications* (pp. 21–38). Paris: TESOL France.

Kellogg, R. (1994). *The psychology of writing.* New York: Oxford University Press.

Krashen, S. (1993). *The power of reading: Insights from the research.* Englewood, CO: Libraries Unlimited.

Lantolf, J. (Ed.). (1994). Sociocultural theory and second language learning. Special Issue, *Modern Language Journal, 78,* 4.

Lantolf, J. & Appel, G. (Eds.). (1994). *Vygotskean approaches to second language research.* Norwood, NJ: Ablex.

Lantolf, J. & Pavlenko, A. (1995). Sociocultural theory and second language acquisition. In W. Grabe, et al (Eds.), *Annual Review of Applied Linguistics, 15.* Overview (pp. 108–124). New York, NY: Cambridge University Press.

Larsen-Freeman, D. & Long, M.H. (1991). *An introduction to second language acquisition research.* New York, NY: Longman.

Leki, I. (1992). *Understanding ESL writers: A guide for teachers.* Portsmouth, NH: Heinemann.

Loban, W. (1976). *Language development: Kindergarten through grade twelve.* Urbana, IL: NCTE.

Martin, J. (1992). *English text: System and structure* Philadelphia, PA. J. Benjamins.

Mathewson, G. (1994). Model of attitude influence upon reading and learning to read. In R. B. Ruddell, M. R. Ruddell, & H. Singer (Eds.), *Theoretical models and processes of reading.* (4th ed.) (pp. 1131–1161). Newark, DE: IRA.

McCombs, B. (1988). Motivational skills training: Combining metacognitive, cognitive, and affective learning strategies. In C. E. Weinstein, E. T. Goetz, & P. A. Alexander (Eds.), *Learning and study strategies: Issues in assessment, instruction, and evaluation.* New York: Academic Press.

McGilly, K. (Ed.). (1994). *Classroom lessons: Integrating cognitive theory and classroom practice.* Cambridge, MA: MIT Press.

McGinley, W., & Tierney, R. (1989) Traversing the topical landscape: Reading and writing as ways of knowing. *Written Communication, 6,* 243–269.

McKenna, M. (1995). Toward a model of reading attitude acquisition. In E. H. Cramer & M. Castle (Eds.), *Fostering the love of reading: The affective domain in reading education* (pp. 18–40). Newark, DE: IRA.

McLaughlin, B. (1990). Restructuring. *Applied Linguistics, 11*, 113–128.

Moll, L. (Ed.). (1990). *Vygotsky and education: Instructional implications and applications of sociohistorical psychology.* Cambridge: Cambridge University Press.

Newkirk, T. (Ed.). (1993). *Nuts and bolts: A practical guide to teaching college composition.* Portsmouth, NH: Heinemann.

Newman, D., Griffin, P. & Cole, M. (1989). The construction zone. New York: Cambridge University Press.

Perera, K. (1984). *Children's writing and reading: Analyzing classroom language.* New York: Blackwell.

Perfetti, C. & McCutchen, D. (1987). Schooled language competence: Linguistic abilities in reading and writing. In S. Rosenberg (Ed.), *Advances in applied psycholinguistics: Volume 2. Reading, writing, and language learning* (pp. 105–141). New York: Cambridge University Press.

Pressley, M., Symons, S., McGoldrick, J. & Snyder, B. (1995a). Reading comprehension strategies. In M. Pressley & V. Woloshyn (Eds.), *Cognitive strategy instruction that really improves children's academic performance* (pp. 57–100). 2nd ed. Cambridge, MA: Brookline Books.

Pressley, M., McGoldrick, J., Cariglia-Bull, T., & Symons, S. (1995b). Writing. In M. Pressley & V. Woloshyn (Eds.), *Cognitive strategies that really improve children's academic performance* (pp. 153–183). 2nd ed. Cambridge, MA: Brookline Books.

Pressley, M. & Woloshyn, V. (Eds.) (1995). *Cognitive strategy instruction that really improves children's academic performance.* 2nd. ed. Cambridge, MA: Brookline Books.

Pulvermuller, F. & Schumann, J. (1994). Neurobiological mechanisms of language acquisition. *Language Learning, 44*, 681–734.

Purves, A., Quattrini, J., & Sullivan, C. (1995). *Creating the writing portfolio.* Lincolnwood, IL: NTC Publishing Group.

Qin, Z., Johnson, D. & Johnson, R. (1995). Cooperative versus competitive efforts and problem solving. *Review of Educational Research, 65*, 129–143.

Raimes, A. (1983). *Techniques in teaching writing.* New York: Oxford University Press.

Raimes, A. (1991). Out of the woods: Emerging traditions in the teaching of writing. *TESOL Quarterly, 25*, 407–430.

Raimes, A. (1992). *Exploring through writing: A process approach to ESL composition,* 2nd ed. New York: St. Martin's Press.

Reed, J. & Schallert, D. L. (1993). The nature of involvement in academic discourse tasks. *Journal of Educational Psychology, 85*, 253–266.

Reid, J. (1993). *Teaching ESL writing.* Englewood Cliffs, NJ: Regents Prentice Hall.

Richards, J. & Rodgers, T. (1986). *Approaches and methods in language teaching.* New York: Cambridge University Press.

Rigg, P. (1991). Whole language in TESOL. *TESOL Quarterly, 25*, 521–542.

Rogoff, B. (1990). *Apprenticeship in thinking.* New York: Oxford University Press.

Scardamalia, M. & Bereiter, C. (1991). Literate expertise. In K.A. Ericsson, & J. Smith (Eds.), *Toward a general theory of expertise: Prospects and limits* (pp. 172–194). New York: Cambridge University Press.

Schinke-Llano, L. (1993). On the value of a Vygotskean framework for SLA theory and research. *Language Learning, 43*, 121–129.

Schumann, J. (1994). Where is cognition? Emotion and cognition in second language acquisition. *Studies in Second Language Acquisition, 16*, 231–242.

Shor, I. (Ed.). (1987). *Freire for the classroom.* Portsmouth, NH: Boynton/Cook.

Shraw, G., Bruning, R. & Svoboda, C. (1995). Sources of situational interest. *Journal of Reading Behavior, 27*, 1–17.

Singer, M. (1990). *The psychology of language: An introduction to sentence and discourse processes.* Hillsdale, NJ: L. Erlbaum.

Silva, T. (1990). Second language composition instruction: Developments, issues, and directions in ESL. In B. Kroll (Ed.), *Second language writing* (pp. 11–23). New York: Cambridge University Press.

Silva, T. (1993). Toward an understanding of the distinct nature of L2 writing: The ESL research and its implications. *TESOL Quarterly, 27,* 657–677.

Slavin, R. (1995). *Cooperative learning.* 2nd ed. Boston: Allyn and Bacon.

Smagorinsky, P. (1992). How reading model essays affects writers. In J. Iwrin & M. Doyle (Eds.), *Reading/writing connections: Learning from research* (pp. 160–176). Newark, DE: International Reading Association.

Spiro, R., Coulson, R., Feltovich, P. & Anderson, D. (1994). Cognitive flexibility theory: Advanced knowledge acquisition in ill-structured domains. In R. B. Ruddell, M.R. Ruddell, & H. Singer (Eds.), *Theoretical models and processes of reading* (pp. 602–615). Newark, DE: IRA.

Stahl, R. (Ed.). (1994). *Cooperative learning in social studies.* Reading, MA: Addison-Wesley.

Stolarek, E. (1994). Prose modeling and metacognition: The effect of modeling on developing a metacognitive stance toward writing. *Research in the Teaching of English, 28,* 154–174.

Swain, M. (1995). Three functions of output in second language learning. In G. Cook & B. Seidlhofer (Eds.), *Principle and practice in applied linguistics: Studies in honour of H. G. Widdowson* (pp. 125–144). Oxford: Oxford University Press.

Swales, J. (1990). *Genre analysis.* NY: Cambridge University Press.

Tierney, R., Carter, M. & Desai, L. (1991). *Portfolio assessment in the reading-writing classroom.* Norwood, MA: Christopher Gordon.

Tobias, S. (1994). Interest, prior knowledge, and learning. *Review of Educational Research, 64,* 37–54.

Tompkins, G. (1990). *Teaching writing: Balancing process and product.* New York: Merrill.

Tremblay, P. & Gardner, R. (1995). Expanding the motivation construct in language learning. *Modern Language Journal, 79,* 505–518.

White, E. (1994). *Teaching and assessing writing* (2nd ed.). San Francisco: Jossey Bass.

White, R. & Arndt, V. (1991). *Process writing.* New York: Longman.

Williamson, M. & Huot, B. (Eds.). (1993). *Validating holistic scoring for writing assessment.* Cresskill, NJ: Hampton Press.

CHAPTER 10

Assessment and Second Language Teaching

Harry L. Gradman and Daniel J. Reed
Indiana University

INTRODUCTION

So often the development of the sorely-needed overall proficiency instrument falls to the newly educated, newly hired language teacher. If for no other reason than that, an understanding of and practice in language testing is a crucial component of second language teacher education. Of course, other reasons exist as well. How do we gauge the effectiveness of our own teaching? How do we conduct trials of new textbooks and educational computer software—and justify related, large expenditures? On what basis do we provide intelligent feedback to the institutions who develop the standardized tests that our students take? Reflection on these important, practical issues brings to mind basic language testing questions. How do we measure what someone else knows? How do we report what someone else knows? How do we translate our impressions of what someone else knows into meaningful statements to a larger population that may not have our same understanding of the complexity of language and the attendant complexity of its assessment?

Decisions are regularly made about one's future, with linguistic skills an important part of that decision, and yet by persons who have little, if any, background in second language acquisition or assessment. Beyond that, but equally as important, statements of theory based on the linguistic acts of second language speakers and learners are regularly made from data collected in assessment exercises of grammatical and discourse features. In important ways, assessment of language skills underlies what we know about language acquisition. All observations about the performance of language users imply a mode of assessment related to an understanding of language.

P*ause to consider . . .*

the range of assessment exercises described in the preceding chapters. Review the experiments reported in VanPatten (Ch. 1, psycholinguistics), Bardovi-Harlig (Ch. 2, second language acquisition), Kasper (Ch. 6, pragmatics), and Lee (Ch. 8, reading).

THE ROLE OF LINGUISTICS

The relationship between linguistic analysis and assessment reports has long been an issue of consideration. Should assessment of skills be reported in linguistic terms. Does terminology influence all assessment? There was a time when people believed that all one had to do was test the sounds, the sound combination principles, the words and word formation principles, and the sentence-level grammar of a particular language via the medium of listening, speaking, reading, and writing (e.g., Lado 1961, pp. 22 ff). The resulting compilation would amount to a statement of language proficiency. This was at a time when people felt more secure about their understanding of language and its definable components. It was, accordingly, reasonable as well to suggest that second language testing should focus on the differences between the language that the person knew well, normally the first language, and the language being learned, the second or foreign language. Many testers and testing instruments still follow this same basic philosophy: Namely, language is the sum of a variety of relatively characterizable parts or features that can be sampled, tabulated, and stated in some set of terms that correspond to greater or lesser proficiency in a language. Such a view is more or less consistent with what has been thought of as "discrete point" language testing, an approach that has been referred to and discussed in many of the language testing overviews published during the past 35 years (cf. Carroll 1961; Cohen 1994; Hughes 1989; Lado 1961; Oller 1979). These tests are sometimes thought of as "objective" tests because a list of specific points can be stated, based on language descriptions, and questions or test items can be written with those specific points as their focus.

As investigators have expanded their view to a broader consideration of language, to a language that is greater than the sum of its more narrowly defined linguistic parts—about which there has never been great agreement anyway—so too have the approaches to the assessment of language skills changed. Given that we are often concerned with how well one can use language in a particular situation (such as how successfully one can order food in a restaurant), as opposed to how accurately one can use linguistic units in isolation, a number of language specialists have suggested that it is inappropriate to characterize language proficiency without taking into account the context in which that proficiency is measured (cf. Carroll 1961; Oller 1979). This has been thought of as a more "functional" approach to language testing and, indeed, as an "integrative" approach, because all of the linguistic components, including more than one skill, may be required in assessment without specific reference to or identification of particular sounds, words, or grammatical rules. In truth, of course, it is difficult to imagine, except when testing learners at the earliest levels, instruments devoid of context, or even situations, where sounds or words or grammar do not dictate differences in the communicative outcome. Nevertheless, broader-reaching tests, those which move beyond specifically-defined linguistic points are sometimes thought of as "subjective" tests, as opposed to the more specific "objective" tests. The relevance of these terms is perhaps most apparent in scoring, which in the former case typically amounts to a judgment by the tester expressed as a rating (e.g., 1 on a scale of 1–5), while in the latter case it is essentially a tally of the number of items to which correct responses were given.

---

*P*ause to consider . . .

the following: Some people say that tests that are easy to make up are hard to grade, and tests that are hard to make up are easy to grade. How may this relate to the contrast between "subjective" and "objective" tests?

TEST CHARACTERISTICS

Testers have often spoken about basic characteristics that define so-called "good" tests, though whether such characteristics can be discussed without considering the purpose of assessment is debatable. Those characteristics, commonly cited as "reliability," "validity," and "practicality" (cf. Bachman 1990; Harris 1969; Lado 1961) are more easily stated than operationally determined. Put simply, one would expect that, all things being equal, one would receive the same score on a reliable test when taken over again. Put more broadly, similar students, with similar skills, would receive similar scores when taking a reliable test. Weaker students would receive poorer scores than would stronger students. However, it is difficult to imagine language learners remaining at the same point of learning over a period of time. We would expect learners' skills to improve with instruction and increased exposure to the language and to deteriorate with time as practice and exposure decreased. Reliability, then, tends to be determined from the performance of larger groups of students rather than the repeat performance of individual students. Other factors, such as the consistency of interview raters or the choice of composition topic, can affect reliability as well.

A "valid" test is one that measures what it is supposed to measure. The determination of what a test should measure, however, is subject to one's broad theory of what language is as well as one's notion of how best to measure those traits or "constructs" once they are established. Language teachers are sometimes in an unusually good position to know the characteristics of a valid test so long as that test is based on what teachers have been doing in the classroom. When the course syllabus defines a content "domain," then a test's content can be examined in terms of its relevance to and representativeness of that domain (aptly termed "content-related validity"). The issue becomes much more complex, however, outside of the language classroom. The set of characteristics that can be called "language," both in the narrowest and in the broadest senses, are elusive enough that language testers often seek additional evidence for the validity of a language test, such as how well that test relates to other tests that are thought to be valid or other activities that are thought to be common reflections of actual language use (sometimes termed "concurrent" or "criterion-related validity"). Both content-related and criterion-related evidence are relevant to the more complex concept of "construct validity," which concerns the patterns of relationships among various measures of different abilities and one's underlying theory of those abilities (Bachman 1990; Messick 1988).

The notion of "practicality," or "feasibility," of test construction and administration seems the simplest of these basic characteristics. However, the selection of a particular test type may be so dependent on the ability of an institution to create or to administer a testing instrument that other considerations may decrease in importance. The necessity of a timely report on the assessment of a large number of language learners at a given point in their instruction may suggest a test format that allows for simple scoring by a small number of minimally qualified people, as opposed to a format that may demonstrate more closely the particular skills or situations in question. Thus, for example, we see the popularity of examinations such as the *Test of English as a Foreign Language (TOEFL)* from the Educational Testing Service (ETS), which can be administered to many thousands of people at essentially the same time with score reports forthcoming with reasonable promptness (Educational Testing Service 1990a). An example of a foreign language multiple-choice test that has been used with a large number of examinees is the *Chinese Proficiency Test* (CPT) developed at the Center for Applied Linguistics (CAL).

Pause to consider . . .

that an advantage of the TOEFL test, and multiple-choice tests in general, is that a variety of points can be covered in a more discrete fashion (even though tests like these are never completely discrete, because items are presented in sentence length contexts at their simplest). With this in mind, examine the following sample vocabulary item:

*The traveler had to **hurry** to the boarding gate, because the plane was about to take off.*

    a.   *walk*   c.   *refer*
    b.   *look*   d.   *rush*

Is testing the word *hurry* in the context of this sentence better than testing it in isolation? Is it possible to respond correctly to this item without knowledge of the highlighted word? If so, what language skills/knowledge does this item test? Alternatively, would knowledge of the word *hurry* be necessary to respond correctly to this item if it were to appear in isolation, with no context? If you wanted to test knowledge of the word *hurry* and retain the context, how could you modify the carrier sentence? What advantages and disadvantages do you see for discrete point and integrative tests based upon these considerations?

Testing Needs and Types

The assessment of language skills is driven by a number of factors: one's view of language, general measurement considerations, and the needs of the consumer of the information. The latter point is one that sometimes tends not to be as important to examiners. However, it is foolhardy to think that someone, such as an admissions officer, who probably sees very few scores and has to make rapid decisions is not influential in the formation of tests or their reports. The same could be said for just about every conceivable score consumer. Hence, the trend towards samples of speech and broader oral interviewing for potential college teaching assistants, in addition to the more standard objective reports of the past, a trend driven by institutional needs as well as current focuses on the nature of language. It is not difficult to think of distinct language uses and ways of measuring those uses specific to the task. It may not, for example, be necessary for a flight attendant to communicate on a wide range of issues or in a broad range of nonaural/oral skills. However, a specific vocabulary and heightened set of listening and speaking skills may well be required of and elicited from future college students in a quite different manner. The size of examinee groups, too, may allow for different methods of examination.

In many ways, language testing has reflected exactly what we have wanted it to over the years. When our view of what it means to "know" another language has been the ability to translate carefully the writings of one language to another, our method of testing has been translation. It would be difficult to argue that the act of translation and the demonstration of that ability was unreasonable when one's tutelage had been primarily in that activity. Buck (1992) presents an analysis of data that suggests that one cannot reject translation on psychometric grounds—though he cautions against the potential undesirable "washback effect" of excessive practice in the classroom. Granted, we may argue that translation may be a narrow and specialized skill, that it is difficult to establish unique equivalencies between languages, and that this is not the primary activity of many second language users: Nevertheless, when a test measures what is taught, then translation is not an *a priori* rejected method of assessment.

Similarly, so-called "grammar tests," a characterization which covers a multitude of activities, often accurately reflect what happens in the language classroom. When students have been laboriously taught how to identify grammatical categories and the functions of various parts of sentences, then it should not seem strange to see a test in which students circle nouns, verbs, or other parts of speech, or underline the subject of the sentence once and the object of the verb twice. Common variations, such as listing word types, selecting ungrammatical versus grammatical constructions, using specific words in sentences, and listing rules with examples are often simply reflections of what has occurred in the language classroom. We may argue that classroom activities do not lead to language proficiency and, at best, foster the memorization of some language-related information, if not some "understanding" of the target language; however, that is a different testing consideration.

> ***P****ause to consider . . .*
>
> Spolsky's (1978, pp. v–x) suggestion that trends in testing follow trends in teaching, a notion that we have followed thus far in our discussions. Some people say, however, that the way we test languages has an effect on the way we teach languages, the so-called "washback" (or "backwash") effect (Hughes 1989, pp. 1–2). Compare the difference in teaching that could result from the difference between a detailed objective examination and an oral interview.

Allowing for disagreement as to the merits of some of the more traditional approaches to language testing, important issues arise when taking into account the level of the language learner, especially in more proficiency-oriented classrooms. Consider, for example, the beginning learner who spends hours listening to the target language and repeating utterances in the classroom with oral production as its goal. It seems obvious that written examinations of such learners, at least as we have already described, are inappropriate. Similarly, comprehensive oral interviews seem out of place. Nevertheless, it does not seem unreasonable to assess such learners in a fashion appropriate to their stage of language learning and in accord with their language learning activities, an understanding necessary for the consumers of this information. In early stages of such assessment, simple tasks are given, such as recognizing sounds as being the same or different, or identifying sounds or words represented in pictures provided for the examinees (Lado 1961, pp. 56–60). It is difficult to imagine complex, meaningful activities beyond identification at the beginning levels of language learning. Of course, as proficiency begins to develop, techniques that are more contextualized and communicative, such as having students read aloud or retell simple stories (Heaton 1990; Morley 1994; Prator & Robinet 1985), become possible.

Vocabulary and reading tests are often considered together. The problem of selecting or "sampling" what is to be tested is a common concern. Neither formal principles nor reliable standard lists exist to guide the selection of the set of words to be tested. Classroom vocabulary testing often draws from words used in classroom activities and assignments, such as reading passages and discussions. Tests for larger populations lack such a well-defined domain. The words themselves may be presented in isolation or in some sort of context, with tasks ranging from identification of synonyms to production of sentences. Although the activities may reflect what happens in the language learning classroom, the question of generalizability remains an issue. Both the form and content of reading passages are subject to similar considerations. What may be appropriate for biochemists may not be for historians. Similarly, the depth of reading passage recall may be affected by prior knowledge and interest (cf. Lee, Ch. 8, "From Misconceptions to Models of Reading Processes").

> ### *Pause to consider . . .*
>
> that the selection of vocabulary items to be tested is neither simple nor straightforward. Extend this concern to reading comprehension passages. Consider the appropriateness of uncommon test items, such as advertisements, graphs, billing statements, and assembly instructions as possible reading comprehension topics. What guides your selection of passage topics?

More General Language Ability Measures

At first glance it seems easy to talk about communicative or proficiency-oriented testing. If we were interested in testing a learner's ability to speak in a foreign language, then we should have a test that requires that learner to speak. Similarly, if we were interested in testing a learner's ability to write in a foreign language, then we should have a test in which the learner must write. In an effort to avoid some of the more obvious difficulties associated with testing, such as the amount of time necessary to administer an oral test, or to read and grade writing samples, and hence associated monetary considerations, other testing methods have been employed. With every method, of course, come additional considerations which tend to muddy the overall assessment picture.

"Dictation" as a testing method has been condemned by its critics and proclaimed by its advocates. Its contribution to the assessment of language skills depends upon our understanding of both the exercise and its employment. What is usually meant by "dictation" is the writing down on paper of what has been heard by the examinee, either as stated by the examiner in person or as played on a recording. As such, dictation is a task that requires higher-level skills: listening, writing, and consequently, reading. Although a dictation test could also require examinees to repeat aloud what they heard either to an examiner or on tape, we reserve evaluation of that format to a broader discussion of oral testing specifically. Perhaps the greatest difficulty in accepting dictation as a legitimate testing method has been the manner in which it is usually administered. The approach most often condemned involves slowly uttering a statement and repeating it in phrasal groups upon request of the examinees. Some critics have suggested that this amounts to no more than a spelling test, something that could be handled more effectively by giving students a list of words to memorize and then simply reading the same list of words aloud for them to write correctly (Lado 1961, p. 34; Oller 1979; Stansfield 1985).

It is difficult to argue against this criticism. Despite the fact that dictation may reflect classroom activities and foster familiarization with correspondences between sounds and symbols, room certainly exists for evaluating its merits as a testing method and modifying the overall approach towards more natural language use. In a more natural approach to dictation, sentences would be uttered once at normal language speed. The examinees would have the task of recording what they hear without the possibility of repetition. In that sense, examinees would be expected to demonstrate the ability—possessed by native speakers—to "repeat" what they have heard. It has been shown that children acquiring a first language can repeat utterances only in terms of the grammars they have developed (Ervin 1964). The same has been demonstrated for second language learners. Insofar as dictation reflects something native speakers of a language are capable of doing (i.e., accurately repeating novel utterances), it is praised by its adherents.

The "cloze test" has been cited by many as a good way to test a variety of points for language learners. It is essentially a test in which words have been deleted from a passage, either on a fixed-ratio or rational deletion basis; the task of the examinee is to fill in the blanks with appropriate words. Because with the fixed-ratio version, every nth word is deleted, it is possible to cover a wide range of grammatical features. In addition, cloze tests usually involve extended passages; thus, for those who are concerned that language tests must reflect natural language as much as possible, contextual focus is maintained. With the rational deletion approach, items belonging to a particular part of speech, such as verbs, could be deleted. Cloze tests were originally designed to test the readability of particular reading passages. As such, caution must be taken in the selection of passages for these kinds of tests. Well-written, easy-to-read passages are typically best to use for cloze tests. Sometimes scores from these tests have been said to reflect academic ability, though in those cases the source of the cloze passages must be carefully examined. It should be noted that it is difficult to develop comparable forms of cloze tests (Alderson 1979) and that at different levels students are capable of different kinds of tests. For example, early learners tend to be better at multiple choice initially, then fill-in-the-blank, and then cloze exercises (Gradman & Hanania 1990).

---

*P*ause to consider . . .

that cloze tests are traditionally thought of as written tests. However, the philosophy on which cloze tests is based, namely, that a number of signals may sometimes provide quite similar information, can be applied to aural materials as well. What are some examples of language use in which it may be difficult to hear complete messages? Can you think of ways that the cloze test may be adapted to an aural test?

SPOKEN PRODUCTION

We are now drawn to the notion of testing one's oral/aural skills through the medium of an oral interview, whether free or guided. The advantages of the oral interview, as suggested above, are obvious. One can observe the examinee speaking the language in what appears at first glance to be a natural situation.[1] Leaving aside the question of naturalness for the time being, we should turn to the administration of the oral interview. How long should the interview last in order to provide the tester with a complete picture of an applicant's abilities? In the case of early language learners, the length of the interview is less crucial. However, in the case of more advanced interviewees, the question has greater consequences. How broad a range of topics should be covered? What opportunities do interviewees have to display grammar, vocabulary, fluency, and so forth? In a class of fifteen students, with a twenty-minute oral interview per student, assessment, changing of examinees, and normal breaks, a minimum of five hours would be required to administer all of the interviews. It is not difficult to imagine the other issues that arise when there is a set routine for the oral interview: the question of security (i.e., preventing examinees from talking to one another); the difficulty in establishing the testing routine; the selection of content that is appropriate to all students; the necessity of fixed rather than spontaneous questions and responses, and so forth. Moreover, we have yet to establish a method for marking or rating the examinees' performance in these interviews, a problem inherent in all subjectively-oriented examinations. Lastly, it is unclear what inferences about present competence or future performance can be drawn from the limited samples available in these restricted settings (Bachman 1990; Bachman & Savignon 1986).

Faced with considerations such as those noted above, some testers prefer more guided oral interviews. Although such tests can be constructed in a variety of ways, they all share the notion that the interview is not a free exchange or discussion of topics between the interviewer and interviewee. As in the case of the *Bilingual Syntax Measure* (Burt, Dulay & Hernandez-Chavez 1975) or the *Ilyin Oral Interview* (Ilyin 1976), for example, the interview is directed towards specific pictures with predetermined questions that require the interviewee to answer within a specific context and, often, within a specific timeframe. The same can be said for the *Test of Spoken English* (TSE), in which some responses are guided by pictures presented to the interviewee as well as by information presented on tape and in the test booklet (Educational Testing Service 1990b). Although these types of guided interviews alleviate some of the content considerations, either an administrator or a facility with tape recorders is required; thus no time savings may be realized. In the case of the TSE, the expense to the individual examinee can be considerable.[2] In each of these exams, knowing what the results mean is less than specific. Whether the score is calculated on the basis of particular errors committed or on the basis of characteristics of groups of speakers, only a general statement about the speaker is generated. The scores will likely not suggest specific areas for study concentration or remedies for score improvement.

Another approach favored by those who desire a more realistic speaking situation is the sort first taken by the United States Foreign Service Institute (FSI) and, after use by various government agencies, later adapted by the American Council on the Teaching of Foreign Languages (ACTFL) and ETS to an oral interview style intended for academic contexts. The *ACTFL Proficiency Guidelines* (ACTFL 1986) serve as the basis for the *ACTFL Oral Proficiency Interview* (OPI). Separate tests are offered to assess listening, reading, and writing ability. The view of "proficiency" reflected in these tests emphasizes not what an individual knows about the target language (e.g., words and grammatical structures), but rather what a person can do with or through it. That is, the test is essentially *functionally* based. It is also "holistically" scored: A single, global rating is assigned and intended to reflect overall language proficiency, based on performance on a range of tasks. A learner at the "Intermediate" level for instance, is able to handle routine transactions, such as ordering a meal at a restaurant and paying the bill afterwards. A learner at the "Advanced" level is able to complete a transaction that has a complication, such as making some special arrangement with the waiter after discovering that he has lost his wallet. These examples usually require a "role play," but many other functions do not, such as describing the house in which one lives or comparing one's home town to some other town or city. When an interviewee sustains the requirements of a level throughout the interview, then it is assumed that this person can perform similar functions in future situations.

One consequence of defining proficiency in this way is that scale levels are broad; learners at the same major level may have different profiles or abilities. In other words, detailed diagnostic information is not provided. However, the goal of the test is to identify certain general abilities that are shared by all examinees at a particular level or higher (but not lower than that level). These abilities are the criteria that form the basis for the ratings and that are reflected in verbal descriptors for each level (published in the *ACTFL Proficiency Guidelines*). Because score interpretation is made with reference to these criteria, the OPI can be thought of as a "criterion-referenced" test, as opposed to a "norm-referenced" test. In norm-referenced testing, a score is interpreted with reference to "typical" performances by other examinees on the same test (e.g., 34% better or worse than the average score, or statistical "mean," for a given test), without direct mention of the general abilities that examinees have, such as the types of tasks or functions that they can perform.

The Simulated Oral Proficiency Interview (SOPI) is a tape-mediated version of the OPI that has been developed by CAL for use in situations where trained testers may not be available. Both the OPI and the SOPI are available for languages other than English, including French, German, Spanish, Japanese, and Arabic.

---

*P**ause to consider . . .*

Young's (1995) suggestion that highly proficient speakers are able to perform such functions as cooperatively establishing conversational topics and making smooth transitions. Young found, however, that the discourse structure of the oral interviews he examined did not provide advanced students with sufficient opportunity to demonstrate such abilities. What are some potential uses for oral interviews in which assessment of higher-level skills may be desirable? Can you think of any oral testing techniques that may allow one to reliably estimate such abilities?

WRITTEN PRODUCTION

Concerns similar to those for oral interviews, such as topic selection, rater reliability, and marking criteria, are also valid for compositions. In both cases, topic selection faces the sampling issues of examinee background, depth of examinee knowledge about the topic, and the degree to which performance on one topic can be generalized to performance on another topic (Reynolds 1996; Tapia 1993; cf. also Grabe & Kaplan, Ch. 9, "Writing and Disciplinary Knowledge"). In contrast to oral interviews, however, where topic shifts are common, essay assignments are often based on a single prompt, which magnifies these concerns. Rater reliability, conversely, appears to be a function of training. Where training is thorough and uniform, reliability tends to be higher. In addition, reliability tends to increase when training sessions are held before each test administration and more than one rater is assigned to each examinee (Lumley & McNamara, 1995).

There are four main types of scoring for written production: holistic, analytic, primary trait, and multitrait (Cohen 1994). Holistic scoring of essays resembles oral assessment, especially in its use of scales, such as those developed by the FSI and ACTFL. A single score is given to reflect overall proficiency in that modality. The *Test of Written English* (TWE), for example, is holistically rated on a scale of 1–6, ranging from incompetent to fully competent. Evaluations are based on reader impressions of essays on both "rhetorical" and "syntactic" levels (Educational Testing Service 1992). Correlations between TOEFL and TWE are only moderate (ibid), which suggests that TWE scores provide information that the regular TOEFL scores do not. However, as with the ACTFL oral proficiency ratings, because the score levels, or bands, are so broad, many students tend to score at the same level, despite the fact that they may have differing writing abilities. Thus, this test provides an additional, if only limited, indication of an examinee's overall writing ability.

More detailed assessment of writing abilities is possible by focusing on specific characteristics using either an "analytic" or a "multitrait" rating scale. Separate analytic scales may be used to evaluate aspects of writing, such as vocabulary, syntax, content, and development. Multitrait scales assess abilities that are more global, more functional in nature, such as the ability to read and respond critically to a text (Cohen 1994, p. 322). "Primary trait" scoring can be thought of as an opportunity to focus on one such trait by carefully selecting a writing topic that requires that particular ability. Thus, in primary trait and multitrait scoring, one has a more specific idea of what is being tested than in holistic scoring. The more narrow aim of such tests may be more appropriate after emphasizing particular abilities in the classroom or when testing for "special purposes" is needed.

Portfolio collections of samples of student capabilities are often an example of statements of proficiency negotiated between the language student and the assessor, an interesting alternative evaluation procedure that somewhat blurs the distinction between traditional testing and regular classroom activities. Student portfolios may include different types of writing, such as descriptions, formal essays, or prose analyses, and drafts in various stages and written under differing conditions, such as in the classroom, at home, or in the library. Thus, a possible argument in favor of the portfolio approach is that traditional essay concerns regarding restricted samples are greatly alleviated by the assignment of a range of topics to be written under a variety of conditions.

Pause to consider . . .

that the portfolio evaluation criteria are subject to a number of interpretations. One may wish to emphasize the quality of final drafts or the improvement from one draft to the next, or weigh assessment of some of the types of writing more heavily than others. Decisions regarding what to include in the portfolio and how to evaluate it could be made by the students themselves, with or without consultation with classmates and/or teachers. Given all of these options, Hamp-Lyons (1993) suggests that the criteria for inclusion and evaluation should be spelled out as clearly as possible from the very beginning of a course. What would you suggest be included in the portfolio of a language learning student? Who should decide what is to be included? How flexible should the criteria be? How is the assignment of overall letter grades to portfolios similar to the holistic rating of oral interviews and written compositions?

Much as notions of language ability have expanded into broader conceptualizations of communicative competence in recent years, so too ideas concerning validity have been extended to encompass concerns such as ethics and social consequences (Chapelle 1994; Chapelle & Douglas 1993; Messick 1988; Spolsky 1981). Identification of "stakeholders," those individuals for whom the test results have importance, and consideration of factors specific to particular testing situations can yield implications for both test development and test use. For instance, Lynch & Davidson (1994) present a criterion-referenced language test development approach intended to create a "positive washback effect" by linking curricula, teacher experience, and tests. Chapelle (1994) appeals to the concept of "consequential validity" in her assessment of measures of vocabulary ability in second language research settings.

Pause to consider . . .

who the "stakeholders" are in each of the following situations. What's at stake? In each case, assume the person in question is a non-native speaker of the language mentioned.

1. A student is applying to study at an English-speaking university and is required to take the TOEFL test;
2. A doctor is moving to Australia and must take an English test before he can practice medicine there;
3. An applicant to become an international flight attendant is asked to take a foreign language test in Italian;
4. A parent's child is taking a French test at school; and,
5. An applicant for a college-level teaching job in Mexico must take a Spanish test.

CONCLUSION

We hope it is clear through the issues raised in this chapter that a prospective teacher can benefit greatly from an understanding of basic principles of language testing. A multitude of issues in the language teaching profession require a knowledge of the multiple approaches to language assessment: There are concerns about how testing approaches influence classroom activities and curriculum design. There are questions regarding the fairness of selection decisions when both the test-taking population and the target language community consist of people from a wide variety of backgrounds, representing many dialects or varieties of the language. In many intensive language programs, a need exists to test students at regular intervals in order to place them into language classes that best suit their level of development; thus necessitating the creation of "equivalent" versions of placement examinations, so that students will not retake the exact same tests.

Underlying all of our efforts to address issues such as these is the recognition that tests are simply tests. There will never be anything totally realistic about a test, so perhaps we should not rely too heavily on any single instrument aimed at describing the characteristics of particular individuals or how individuals relate to larger groups. Test results can be valuable when decisions that involve language abilities need to be made, but the decisions themselves are made by humans, not by the tests, and may require the language teacher to consider matters both within and beyond the realm of language testing.

---

*P*ause to consider . . .

how knowing more about language assessment will help you as a language teacher.

NOTES

[1] See Hartford (Ch. 5) and Kasper (Ch. 6) for a discussion of the factors that define a natural situation.
[2] Although a version of the TSE is available that can be graded locally, the expense is passed on to the institution administering the exam in terms of time spent in evaluating and reporting the responses.

KEY TERMS, CONCEPTS, AND ISSUES

assessment
language proficiency
testing instruments

objective tests
subjective tests
grammar tests

cloze tests
discrete point testing
communicative testing
proficiency-oriented testing
oral interviews
   guided
   free
functional approach to language testing
integrative approach
portfolio assessment
reliability
validity
   content-related
   concurrent
   construct

practicality
context
   linguistic context
   nonlinguistic context
stakeholders
rating
scoring
   holistic
   analytic
   primary trait
   multitrait
   norm-referenced
   criterion-referenced
   rater reliability
   washback (or backwash) effect

Exploring the Topics
Further

EXPLORING THE TOPICS FURTHER

1. *General Overviews.* Cohen (1994) and Oller (1979) thoroughly address a wide range of issues related to classroom testing. Cohen's text covers recent topics, such as portfolio assessment and the use of computers, and is easily readable for persons without a strong background in language testing. Oller's book contains an in-depth treatment of discrete point versus pragmatically-oriented approaches. Alderson, Clapham & Wall (1995) provide a step-by-step look at the phases of the test development process. Bachman (1990) discusses considerations that underlie nearly all cases of testing research, test development, and test use. His framework encompasses concerns related to testing context, language abilities, and measurement principles. Other surveys of interest include Davies (1990), Harris (1969), Hughes (1989), and Valette (1977). For an earlier perspective, see Lado (1961).

2. *Proficiency testing. Studies in Second Language Acquisition, 10(2), (1988)* is devoted to the assessment of oral language proficiency. This entire journal issue and Bachman (1990) offer thorough, critical discussions of proficiency testing from a number of viewpoints. McNamara (1996) presents a valuable introduction and informative critique of "performance-based assessment" in second language contexts.

3. *Future research directions.* Several sources report on new uses of computer technology, applications of more sophisticated measurement theories, and on other innovations. For starters, we would suggest looking at Stansfield (1986), Portal (1986), and Douglas & Chapelle (1993).

4. *Internet.* Access to information from major testing centers has been increased with the development of the Internet. There is now a "Resources in Language Testing Page" on the World Wide Web (http://www.surrey.ac.uk/ELI/ltr.html). Information on TOEFL and other ETS programs can be found on the ETS web page (http://www.ets.org). CAL (http://www.cal.org) has information on tests for languages other than English.

5. *Journals and newsletters of interest. Language Testing* is the academic journal for language testers. Another useful publication is *Language Testing Update,* the official newsletter of the International Language Testing Association (ILTA). Information regarding ILTA membership may be obtained by writing to: International Language Testing Association, Tim McNamara, Department of Applied Linguistics and Language Studies, University of Melbourne, Parkville, Victoria 3052, Australia.

REFERENCES

ACTFL (1986). *Proficiency guidelines.* Hastings-on-Hudson, NY: ACTFL.

Alderson, J.C. (1979). The cloze procedure and proficiency in English as a foreign language, *TESOL Quarterly, 13,* 219–227.

Alderson, J.C., Clapham, C. & Wall, D. (1995). *Language test construction and evaluation.* Cambridge: Cambridge University Press.

Bachman, L.F. (1990). *Fundamental considerations in language testing.* Oxford: Oxford University Press.

Bachman, L.F. & Savignon, S.J. (1986). The evaluation of communicative language proficiency: A critique of the ACTFL oral interview. *Modern Language Journal, 70,* 380–90.

Buck, B. (1992). Translation as a language testing procedure: does it work? *Language Testing, 9,* 123–48.

Burt, M.K., Dulay, H. C. & Hernandez-Chavez, E. (1975). *The bilingual syntax measure.* New York: Harcourt, Brace, and Jovanovich.

Carroll, J.B. (1961). Fundamental considerations in testing for English language proficiency of foreign students. In *Testing the English proficiency of foreign students.* Washington, D.C.: Center for Applied Linguistics, 31–40. Reprinted in H.B. Allen and R.N. Campbell (Eds.) *Teaching English as a second language: A book of readings.* (pp. 313–320). New York: McGraw-Hill, 1972.

Chapelle, C.A. (1994). Are C-tests valid measures for L2 vocabulary research? *Second Language Research, 10,* 157–187.

Chapelle, C.A. & Douglas, D. (1993). Foundations and directions for a new decade of language testing. In D. Douglas & C. Chapelle (Eds.), *A new decade of language testing research.* (pp. 1–22). Alexandria, VA: Teachers of English to Speakers of Other Languages, Inc.

Cohen, A.D. (1994). *Assessing language ability in the classroom.* Boston: Heinle and Heinle.

Davies, A. (1990). *Principles of language testing.* Cambridge, MA: Blackwell.

Douglas D. & Chapelle, C. (Eds.). (1993). *A new decade of language testing research.* Alexandria, VA: Teachers of English to Speakers of Other Languages, Inc.

Educational Testing Service. (1990a). *TOEFL test and score manual,* 1990–1991. Princeton, NJ: Educational Testing Service.

Educational Testing Service. (1990b). *Test of spoken English manual for score users.* Princeton, NJ: Educational Testing Service.

Educational Testing Service. (1992). *TOEFL test of written English guide* (Third Edition). Princeton, NJ: Educational Testing Service.

Ervin, S. (1964). Imitation and structural change in children's language. In E. Lenneberg (Ed.), *New directions in the study of language.* Cambridge, MA: MIT Press.

Gradman, H.L. & Hanania, E. (1990). Discrete focus vs. global tests: Performance on selected verb structures. In J.H.A.L. de Jong and D.K. Stevenson (Eds.), *Individualizing the assessment of language abilities* (pp. 166–176). Clevedon: Multilingual Matters LTD.

Hamp-Lyons (1993). Components of portfolio evaluation: ESL data. Paper presented at the annual AAAL Conference, Atlanta, GA, April 16–19.

Harris, D.P. (1969). *Testing English as a second language.* New York: McGraw-Hill.

Heaton, J.B. (1990). *Classroom testing.* London: Longman.

Hughes, A. (1989). *Testing for language teachers.* New York: Cambridge University Press.

Ilyin, D. (1976). *Ilyin oral interview.* Rowley, MA: Newbury House.

Lado, R. (1961). *Language testing.* New York: McGraw-Hill.

Lumley, T. & McNamara, T.F. (1995). Rater characteristics and rater bias: Implications for training. *Language Testing, 12,* 1, 54–71.

Lynch, B.K. & Davidson, F. (1994). Criterion-referenced language test development: Linking curricula, teachers, and tests. *TESOL Quarterly, 28,* 4, 727–743.

McNamara, T. (1996). *Measuring second language performance.* London: Longman.

Messick, S.A. (1988). Validity. In R.L. Linn (Ed.), *Educational measurement.* Third Edition (pp. 13–103). New York: American Council on Education/Macmillan.

Morley, J. (Ed.). (1994). *Pronunciation pedagogy and theory: New views, new directions.* Alexandria, VA: Teachers of English to Speakers of Other Languages.

Oller, J.W. Jr. (1979). *Language tests at school: A pragmatic approach.* London: Longman.

Portal, M. (Ed.). (1986). *Innovations in language testing.* Philadelphia: NFER-NELSON.

Prator, C. & Robinett, B.W. (1985). *Manual of American English pronunciation.* 4th ed. New York: Holt, Rinehart and Winston.

Reynolds, D. (1996). *Repetition in second language writing.* Unpublished Ph.D. Dissertation, Indiana University.

Spolsky, B. (1978). Introduction: Linguistics and language testers. In B. Spolsky (Ed.), *Advances in language testing* (pp. v–x). Arlington: Center for Applied Linguistics.

Spolsky, B. (1981). Some ethical questions about language testing. In C. Klein-Braley and D.K. Stevenson (Eds.), *Practice and problems in language testing I.* Frankfurt am Main: Peter D. Lang.

Stansfield, C. (1985). A history of dictation in foreign language teaching and testing. *Modern Language Journal 69,* 121–128.

Stansfield, C. (Ed.). (1986). *Technology and language testing.* Washington, D.C.: Teachers of English to Speakers of Other Languages.

Tapia, E. (1993). *Cognitive demand as a factor in interlanguage syntax: A study in topics and texts.* Unpublished Ph.D. Dissertation, Indiana University.

Valette, R.M. (1977). *Modern language testing* (2nd ed.). New York: Harcourt, Brace, and Jovanovich.

Young, R. (1995). Conversational styles in language proficiency interviews. *Language Learning, 45,* 3–42.

About the Authors

KATHLEEN BARDOVI-HARLIG is Associate Professor of TESOL and Applied Linguistics at Indiana University. She received her Ph.D. in Linguistics from the University of Chicago in 1983. Her main areas of research interest are the development of grammatical and pragmatic competence in second language acquisition. She has taught courses in second language acquisition designed for language teachers as well as doctoral seminars for future researchers in the United States, Hungary, and Japan. She has also taught courses in TESOL methods, interlanguage pragmatics, and discourse analysis. Her research in second language acquisition has appeared in journals such as *Studies in Second Language Acquisition, Language Learning*, and *TESOL Quarterly*. Her work on language-teacher preparation has been published in TESOL Journal and *ELT Journal* and in various books.

MARIA-LUISE BECK is a faculty member in the Division of German, Department of Foreign Languages and Literatures at the University of North Texas. She received her Ph.D. from the University of Texas at Austin and has taught language classes in German and ESL as well as courses in ESL methods and in linguistics. Her primary research interest is the representation of second language knowledge among adult learners. She also works on materials development for all levels of language instruction. Most recently, she has been involved in the creation of uniform perfomance standards for second language teachers and for teacher training programs in the state of Texas.

KIMBERLEY BROWN is Associate Professor of Applied Linguistics and International Studies at Portland State University. She received her Ph.D. in Second Languages and Cultures Education from the University of Minnesota in 1988. Her areas of research are World Englishes, teacher education, and culture learning in the language classroom. She teaches courses ranging from TESOL methods and social dimensions of language contact (bilingualism, language planning, World Englishes) to introductory International Studies courses. She is a frequent presenter at regional and national TESOL and NAFSA: Association of International Educators meetings and has played leadership roles in both organizations throughout the last decade.

WILLIAM GRABE is Associate Professor in the English Department at Northern Arizona University. He received his Ph.D. from the University of Southern California in 1984 and has been at Northern Arizona University from 1984 to the present. His research interests include the development of L1 and L2 reading and writing abilities, literacy, sociolinguistics, written discourse analysis, and language policy. He has published in a number of journals and anthologies. His most recent book, *Theory and Practice of Writing* (co-authored with Robert Kaplan) was published in 1996 (Longman). He is currently working on a book on reading in a second language. He is also currently Editor-in-Chief of the *Annual Review of Applied Linguistics* (Cambridge).

HARRY L. GRADMAN, Professor of Linguistics at Indiana University, chairs the Program in TESOL and Applied Linguistics and directs the Center for English Language Training. His professional interests include language program management, program evaluation, and student recruitment and retention. He received his Ph.D. in Linguistics from Indiana University in 1970. In addition to his regular duties as chair and director, he currently teaches graduate courses in English linguistics and language assessment, and he has directed many Ph.D. dissertations. His areas of research are language testing and second language acquisition. He has published numerous articles based on empirical research on reduced-redundancy testing, closed versus open response testing formats, and the relationships among language learning background variables and performance on tests of general proficiency, overall writing ability, and globally-assessed speaking ability.

BEVERLY S. HARTFORD is Associate Professor of TESOL and Applied Linguistics at Indiana University. She received her Ph.D. from the University of Texas at Austin. Her main areas of research are the development of pragmatic competence and language contact. She teaches courses in sociolinguistics, including language and society, bilingualism and language contact, World English, and language attitudes. She also teaches applied linguistics courses in the areas of pedagogical grammar, second language acquisition, and intercultural pragmatics. She has trained English teachers at universities in both Poland and Nepal, as well as conducted numerous workshops for language teachers throughout the world, including Malaysia and Venezuela. Her publications have appeared in *World Englishes*, *Language Learning*, *Studies in Second Language Acquisition*, *Discourse Processes*, and *ELT Journal*.

ROBERT B. KAPLAN is Emeritus Professor of Applied Linguistics at the University of Southern California. He received his Ph.D. from the University of Southern California in 1965 and remained at USC until his official retirement in 1995. His research interests center on written discourse analysis, contrastive rhetoric, the development of writing abilities, ESL program administration, language policy and planning, and language teaching for scientific, professional, and academic purposes. He has been president of a number of major applied linguistics organizations in his career (TESOL, CATESOL, NAFSA, AAAL). He has published numerous journal articles and anthology chapters and has authored or edited more than ten books. His most recent book, *Theory and Practice of Writing* (co-authored with William Grabe) was published in 1996 (Longman). He is currently completing a volume on language policy and planning (with Richard Baldauf) and a second volume on language learning and language teaching.

GABRIELE KASPER is Professor in the Department of English as a Second Language at the University of Hawai'i at Manoa, where she teaches in the M.A. program in ESL and the Ph.D. program in Second Language Acquisition. Before coming to Hawai'i, she taught at universities in Germany and Denmark and more recently in Japan. Her main research interests are sociolinguistic and psycholinguistic aspects of interlanguage pragmatics and discourse. Her most recent book is on communication strategies, co-edited with Eric Kellerman.

JAMES F. LEE is Associate Professor of Spanish at the University of Illinois at Urbana-Champaign. He served as the Director of Basic Language Instruction in the Department of Spanish, Italian and Portuguese from 1986 to 1993 and as the Director of the Office of Lesbian, Gay, Bisexual and Transgender Concerns from 1993 to 1996. He received his Ph.D. in Hispanic Linguistics from the University of Texas at Austin in 1984. His primary research interest is reading in nonnative languages, and he has published many articles and chapters in this area. He is also very concerned with language teaching and has published a monograph on TA training, several textbooks with McGraw-Hill, and co-authored (with Bill VanPatten) *Making Communicative Language Teaching Happen.*

MARTHA C. PENNINGTON holds a Ph.D. in Linguistics from the University of Pennsylvania and is the Powdrill Professor of English Language Acquisition at the University of Luton, where she conducts research on bilingualism and language learning and teaching. She has published widely in the field of ESL, including her recent book, *Phonology in English Language Teaching* (Longman, 1996) and her forthcoming books, *Language Learning: An Introduction* (Arnold) and *Phonology in Second Language Acquisition* (Arnold). She has also published in ESL and applied linguistics journals in the areas of phonology and language teacher education.

DANIEL J. REED is Research Associate and Assistant Professor in the Program in TESOL and Applied Linguistics at Indiana University. He is currently president of the Indiana State Affiliate of Teachers of English to Speakers of Other Languages (INTESOL). He also is a member of the International Language Testing Association (ILTA) and the American Council on the Teaching of Foreign Languages (ACTFL). He has been certified by ACTFL to administer the ACTFL Oral Proficiency Interview (OPI), and he now conducts research on that test. He received his Ph.D. in Linguistics from Indiana University in 1991. The courses he teaches include Transformational English Grammar, a Survey of Applied Linguistics, and Language Testing. His research interests primarily lie in the area of language assessment, and he has published articles on topics which span the traditional linguistic levels from the details of pronunciation to the holistic assessment of overall, functional language proficiency. His experience with quantitative research designs includes a large-scale, comparative analysis of performance on the Test of English as a Foreign Language (TOEFL) and the Test of Written English (TWE). His most recent work is based on detailed analyses of oral proficiency interview transcripts.

BILL VANPATTEN is Professor of Spanish and Second Language Acquisition at the University of Illinois where he is also the Director of Graduate Studies in Spanish, Italian, and Portuguese. He received his Ph.D. in Hispanic Linguistics from the University of Texas at Austin in 1983. His main areas of interest are psycholinguistic processes in second language acquisition, especially input processing and the implications it has for second language instruction. He has taught a wide variety of courses, from basic Spanish to doctoral seminars in second language acquisition. In addition to his many articles, chapters in books, and textbooks, Professor VanPatten is the author of *Input Processing and Grammar Instruction: Theory and Research* (Ablex) and is the co-author (with James F. Lee) of *Making Communicative Language Teaching Happen*.

Index